D0046056

STRATEGIC DIGITAL MARKETING

CONTENTS

INTRODUCTION

The digital age is here—and it's developing rapidly. Even though I keep up with the latest hardware and software advances more diligently than most, I'm constantly amazed at how quickly the world is changing. For the first time in history, we can all feel just how profoundly the evolution of technology is impacting our daily lives—and that change is only accelerating.

I graduated from Wharton in the late 1980s, and started my own marketing firm after graduating from NYU law school in 1991. This was a time before digital media, before cell phones, and even before the introduction of the Internet. Our firm used landline telephone technologies and a whole lot of human capital to generate sales for our clients. In the 1990s, people could actually be convinced to buy products with a personal phone call—at least at a high enough rate to generate significant returns for our clients. It was a different world.

With the advent of the Internet, that world soon faded away. We rode the leading-edge of the first technological revolution, transformed into a full-service CRM company, and became one of the first firms to integrate digital marketing into our activities. During my tenure as CEO, we grew the organization to more than 5,000 employees, and became one of the world's largest privately owned marketing companies.

I sold and exited the company just before the burst of the Internet bubble in 2001, and started my own consulting company. I also began teaching collegiate marketing courses at Rutgers University as a way to give back to the community, and really enjoyed students' hunger to understand technology and the changing business landscape. My courses explored how companies failed to keep pace with technological advancement for the first time in 2001, and students couldn't get enough.

I was asked to teach more regularly, and eventually to design entire marketing curricula that sought to educate students and executives about coping with our evolving digital world. Years later, I formally joined the Rutgers Center for Management Development as managing director and began to develop digital marketing programs and corporate training in full force.

Over the past several years, I've had the privilege of working with some of the best and brightest minds in digital marketing. These thought-leading practitioners joined my cause and have helped us develop a world-class digital marketing curriculum for our executive education programs at Rutgers. We've integrated iPads and other forward-looking technologies into our programs to develop a unique and hands-on method of training executives.

Our digital marketing offerings are growing at 300 percent per year, and we now consistently run programs for executives on five different continents. We spread this innovative curriculum to corporations as well, offering custom training for several Fortune 500 companies and some of most recognizable brands in the world. I partnered with Alexander Kates, one of the most brilliant and innovative young minds in digital today, to expand our digital offerings to these top brands.

In working with these companies, we've noticed common themes and trends in how they react to the digital world, irrespective of their industry, sector, or geography. We often spend weeks customizing training content for clients to take into account industry considerations, functional needs, or strategic marketing approaches. However, when we deliver the training, I am astonished at how often the exact same questions, hurdles, and frustrations arise—whether we're in Singapore, Prague, Sydney, or New York.

This book serves a dual-purpose: To address where companies are failing to cope with our digital world, and to spread the tried-and-true approach to digital marketing education we've developed, honed, and successfully deployed over these last several years.

To begin to fully grasp digital marketing, one must first understand how our world has changed, where it's headed, and how that affects the realm of marketing. In the first part of the book, we explore the new digital paradigm in full, and using case studies from personal experience, help you to develop an intimate understanding of our new digital world. We examine a new approach to analyzing the world of marketing, through a *digital lens*, using Return on Investment (ROI) as the benchmark for comparison. You'll also gain an understanding of the modern digital ecosystem, what companies are doing right, and where they're falling short. Finally, we introduce a new digital marketing strategy framework that provides a sound basis for business units approaching digital marketing initiatives.

In our time educating executives about digital marketing, we've become intimately familiar with each digital marketing channel. However, as quickly as our digital world evolves, we firmly believe that no one person is an up-to-date world expert on each and every digital media channel. For that reason, we've partnered with many of the most eminent and respected specialists in each area of digital marketing to share their knowledge, innovative tips, and real-world case studies. Each of these experts consults for top brands around the world and guides executives toward success in our corporate training programs. They are also reputed authors in their own right, having published best-selling books in their digital marketing areas of expertise. We wholeheartedly believe that they provide the most inventive and up-to-date introductions to each digital marketing channel. We're very fortunate to have had the opportunity to work with each of them in putting together this compilation.

As colossal a problem as lack of digital knowledge is in corporations today, we've found that the inability to actually apply this knowledge is their greatest hurdle to change. Companies fail to put together the necessary structural, cultural, and logistical pieces to transform the organization into one that can cope—and thrive—in this digital world. In the final part of this book, we introduce a new pragmatic framework for effecting change within modern organizations, and discuss strategies for implementing that change.

This book is intended for marketing veterans, budding enthusiasts, and C-suite executives alike. We firmly believe that this knowledge is useful to not just marketers, but also human resource managers, legal and compliance departments, creative engineers, and general managers of all types. All corporate training we run is cross-functional too, because today's rapidly-evolving marketing environment demands organization-wide collaboration. Whether you're looking to be the agent of change within your organization, or further your personal career path, we hope you find *Strategic Digital Marketing* to be exceptionally useful in acquainting you with the brave new world of digital marketing.

—*Eric Greenberg*

PART 1

OUR NEW DIGITAL WORLD

CHAPTER 1

THE DIGITAL PARADIGM

—by Alexander Kates and Eric Greenberg

In the not-too-distant past, *advertising simply worked*. Brand messages, crafted by the brilliantly creative, could be pushed to consumers through various forms of media—TV, print, and eventually online. The consumer, becoming familiar with your brand through these media, would choose to buy your product or service among few available choices. Instinct and familiarity drove sales. After all, consumers had very little information at their fingertips to make rational decisions. People would look at comparable products on a store shelf, and pick the brand that just *felt right*. Purchasing was a result of sentiment-backed guesswork.

Striving to be the result of that consumer guesswork, the advertising industry used surveys and studies to create generally accepted formulas that sought to determine the best ways to reach consumers. Proxy measurements, such as *gross rating points* (GRPs), often provided enough insight to make intelligent decisions about marketing-campaign potential. These methods served as a substitute for true campaign tracking, which was all but impossible before the dawn of the digital age. Marketers didn't always understand why these methods worked—but they did. In essence, advertising too was guesswork—it was just smarter guesswork, backed by a thoroughly researched and refined methodology.

The end result of this mutual guesswork is that big brands came out on top. Consumers' limited information gave companies the power to influence sentiments and choice by garnering eyeballs and attention through TV, radio, print, and the early Internet. Companies held all the cards in the company–consumer relationship.

Under this old paradigm, marketing was about pushing your message to consumers, and getting them to hear it. Your competition was other brands' messages, and anything else consuming your target customers' attention that prevented them from falling in love with your brand at first sight. It was the marketer's job to cut through this background clutter present in the marketing universe. This was generally done by throwing a profusion of advertising dollars behind brand messages to push them through these traditional media channels, as shown in Figure 1.1.

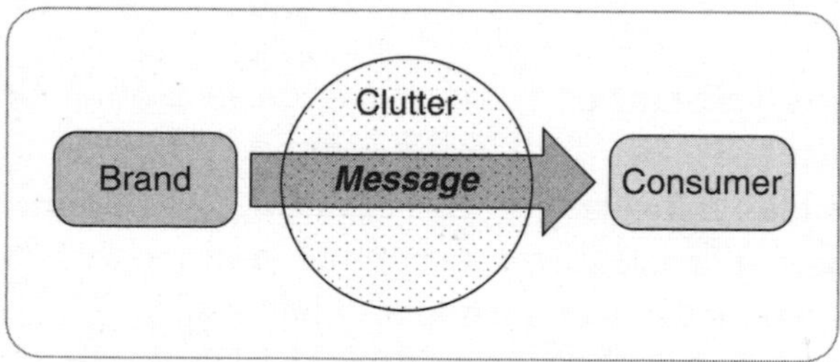

FIGURE 1.1 The Old Marketing Paradigm: Marketing was about pushing messages through background clutter to reach consumers and ultimately influence their purchase decisions.

THE NEW WORLD OF MARKETING

Today, there is a whole lot more background noise than there used to be. For starters, consumers have a nearly unlimited amount of information at their fingertips. There is also more competition on nearly every front: more competitive products and services, more channels to compete in, and more considerations in the consumption process. Pushing a message through this increasingly dense noise is becoming an exercise in futility.

Fortunately, the information age has created new, bidirectional channels that cut directly through the noise. These channels can be utilized to carry messages effectively through to the consumer. To focus our message into these channels, we use the metaphor of a giant lens that focuses the message and then disperses it into each of these digital channels, as shown in Figure 1.2. We have to place this lens over our traditional marketing methodology and view the digital world of marketing in a brand new light. Accepting our near-blindness, and putting on our digital glasses, is essential to getting our messages through these digital channels—and into the ears and hearts of our consumers.

However, the messages cannot simply be pushed through all of these channels by marketers as they used to be. In some channels, the message needs to be *pulled* from the other end; in others, you need to find a group of peers to push the message for you. And in still others, you need to entice the consumer to discover your message on their own, or to let consumers decide among themselves how to get the message through the channel. Information now flows both ways, and consumers themselves feed information into these channels. Things are a lot more complicated than they used to be. The more complex digital lens diagram shown in Figure 1.2 would not look out of place in an advanced physics textbook, and if anything, is a grave oversimplification of how marketing works in the twenty-first century.

We're in a different world today. It's unfortunate for us marketers sometimes, but consumers these days actually know things. In fact, they know a lot. Google connects potential customers with countless third-party opinions, articles, and reviews from around the web. Communications between customers, as well as a customer-service experiences, are entirely public on Twitter. Brand interaction and sentiments, including what our personal acquaintances think, are freely available on Facebook. Photos and video clips, helpful or harmful to a brand, circulate Instagram and Vine. If one customer has a less-than-perfect experience with your product in Winstonville, Mississippi, the entire world will know about it in minutes. The hyper-informed consumer knows everything about your brand—the good, the bad, and the ugly. Our brands have been stripped of their warm, protective clothes. They stand naked in the cold to be judged by the eyes of the world.

Fortunately, there is a silver lining to be found in all of this dismal complication. Digital media channels afford an opportunity to develop deep connections with consumers beyond what was ever previously possible. When your naked brand can be

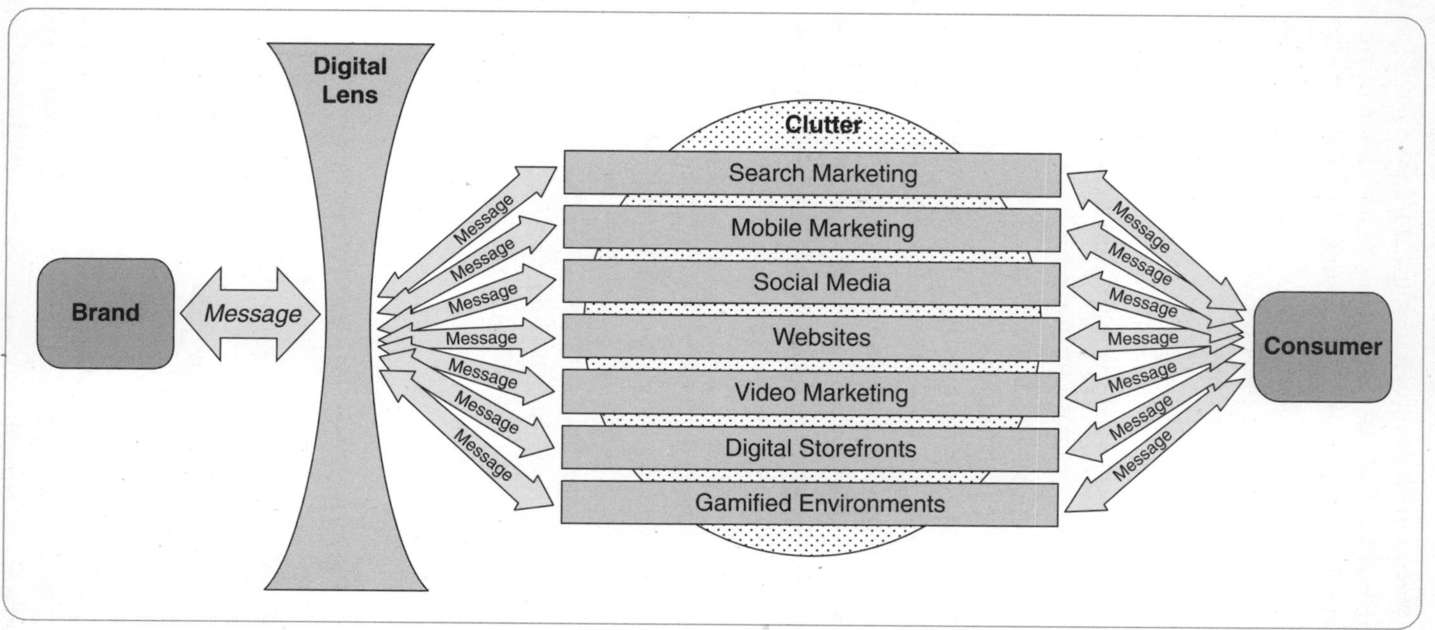

FIGURE 1.2 The New Digital Paradigm: Marketing messages must be fragmented and creatively fed into various digital channels to reach consumers at the correct moment.

judged completely, without hiding behind your unverified claims and pushed messages, customers come to truly know your brand. If they still like what they see, the relationship, trust, and devotion are deeper than ever before. Brand evangelists will champion your brand for you, feed media channels, and facilitate getting your message through to consumers. The most innovative brands not only push creative messages, but allow consumers to absorb those same messages via osmosis from the rest of the world. Many companies have done this with great success. For instance, Nike involved consumers directly in developing complementary wearable fitness bracelets and mobile apps. Early adopters cultivated a brand image that Nike actually cares about health and fitness, and that's something that customers really got behind and spread the word about. Brand image is no longer something marketers create: It's something marketers seed, media channels fertilize, and consumers themselves grow.

The new digital paradigm has also created a world that demands brutal honesty, full accountability, and complete transparency from product and service brands. We will be punished more severely for our mistakes, and will be scrutinized more acutely for how we deal with them. Success stories will spread more quickly and more widely than ever before, too. Marketers shape and facilitate brand messages through media channels, and must be diligent about their messages being everywhere that consumers are looking for them. In this commoditized digital world, the role of the marketer has never been more complicated—or more important.

THE MODERN DIGITAL CONSUMER

You no longer know your consumer. You think you do, but you don't. You've been left in the dust. All of the research and data collection you've done over the past several years doesn't begin to paint a picture of the modern consumer. The truth is: the consumer is evolving much faster than you are. Today's world is one in which technology and free information flow enable the consumer to always stay several steps ahead of large organizations seeking to sell their products and services. By failing to act swiftly, companies are only driving nails into their own digital coffins. Examine the following fictional scenario:

> A young man strolls into a Walmart retail store. As he passes through the automatic sliding doors, he is identified through a unique ID chip in his smartphone: He is Joe Davis, a 35-year-old male from Manalapan, New Jersey. The Walmart database shows that he spent an average of $93 per month at this retail location over the last 12 months, 45 percent of which was clothing, 23 percent was sporting goods, and 22 percent was personal care. All of the Walmart employees have this information on their point-of-sale tablets and are ready to assist him, should he require it.
>
> Earlier this week, Joe received an automated 15 percent off dental products coupon by e-mail because his purchases in that category have dropped off dramatically over the last three months. When Joe enters the store, the coupon pops up on his smartphone as a reminder, along with some loyalty points he's earned just by walking in.
>
> Joe makes his way to the dental products, and begins to examine the electric toothbrushes offered by several competing manufacturers. One of the products from Oral-B catches his eye—he vaguely remembers a TV commercial he saw about it that intrigued him. Joe pulls out his smartphone and scans the barcode on the back of the Oral-B box using a price-check application.
>
> The product pops up immediately on his phone, citing 253 reviews from confirmed Amazon.com customers. The reviews are lukewarm at best—3.2 out of 5 stars. The most *up-voted* review indicates that many customers feel the rotating mechanism makes their gums feel numb. The shopping site recommends several better-rated alternatives from competing brands, including a popular Philips Sonicare brush that received 4.4 out of 5 stars across 942 reviews.
>
> Joe looks up from his phone, and takes one large sidestep to position himself in front of the Sonicare toothbrush. He inspects the packaging briefly, and returns his attention to his phone. Using his social shopping app, he finds that Sonicare is *liked* by 355,000 people on Facebook, including several of his closest friends. Several of his followers also follow the Sonicare brand on Twitter. The top

three Amazon reviews (two of which are from dental professionals) are glowing, and recommend the product over competing brands' products. One of Joe's Facebook friends even reviewed a similar Sonicare model on Amazon, giving it a five-star rating.

Joe then performs a voice search for the best electric toothbrushes and he finds that the Sonicare website is the first link to show up in Google. A second link on Google's first page of results compares Sonicare's top offerings to those of Oral-B's and two other competitors, and concludes that Sonicare fared better in a clinical test. As the icing on the cake, Joe also notices a paid search ad stating that Sonicare is currently running a coupon promotion for a free set of replacement brush heads with the purchase of this toothbrush line.

In ninety seconds of brief research, Joe has made his purchase decision—the Sonicare toothbrush is the clear winner. It may not have been the first brand he identified with, but the social sentiments and data at his fingertips have influenced his decision. Let's continue Joe's journey:

Joe's social shopping app indicates that the price is $12 cheaper on Amazon.com, $16 cheaper on eBay, and the same price at the Target store down the street. Although he can place the order online with his phone with a single click and receive it at his front door in two days, he decides the immediate gratification of using his new toothbrush tonight outweighs the cost savings. Joe puts the Sonicare toothbrush in his Walmart shopping cart.

As he continues down the dental isle, his *smart shopping cart* recognizes the toothbrush by its RFID product tag. Automatically, the top-rated and most-purchased complimentary toothpaste for that toothbrush pops up on his smartphone screen, along with an additional 10 percent off coupon if he buys both together. Who doesn't need more toothpaste? Joe decides to buy the toothpaste too. His intelligent shopping list app recommends a few additional products that are verified to be currently in stock at this Walmart, and he drops by those aisles to pick those items up too before heading to checkout. He checks out at the register by quickly swiping his phone over a scanner—earning more store loyalty points in the process—and off he goes, toward a future of improved dental hygiene.

This may seem like a scene from the distant future, or some sci-fi TV show depicting the year 2034, but it isn't. All of the above technologies are readily available today and are in use, though as of this writing not necessarily by Walmart. In fact, the entire consumer side of the experience, including real-time product and price comparisons, social data, recommendations, and intelligent mobile shopping apps, is becoming the status quo for the new digital consumer. Brick-and-mortar stores are struggling to cope with the flux of tech-savvy customers shopping this way. Many young people are utilizing Amazon's Price Check app in stores, which allows them to explore products in person, scan the barcodes, and then order the identical products cheaper on Amazon with a single click (with free two-day shipping and generally no tax to boot). Retail stores in several U.S. cities are outraged at the loss of sales and have banned use of the app in their stores. This is not the *future* of the in-store shopper. It's him in the present. This is how consumers shop today.

Conversely, although every one of the retail store technologies mentioned are available, it is nearly impossible to find a retail establishment that's implemented all of them—or even one of them. This is because the consumer is evolving much faster than retail stores, and faster than even the most agile large organization. As soon as new technologies and tools are available, consumers are using them within days. On the other hand, businesses have to wait for project proposals, management approvals, budget allocations, and partner contracting. It takes businesses months, and sometimes years, to make the equivalent infrastructure changes. The digital train has already left the station, and we marketers are all running to catch up to it.

Brick-and-mortar retailers may be lagging behind, but eRetailers are doing a much better job innovating. Digital storefronts like Amazon and Zappos are redefining standards in customer service over the web. eBay is creating unprecedented marketplace efficiency and virtually eliminating the barriers between buyers and sellers. Woot and other daily deal sites are making online shopping more exciting than ever, and Groupon and LivingSocial are making the concept of online shopping local again. Apple and

Google are changing the way we purchase and consume media. Still other storefronts utilize crowdsourcing, social buying, and new levels of customer interaction to bridge the gap between the online and in-store experience. As mobile technology advances, and as online retailers evolve their platforms to incorporate the latest intelligence engines and tracking technologies, we expect that the fine line between online shopping and brick-and-mortar shopping will blur even further, and eventually, will disappear completely.

The bottom line is that the world, and the marketing universe by necessity, is evolving faster than any of us realizes. This rate of change is only going to accelerate in the coming years.

THE NEW CONSUMER'S JOURNEY

Joe's journey epitomizes the innovative modern consumer in the real world. However, to truly understand the full spectrum of consumers' purchase decisions more generally, we think it's helpful to visualize the process. In 2009, McKinsey and Company developed a diagram to help marketers understand this journey:

> The consumer begins with a need or desire to buy a type of product. At this time, the consumer may have some preconceived notions about product specifics she deems important, and is perhaps even considering particular brands. From there, she does research and considers her options, eventually leading to a moment of purchase. Post-purchase, the consumer evaluates her experience with the product, until the moment that the need or desire arises to purchase this same category of product again—coming full circle back to where she started.

All consumers, however loosely, follow this cycle during their first purchase of a product category. However, at that moment when the customer feels the need or desire to purchase another product for this function, she must choose one of two distinct paths: The first is taken by consumers who are thoroughly satisfied with their purchase and do not seek to consider alternatives, ultimately purchasing the same exact branded product again. The second is followed by consumers who are not wholly satisfied, and who therefore reenter the research phase leading up to this second purchase decision.

This cycle makes perfect sense, and for the most part accurately describes the general thought process consumers go through with regard to purchases and brand loyalty. However, the last several years have seen a rather frightening trend that all marketers need to be aware of: Brand loyalty, traditionally one of the most crucial goals of marketing, is decreasing in developed countries. Some say it is dying a slow, painful death, and that consumer behavior has changed beyond recognition.

The data backs this assertion. According to a comprehensive global study conducted by Ernst & Young last year, only 25 percent of American consumers (and 24 percent of Western European consumers) are swayed by a brand's reputation when making a product purchase. The trend shows that over the past decade, loyalty has been steadily decreasing in highly developed nations, and conversely, has been increasing in developing nations where reliance on modern technology lags behind.[1]

This trend hints at an increasingly commoditized world, where purchasing is fueled more by *the best deal* than *the best brand*. It runs counter to the fundamental concept of branding that we marketers have relied on for so many years. Why is this happening?

The short answer: Our quick and easy access to information brought about by modern technology. Consumers these days have an incredible amount of information at their fingertips, both at home and on the go via their mobile phones. Brand information, history, and statistics can be obtained at any time. Aggregated product reviews and scores, from professional reviewers and real purchasers alike, are easily accessible. Recent product news, releases, and hiccups, can be found instantly with a simple search. Even opinions from our trusted peers about a brand or product (via social media) can be utilized to help us make purchases. Furthermore, the best deals, sales, and coupons are aggregated for us and at our fingertips at all times. Trends show that all of these factors are starting to chip away at blind brand loyalty that has been the marketer's instrument since, well, the term *marketing* was first coined.

The modern consumer is confident. He has all the information he'll ever need to make good decisions, and he knows it. The modern state of the web has completely obliterated the fear of the unknown consumers have faced for centuries. When a consumer is comparing two products, one from a top brand with tens of millions in advertising behind it and another he has never heard of, for the first time in history the two products are (almost) on an equal playing field. And it doesn't matter whether the comparison takes place on the web or in a store. The always-connected consumer has the information to help him decide either way.

For these reasons, we feel the prior models of the consumers' purchase decision journey are incomplete. They fail to account for these trends and this phenomenon. Instead, we propose the diagram shown in Figure 1.3.

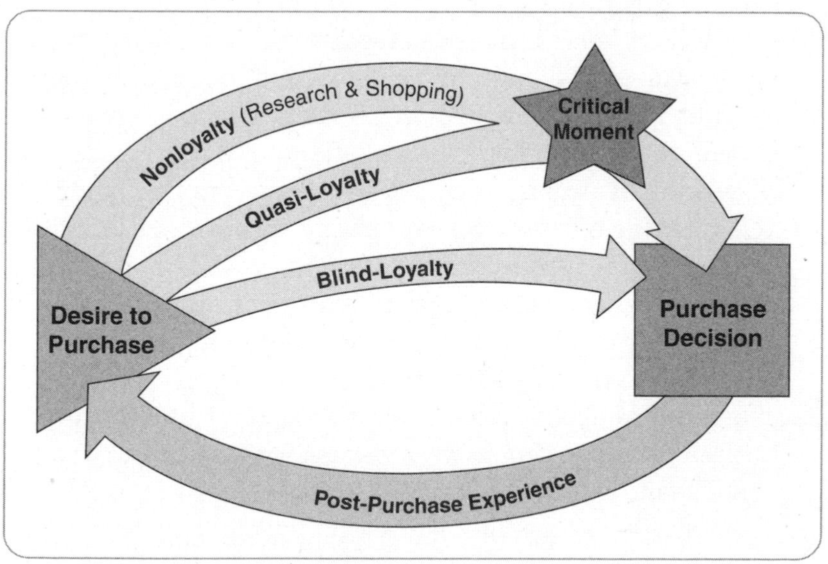

FIGURE 1.3 The New Consumer's Decision Journey: With brand loyalty diminishing, purchase decisions are increasingly driven by a single *critical moment* that is generally influenced by digital channels.

As a result of the modern digital ecosystem, consumers with the intention to buy now have three distinct paths when deciding to repurchase a given type of product:

1. **Nonloyalty:** Consumers dissatisfied with a previous purchase, just like first-time buyers of a particular product type, engage in thorough research using all information available to them in order to help make a good decision. Digital and traditional marketing channels together culminate in a single value proposition that influences the consumer at the moment of purchase.
2. **Blind-Loyalty:** Some consumers, due to lack of access to (or desire to use) technology, or due to absolute brand loyalty, will continue to repurchase the same brand's product over and over without ever considering alternatives. They enter the *blind-loyalty loop* and stay there until they feel their brand disappoints them in some way. Through quality products, excellent customer service, and a complete brand experience, all brands should strive to put their customers here. That said, a rapidly shrinking percentage of consumers fall into this category, and in today's digital world, relying on blind loyalty is dangerous and often more than we can hope for.
3. **Quasi-Loyalty:** In today's digital world, an increasing percentage of consumers are happy with the last brand purchase they made, but can still be swayed by various factors to try a different brand's product instead. Just a decade ago, most of these consumers would have likely fallen into the blind-loyalty loop and repurchased a brand's product without question. Today, these consumers often have a *critical moment* just prior to purchase. Using the abundance of information available to them at this moment, the consumer will either decide that they are happy repurchasing the same product, or can be swayed by one or more factors to purchase a different brand's product. For quasi-loyalists, it can be negative information about your brand, or positive information

> about another brand, that determines the outcome. Google calls this critical moment the *Zero Moment of Truth* (ZMOT). Whatever you call this critical moment, the factors that determine its outcome are driven by—you guessed it—digital marketing.

At the critical moment, the consumer may visit your website from her laptop at home or her mobile device. She may access social sentiments from her peers on Facebook and Twitter. She may look at real-time pricing information at local stores and on the web, or access available coupons for this particular product type. She may also run a search that reveals the latest news about your product or product category, or recent reviews posted by purchasers. At this critical moment, she may even be recommended similar or better-rated products by an eRetailer or mobile shopping app. All of your digital properties, paid, owned, and earned, as well as those of your peers, are fair game at the critical moment. News, posts, tweets, pricing, coupons, reviews, product releases, and viral media—all accessible in 60 seconds or less—can impact the consumer's decision to remain loyal to your brand or ditch it for something else. For this reason, it is absolutely crucial that brands have their digital ducks in a row to be prepared for that critical moment, else these otherwise loyal consumers will be swayed by the plethora of real-time information at their fingertips.

Marketers are beginning to understand the impact that digital channels have on consumers in the active evaluation phase. Those who understand only that much are on the right track, but are missing the true value of digital marketing. The ability to influence critical moment outcomes will undoubtedly separate brands that will persist into the 2020s from those that will slowly sink into the annals of history.

Digital marketing can (and must) be used in the traditional sense to help create, solidify, and perpetuate a cohesive brand image. However, we must remember that digital channels are generally on-demand, and often reach our consumers at the critical time in their purchase cycles. Most brands underinvest in digital strategies, and for them digital investments will garner better returns, dollar for dollar, than traditional alternatives. How do we as marketers utilize digital channels to accomplish these two goals? The next chapter explores necessary principles for marketing success in our digital world.

ENDNOTES

1. "This Time It's Personal: From Consumer to Co-Creator." Ernst and Young, March 2012.

CHAPTER 2

MARKETING STRATEGIES FOR A DIGITAL WORLD

—by Alexander Kates and Eric Greenberg

STATE OF THE MODERN DIGITAL ECOSYSTEM

Enter the digital age. The new digital consumers are super-empowered, ultra-informed, and hyper-connected. The information they seek is perpetually at their fingertips. Any questions they seek to answer, or any information they wish to obtain to aid in making a purchase decision, are a mere few clicks away on their always-connected devices. How do today's brands build awareness, foster loyalty, and fabricate a positive image in a world where consumers hold all of the cards?

The role of the marketer has traditionally started with creative excellence. Marketing teams would fabricate a tangible and unified brand image they felt consumers would identify with. Creative content would be tailored around this image. Following the fabrication of creative, the marketer's role centered on efficient allocation of budget into media channels. Allocations were typically based on market research and historical data. The brand image would then be pushed through these channels to reach consumers.

Currently, organizations are being rapidly educated about the importance and scale of digital channels. They are learning about the multitude of new platforms spanning social and mobile platforms, and the colossal impact these platforms have on the modern consumer. Companies are slowly but surely coming to terms with the reality that these technologies and platforms are here to stay. The strategic answer, companies seem to conclude, is to embrace these new technologies by devoting a portion of their marketing budgets and human capital to each of these channels (see Figure 2.1).

However, companies are riddled with stodgy traditional marketers skeptical of anything digital, and taking this step is a slow and cumbersome process. Nevertheless, getting a company's brand image in front of consumers where they spend their time has always been the marketer's task, so expanding the brand's reach into these new channels makes perfect sense. Today, even

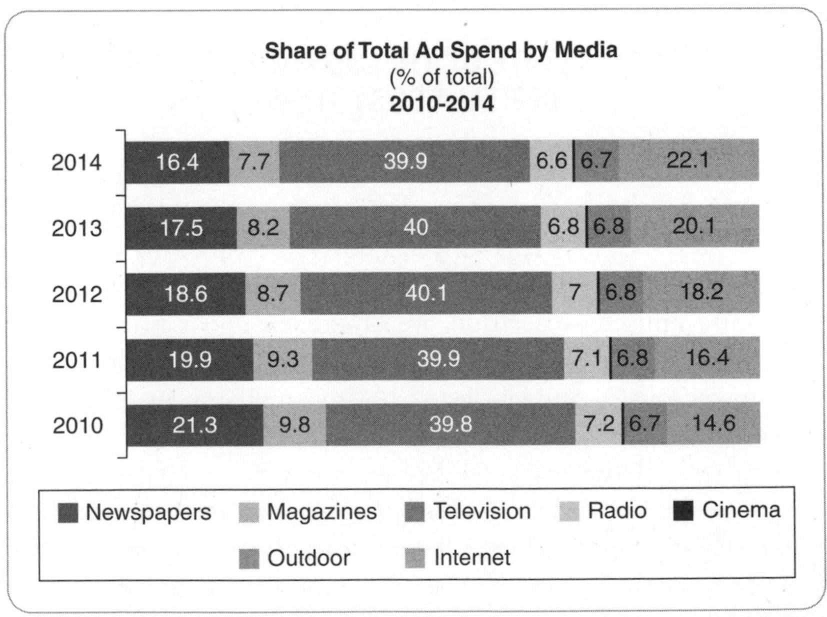

FIGURE 2.1 Marketing Investments: Digital strategies have a rapidly growing share of the total marketing spend, but it is still dwarfed by dollars spent in traditional media.[1]

the most dogged senior marketers are beginning to accept that digital strategies are important, even if they haven't yet taken action to reflect the pervasiveness of the digital world.

That said, most studies conclude that brands, including large Fortune 500 brands, don't have clearly defined strategies for digital channels. Many of the brands that do attempt to employ digital jump into it blindly and in a piecemeal fashion, without a clear overarching plan. They don't dive in hastily because they embrace a test-and-learn or fail-quickly methodology, but rather because they feel the need to quickly catch up and reside in channels where consumers spend their time. While the attempt is commendable, it often ends in a cornucopia of wasted advertising dollars. If the campaign had been planned correctly and holistically, it could have resulted in a great success for the brand.

On the other hand, some innovative marketers at top firms are taking considered action. They recognize that each of these new digital channels is unique, and requires a unique strategy to attack effectively. Keeping the overall goals of marketing in mind, these marketers understand that digital channels need to be leveraged together as a whole to promote a unified brand image to consumers.

Perhaps this is a good start, but it's *only* a start—the tip of a colossal digital iceberg that few companies have explored beneath the water's surface.

BEING LIQUID: THE MARKETER'S NEW ROLE

The answer is not simply to fabricate a solid and cohesive brand strategy that leverages digital channels as a medium. A unified brand strategy is important, but in this new digital world, it is no longer solely the marketer's job to craft that image.

Today, marketers share responsibility for the creation of the brand image with their own public relations departments, legal and compliance teams, and sales forces. They share it with their chief executives and first-year employees. But most importantly, they share this responsibility with their consumers and clients, including brand advocates and critics.

A clear division of roles within the organization is still incredibly important, but today every stakeholder of an organization plays a role in crafting, shaping, and perpetuating a brand image. Companies like Zappos have done this incredibly well by creating a culture in every part of the organization that always seeks to exceed expectations.

So where does this leave the role of the marketer? Is the marketing department less important in this new digital world?

It's actually quite the opposite. The role of the marketer has changed—or rather—has *expanded.* Crafting a brand image, and pushing that message through channels, was the marketer's role under the old paradigm. Unfortunately, this no longer garners results the way it used to. Today, marketers are the seeds of a brand's image. They are storytellers, curators, perpetuators, and enthusiasts. They feed messages into channels in a natural way and let the other stakeholders run with them. They listen to and facilitate conversations, and optimize and share them strategically to maximize impact. Lastly, they analyze the reach of those conversations using data, and further optimize their behaviors accordingly.

Bruce Lee, the sensational martial arts icon of the 1970s, said this:

> Don't get set into one form. Adapt it, and build your own. Let it grow, and be like water. Empty your mind, be formless, shapeless —like water. Now, you put water in a cup, it becomes the cup; You put water into a bottle, it becomes the bottle; You put it in a teapot, it becomes the teapot. Now water can flow or it can crash. Be water, my friend.

It turns out the same mindset that makes a great Jeet Kune Do practitioner also makes a great digital marketer. Marketers in the digital age must be *like water.* They must ebb, flow, and adapt their roles and behaviors on a constant basis. They must spread their activities over a wide range of channels and content types, see which attract the most interest, and run with what works. Planning exact channel strategies, and deciding which content must be poured into which channels beforehand, is a mistake. Instead, it is the marketer's role to test everything, measure where

the stakeholders take things, and allocate accordingly. It's all about testing, gathering data, refining strategy, and finally retesting—and it must be done constantly, consistently, and in very small increments. This concept forms the basis of what we call the modern *liquid marketer.*

Content strategy must also be liquid, like water. Coca-Cola was the first company to embrace the concept of *liquid content.* According to Coke executives, the job of the marketer starts with dreaming up or discovering small bits of content that are so interesting and viral, they simply beg to be shared. When bits and pieces of this content become hits among the general public and go viral, they often grow into something far bigger than the marketer ever imagined. Furthermore, despite marketers directing the conversations, the channels this spreads to and gains traction in are often unpredictable. The marketer can steer things in a desirable direction, but it is often beneficial to let this liquid content flow where it may to some extent.

Individually these bits of liquid content don't usually say too much. They may only represent a fraction of one dimension of the brand's image, and even that may take a backseat to the interesting nature of the content itself. For instance, for Coca-Cola, that dimension may be that "Coke makes people happy." There may be many bits of content spread around the web to demonstrate this: from stories, to user-generated videos, to creative company-crafted clips, to contests and giveaways. A few will work, and others will not—the marketers just run with those that do. They do this by curating the message, stirring up conversation, and directing the conversations into directions and channels that will perpetuate that message. Under a liquid mindset, the marketer is more of an active facilitator than an all-powerful monarch, but the role is just as important.

However, a single piece of viral content only demonstrates, and perhaps indirectly, one dimension of the complete Coca-Cola brand image the company wants to portray. Coke may also want to remind people that their product tastes good, is manufactured to the highest quality, or is environmentally friendly. These messages can come from different content seeded throughout the web that, hopefully, catches on as well. Together, these pieces of liquid content obtained from various sources and channels all come

together in the consumer's mind to form the solidified brand image that the company was going for the entire time. The liquid marketer's role is to nurture and mold the conversations surrounding liquid content, and ultimately to help consumers form the intended brand image on their own. Clever, isn't it?

Best of all—since the information comes from natural consumer channels, and much of it can be user-generated, the message seems more trustworthy. User-generated content, along with effective use of digital channels, can help build trust by making the messages appear less forced than those pushed through traditional channels. Furthermore, the immense reach of content under this schema often results in a brand gaining a disproportionate share of popular culture—much like it has for Coke.

Asidc from marketers and content adopting liquid properties, companies themselves must adopt liquid principles at the very core of their operations to make it all work. Organizational structures, budgeting procedures, HR compensation polices, legal and compliance principles, and upper-management philosophies must all be reformed to operate in this fast-paced digital world. Thinking that worked under the old paradigm may not anymore. The best organizations today rely on continuous, data-driven testing and refinement, and remain as flexible as possible to account for the results of that testing. It's certainly easier said than done, but the more an entire organization is *like water*, and can overcome its size to embrace agility, the more likely it is to survive and thrive in the modern digital ecosystem.

A liquid mindset—liquid content, curated by liquid marketers, within a liquid organization—is a great foundation for creating effective digital strategy in today's digital world.

GETTING STARTED: LEARNING BY EXAMPLE

We marketers are not always so keenly aware of just how fast the world is changing, but we are all indeed aware of the changes. They are impossible to ignore, after all. Every book, newspaper article, and blog entry highlights how crucial digital channels have become

to business and consumption. These sources inform us how behind the times our organizations are. They urge us to act, and swiftly, lest we be left in the dust by the competition. In response, companies have scrambled to jump on the digital bandwagon.

And jump we must. But leaping whole hog into digital, simply by dumping resources and human capital into digital channels, is not the answer. It is certainly true that digital media will continue to play a colossal role in business, and that the proportion of interaction in digital channels will continue to accelerate. We hope that all companies, large and small, will begin to put more emphasis and resources toward digital strategies once they learn about how to effectively utilize these channels. However *doing it right* and simply *doing it* are worlds apart, rather than degrees of the same continuum. The most alarming observation is just how few companies are doing it right.

We'd like to share a small example with you from our personal experience—not from a consultant's point of view—but rather, from a consumer's.

> For *Small Business Saturday* this past year, FedEx wanted to show its support of small businesses by offering American Express gift cards, in $25 denominations, to the first 30,000 people to "like" its Facebook page and fill out a short form. Including logistical expenses, FedEx invested a cool $1 million in the campaign. When companies are giving away free cash these days, word travels around the web, and *fast.* Blogs, news sites, and social deal and coupon sites all raved about FedEx's generosity and support of small business. FedEx assumed it would garner as many as 30,000 new *likes*, enjoy some great press, and build brand loyalty among new and existing customers. Sounds like a great move for FedEx, doesn't it?
>
> On November 26th, FedEx announced that it would open up the contest at sharply 1:30 p.m. EST. Chatter (and *likes*) began to rapidly increase leading up to the 1:30 p.m. *golden time.* When 1:30 p.m. rolled around, it was estimated that nearly 300,000 people were trying to access the form at once. The servers FedEx was using were not nearly prepared for that kind of traffic. They crashed almost immediately.

> Hundreds of thousands of disgruntled visitors, many of whom had shifted around their Saturday schedules in hopes of obtaining free cash, fanatically tried refreshing their browsers for nearly forty minutes. The hopeful gift-card receivers began to express their frustration and discontent at 1:30 p.m., and over the course of the next hour, the comments on the FedEx Facebook page went from frustrated to hateful. Many angered visitors seized the opportunity to post their FedEx horror stories and bash the brand on its own turf while sentiments were low.
>
> At around 3:00 p.m., FedEx made a post to their page announcing that all 30,000 gift cards had been claimed. Even those who received the gift cards felt that the promotion was poorly run and required a great deal of hassle. Many others complained on the FedEx page months later, claiming that they never received the gift cards they were promised.

The real question here is: What did this campaign do for the FedEx brand? They spent $1 million, plus the resources to ship 30,000 gift cards, not to mention the labor required to put together the campaign. At the end of the day, FedEx was left with approximately 20,000 gift-card receivers whose sentiments ranged from neutral to grateful (many were not received, and many Internet-savvy folks received more than one). FedEx was also left with about 280,000 extremely frustrated and disgruntled people who felt that the company had cheated them and wasted their time. In total, about 15,000 of these frustrated individuals made snarky or hateful comments on the FedEx Facebook page, which were collectively viewed by several million visitors. Many more of those 280,000 tweeted about it or shared their discontent via some other social media channel.

The real kicker is that the campaign likely did absolutely nothing to build brand loyalty. The majority of those attempting to acquire gift cards were not brand evangelists or even loyal FedEx customers; they were bargain hunters, deal-forum goers, social news readers, and Facebook junkies looking for a free handout. The gift cards were not FedEx branded, and carried no restrictions on how the money could be spent. The error was both in the design of the campaign, and in the execution. In the end, the campaign was a complete bust for FedEx and its brand image (albeit a small one). It did nothing to secure new customers or cultivate brand loyalty, and caused a lot of negative sentiment and social chatter.

So, what could FedEx have done with their $1 million for *Small Business Saturday* that would have been an effective social media campaign for the brand?

Perhaps they could have held a one-day contest in which participants submitted their story about how they use FedEx services to further their small business or cause. Stories could be submitted via photo, video, or written text using a form on the FedEx Facebook page. The top 20 stories, chosen by qualified FedEx employees, could be posted to the Facebook Page to allow page visitors to vote (via *likes*) on their favorites. The authors of the stories receiving the most votes could receive something nice, like an all-expenses-paid vacation that includes a trip to FedEx headquarters, or perhaps a lifetime's worth of shipping credit with FedEx. We recommend making the remainder of the top 20 instant winners for larger-denomination gift cards. Additionally, everyone who submitted a story that didn't make the top 20 would be entered into a drawing to win one of a several thousand larger-denomination branded FedEx gift cards.

In a scenario such as this, there will always be the large majority that submit their stories but don't win the voting contest or the drawing. For such individuals, we'd recommend sending them small-denomination FedEx gift cards anyway (maybe $10 or $25). Everyone who votes on stories could receive an exclusive discount coupon by e-mail or via Facebook, reiterating the winning stories/quotations and thanking them for their loyalty and support.

Using this new strategy, FedEx wins all around. The entries are limited primarily to FedEx customers, and the FedEx Facebook page gets flooded with twenty glowing stories, photos, and quotations for an entire day. FedEx page visitors get to read these warm stories and vote on their favorites, engaging them and simultaneously promoting the brand to them via their peers.

The chance to win gift cards in a drawing is enough to dramatically improve traffic and submissions—and the winning recipients will be thrilled with their gift cards. The story submitters that didn't win—all loyal FedEx customers submitting success stories—will be delighted to receive a thank-you letter and gift card in the mail that they didn't expect. People love nothing more than unexpected free cash in the mail, and would never forget the company that sent it to them (especially if the gift card is company-branded). It's a nice way of rewarding loyal customers and helping to recruit new brand champions, while simultaneously promoting brand goodwill.

Perhaps most importantly, with this approach no one feels cheated. Everyone submitting stories is a winner to some degree, and the entire group is segmented (and rewarded) based on their engagement level in the campaign. Not a single person feels like their time was wasted with technical or logistical bottlenecks.

This type of campaign would likely identify and develop new brand evangelists and forever-loyal FedEx customers who would spread positive brand sentiment. After all, it is always good practice to nurture and reward evangelists who collectively do so much good for your brand. The end result, without a doubt, is long-term Return on Investment (ROI) on the $1 million spent for this small campaign. Using social media (or any digital channel) correctly is simply a matter of careful campaign design, solid execution, and planned measurement techniques.

THE ULTIMATE GOAL OF DIGITAL MARKETING: ROI

Effective design of digital marketing campaigns is only one piece of the pie—and it's not the only piece companies should be putting on their plates at the outset.

Company decision-makers must have a solid method of deciding what types of campaigns are worth pursuing, and which digital strategies should garner initial investments. Deciding where to allocate budget requires a way to determine comparative effectiveness among other digital (and traditional) campaign options. Some sort of universal measure must be instituted across the entire organization to effectively allocate resources. Although this seems obvious, few companies actually do this in practice. According to a Columbia University study, 65 percent of marketers at Fortune 500 companies say that comparing effectiveness of digital media campaigns is "a major challenge" for their business. While proper measurement may not be easy, it is absolutely critical to marketing success.

Just as digital marketing is still marketing, it is important to remember that marketing investments, whether they're made in digital channels or otherwise, require a positive return on those investments. ROI is the ultimate goal of any digital marketing campaign, just as it is the goal of any traditional marketing campaign or investment. Justification for initial investment in digital initiatives should be crafted and judged in much the same way as traditional ones—using ROI.

Most digital marketers, including many seasoned digital experts, do not use ROI as the lowest common denominator for comparison. According to the Columbia University study, only 43 percent of large organizations base their marketing budgets on some sort of ROI analysis;[2] for digital initiatives, that percentage is much smaller —most likely in the single digits. Many marketers believe that reasonable goals for a Facebook campaign are to garner "likes," generate leads, build brand loyalty, or stimulate product trial. Twitter campaigns often seek to obtain followers or raise awareness. Search campaigns often attempt to increase traffic to the company's webpage or get more blog subscribers. No wonder companies have trouble comparing the relative effectiveness of digital initiatives!

To make matters worse, marketers make the mistake of trying to use these nebulous goals to justify digital marketing spending to management. Many projects get approved that shouldn't be due to digital marketing hype, and many more potentially lucrative projects get rejected because management feels it cannot justify the resource allocation.

Senior management might not understand digital marketing—they may not even be able to distinguish an iPad from a Kindle in some cases—but they are keenly aware of something many marketers forget: Shareholders are not going to be appeased by growth in Twitter followers. Owners won't be happy with vague measures of increased awareness. Company expenses can't be offset with any number of Facebook "likes." Senior management wants to know how spending on a campaign is going to impact sales, and ultimately, the bottom line. Marketers and management are saying the same thing, but the message isn't coming across. If increasing sales is the ultimate goal, shouldn't we always evaluate digital marketing, and all marketing for that matter, through an ROI lens? It's the universal language that marketers, management, and shareholders can all understand. We could refine our earlier digital glasses analogy by saying that the new digital paradigm requires that we view marketing through digital, *ROI-tinted* lenses.

Critics of this approach cite how traditional ROI metrics and formulas fail to account for the complexity and unknown variables inherent in many digital strategies. They aren't wrong. Correctly evaluating ROI with any degree of accuracy requires a great deal of measurement, a slew of tools, some complicated math, and a lot of out-of-the-box thinking. We could devote an entire book to this topic alone. That said, attempting to measure ROI is an absolutely essential step toward effective digital decision-making.

Estimates for ROI should be built directly into campaign design from the outset. For instance, if a campaign involves garnering Facebook *likes*, the value of an incremental *like* should be estimated. Conversion data from your brand's previous Facebook campaigns, comparable third-party campaigns, or campaigns utilizing other channels, might shed light on the probability of a Facebook *like* or impression converting to a sale. By estimating this probability of turning a *like* or impression into an actual customer, your customer cost of acquisition (COA) for this campaign can be set against customer lifetime value (CLTV) estimates to evaluate part of this campaign's ROI. In essence, using what you *can* measure to estimate what you *can't* can help project and measure ROI to some extent. Building measurement and tracking into digital campaigns will help tremendously in backing into ROI estimates, improving projection accuracy, and justifying campaign potential to senior management.

Channel Interaction as a Part of ROI Calculation

Another important component of estimating and measuring campaign ROI is *channel interaction. Interaction* is a term commonly used in statistics to demonstrate the impact multiple variables have on one another. In the case of marketing measurement, these variables are the various digital marketing channels. No individual channel operates in a vacuum. For example, to estimate the impact of a video posted on a brand's YouTube channel, we certainly must estimate how the number of views or shares translates into sales using the aforementioned methodology. However, we must also ask: How are users getting to this video? Which media is the traffic coming from? After viewing the video, where do the users head next?

Views of this video can lead to visits to the brand's Facebook page, and perhaps posts or *likes*. They might lead to searches on Google, followers on Twitter, or visits to the brand's website. The trail of actions users take must also be quantified to accurately assess the ROI potential of a given investment in any particular channel.

All channels, including traditional channels, are linked to every other in some way (though traditional media advertising generally links forward to digital properties, and not vice versa). Our data analyses show certain general trends about how actions in each channel lead to specific actions in other digital channels, but specific campaign design also plays a crucial role in how one channel interacts with another. Using collected data in conjunction with typical interaction paths, the entire marketing ecosystem of a brand can be modeled and mapped visually, showing how channels interact with one another. The result is a complicated and irrevocably intertwined network of interactions between channels that provides a complete picture of how investments will impact the entire ecosystem. Once modeled in this way, it is much easier to estimate how a particular campaign or investment might impact overall results. This is marketing mix modeling for the digital age, and is more important than ever for today's brands.

Case Study: Measuring ROI of a Digital Campaign

To give an example, let's recall the recommendation we made for FedEx's *Small Business Saturday* $1 million Facebook campaign. We'd expect the campaign to receive a total of 7.5 million impressions, based on publicly available data for Facebook campaigns undertaken by other brands, adjusted for the reach of FedEx's 375,000 current *likes* and the average virility of this type of campaign. We're keeping in mind that if many more news outlets than we project pick up on this campaign, the number of impressions could grow well beyond this estimate—but the 7.5 million impressions is a good starting point. Fortunately, accuracy in the number and flow of impressions can be measured post-campaign using Facebook's built-in analytics. We'd project receiving 7,500 story submissions and 2.5 million votes on top stories from 1 million voters, again using internal and external data for Facebook contest conversions, and keeping in mind the time and effort related to participation in this particular campaign on behalf of page visitors.

Recall that all of these 7,500 story submitters will receive a gift card in some denomination, whether they were voting winners, drawing winners, or neither and hence unexpected small-denomination gift card recipients. Let's estimate the ROI from these 7,500 recipients: Internal data shows that brand *loyalists* spend $250 each year on FedEx services, and brand *evangelists* spend twice that on average in addition to converting 20-or-so fence-sitters to loyalists each year. If we estimate that the probability of turning one of those 7,500 gift-card recipients who isn't already a loyalist or evangelist into one of these two categories (let's say 200 evangelists and 1,500 loyalists), then we expect ~$1.5 million in incremental sales over the next 12 months due directly to these 7,500 customers who received gift cards.

For the one million visitors who voted and didn't submit stories or receive gift cards, but instead got an e-mail coupon, we can begin our calculation using data that shows previous targeted e-mail campaigns involving discounts resulted in 9 percent conversion. After one-third of this is subtracted for cannibalization of existing business, this translates to about 60,000 conversions at an average FedEx spend of $17 each, or about $1 million in incremental revenue. Adding the $1.5 million from gift-card recipients to the $1 million from the e-mail endeavor, we'd expect a total of $2.5 million in incremental revenue in this next year alone from this campaign. This translates to an ROI of 150 percent on the initial $1 million investment.

We can go a step further to tie in customer lifetime value (CLTV) and project the present value of future sales made by newly acquired customers. To do so, we can use typical numbers like 10 percent yearly customer churn in conjunction with discounted cash flow models to determine how much more we'd hope to gain in the long run from this campaign. We should also account for channel interaction by tracking the expected and actual flow of these 7.5 million impressions into other digital channels, and add the revenue potential garnered by those secondary channels to the aforementioned $2.5 million. Keep in mind that the above ROI calculation also ignores goodwill generated by the campaign among nonparticipants who read or hear about it afterward, which we'd hope to turn into even more sales over the long term. With additional effort to quantify a few assumptions, intangibles like goodwill can also be internalized in the ROI calculation. Thus, using a combination of internal data, external studies, and some marketing logic, we have some general numbers to work with and a basis for comparing this campaign with other campaign options.

The ROI Approach in Practice

In a perfect world, digital initiatives would be launched quickly, and budgets and strategies would be continuously refined. However, we don't live in a perfect world. Established procedures at companies necessitate navigating many hurdles to get an initial green light, and budgets must be set aside long in advance to even get started. Marketers must adjust their pitches to senior management in order to even allow digital strategies to be considered.

Those pitches should absolutely, without exception, include ROI estimates. We urge senior managers to consider these estimates carefully, and to understand that projected ROI will be adjusted as the campaign progresses.

We wouldn't expect laser-accurate ROI estimates, and neither does your senior management team. Our solemn advice to marketers everywhere is to do everything possible to start using ROI as the lowest-level basis for comparison. When beginning to utilize this approach, the technique will be immediately useful, but confidence in your ROI estimates may be relatively low. However, a focus on building measurement into digital campaigns, and examining this internal data over time, will continually improve accuracy. Incorporating proxy measurements and external findings will further augment the efficacy of your predictions, especially when internal data is sparse.

It's important to keep in mind that not every company should be in every digital channel, and not every investment in the proper digital channel is justified. Using projected ROI as the lowest common denominator will help management decide which digital channels to focus on, how to allocate resources, and which campaigns to pursue as a part of the overall marketing mix. Furthermore, you'll be speaking a language management can understand, which is an essential step toward generating results from your marketing ideas. Again, the goal isn't perfect accuracy, but rather an estimate that can be compared, apples-to-apples, to all other marketing opportunities. The result is smarter decision making, which should lead to greater marketing ROI in the long term for your business. Making these estimates better than other brands will undoubtedly allow you to stay one step ahead of the competition.

A FRAMEWORK FOR DIGITAL SUCCESS

Now that you've gotten a feel for both qualitative and quantitative strategies for digital marketing success, it's time to pull it all together strategically to garner real results. Before jumping into any campaign, however, it is absolutely essential to understand your customer through thorough research and analysis. You will gain a better understanding of the people purchasing your products and services by using the data collected from your marketing campaigns, but without a comprehensive understanding of your customer from the outset, your first attempts are far less likely to see positive results. The framework for strategic digital marking success includes four fundamental steps toward a complete digital marketing strategy:

1. **Create stories for your brand:** Using liquid principles, merge your marketing creativity with ideas garnered by listening to your community to create stories that stick.
2. **Feed and curate digital channels:** Strategically place, manage, and perpetuate the stories in several digital channels. Combine planned campaigns with unplanned virility and direct both toward your desired brand image goals.
3. **Determine ROI of strategies:** Estimate sales using collected data and industry insights. Determine channel interactions and long-term gains from customer acquisitions, and add them to estimated sales to determine ROI.
4. **Test, measure, and refine:** Use analytics to measure impressions, results, and traffic flows. Manage stories, refine channel allocations, and improve ROI estimates using the collected data.

These steps are listed numerically to give you a sense of their typical flow, but in reality all four happen simultaneously and continuously, as shown in Figure 2.2. Testing, measurement, and refinement are at the center of the diagram because all three of the other stages should be constantly and consistently measured and improved. This simple model can be used as a starting point for beginning to understand and plan digital strategy.

In Chapter 3, we delve deeper into content marketing strategy, and demonstrate how brands can create viral and sticky stories in today's digital ecosystem.

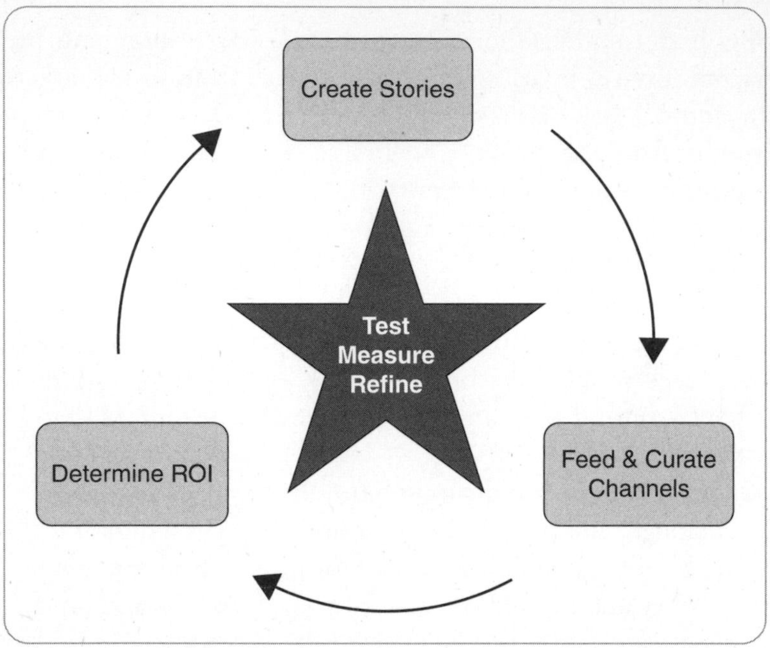

FIGURE 2.2 Liquid Digital Strategy Framework: Marketers today must create sticky stories, feed and curate channels, and measure ROI of investments, all while testing, measuring, and refining.

ENDNOTES

1. http://www.marketingcharts.com/wp/television/tvs-share-of-global-ad-spend-to-stall–20265/
2. http://www.iab.net/media/file/2012-BRITE-NYAMA-Marketing-ROI-Study.pdf

CHAPTER 3

MANAGING CONTENT IN A DIGITAL AGE

—by Neil Perkin

The model of paid, owned, and earned media has rapidly become the default way of viewing the communications landscape amongst clients and their agencies alike. In this useful model, *paid media* can be understood to be paid-for communication that is placed in third-party digital and nondigital channels. *Owned media* defines those brand assets established by brand owners that can enable direct contact with consumers (including corporate and brand websites, customer databases and CRM practices, and brand communities, including those established on social networks). Lastly, *earned media* relates to the content, data, and conversation created by the brand's customers' word of mouth and brand advocacy, and endorsements and reviews from other third parties.

There can be little doubt that whilst paid media remains a critical part of the media mix, there has more recently been a growing focus of brands on the owned and earned elements of this model. As an example, a recent Forbes article on Nike's often-revolutionary marketing approaches[1] notes how Nike's U.S. spending on TV and print advertising had dropped by 40 percent in just three years, even as its total marketing budget has increased to a record $2.4 billion. Meanwhile, according to *AdvertisingAge* estimates, in 2010 Nike spent a greater proportion of its U.S. advertising budget on "nontraditional" advertising than any other top 100 U.S. advertiser (a spend of nearly $800 million). Much of this nontraditional spend was focused on creating owned assets that facilitate an ongoing relationship with the Nike customer. Similarly, the rapid growth in advertiser focus over recent years on creating content, brand equity, and value through social media channels is evidence of the growth in importance of earned media.

While paid, owned, and earned is a useful framework for categorizing media channels and activity, the most interesting spaces in modern media occur where they overlap and are structured to work seamlessly together so that content, conversation, and data can flow smoothly.

Rapidly developing channels, such as so-called "native advertising," that cross the realm between paid and earned media, are just one example of this. In late 2012, digital advertising firm Solve Media defined native advertising as: "…a specific mode of monetization that aims to augment user experience by providing value through relevant content delivered in-stream."[2]

In effect, native advertising utilizes formats that reference the unique editorial and design features of the host site or channel in order to integrate commercial messaging within news and content streams. The growth in native formats, such as Facebook-promoted posts (which enable advertisers to amplify their own posts so that they appear in a greater number of users' newsfeeds) illustrates their potential, particularly in mobile applications where the integration of commercial formats within content feeds makes for an effective small-screen format.

Similarly, Buzzfeed, working directly with advertisers to create customized commercial content that integrates into the wider flow of noncommercial content, has shown the potential of creating unique formats using this native concept. Native advertising is a new, digitally native form of advertorial advertising that can be used both to generate and amplify earned media conversation through paid-for advertising formats.

As far back as 2003, Seth Godin was writing (in *Purple Cow: Transform Your Business by Being Remarkable*[3]) about how, if the web is a mass of conversations, the way in which you market in that environment is to create content that is remarkable, worth talking about, and spreading. Much has been said around this basic concept since then, but we're now seeing an increasing number of intelligent executions that bring it to life—notably through adept forms of curation, dynamic content, widgets, mashups, and visualizations that amplify paid and owned media through earned media.

In a research report entitled "The Converged Media Imperative" published in mid-2012, "Altimeter group describes how the paid media, which has traditionally taken a front seat in marketing initiatives, now requires the integrated support of owned and earned media channels in order to optimize effectiveness:

> While consumers distinguish less and less between these channels, marketers remain specialized in one medium at the expense of the others. Rather than allow campaigns to be driven by paid media, marketers must now develop scale and expertise in owned and earned media to drive effectiveness, cultivate creative ideas, assess customer needs, cultivate influencers, develop reach, achieve authenticity and cut through clutter.[4]

Many of the most innovative modern marketing and media solutions are derived from an in-depth understanding of not just one of these constituent parts, but all three. Such solutions capitalize on an adept use of the one thing that sits at the nexus of all three elements: content.

THE IMPORTANCE OF CONTENT MARKETING

With content increasingly positioned at the center of the digital marketing universe, its ever-growing significance to marketers is reflected in an increasing focus on the emerging discipline of content marketing. The Content Marketing Institute has derived a pithy one-sentence definition of this emerging field:[5] "Content marketing is a marketing technique of creating and distributing relevant and valuable content to attract, acquire, and engage a clearly defined and understood target audience—with the objective of driving profitable customer action."

Data from Econsultancy demonstrates just how important content marketing now is. A survey of 700 marketers and business

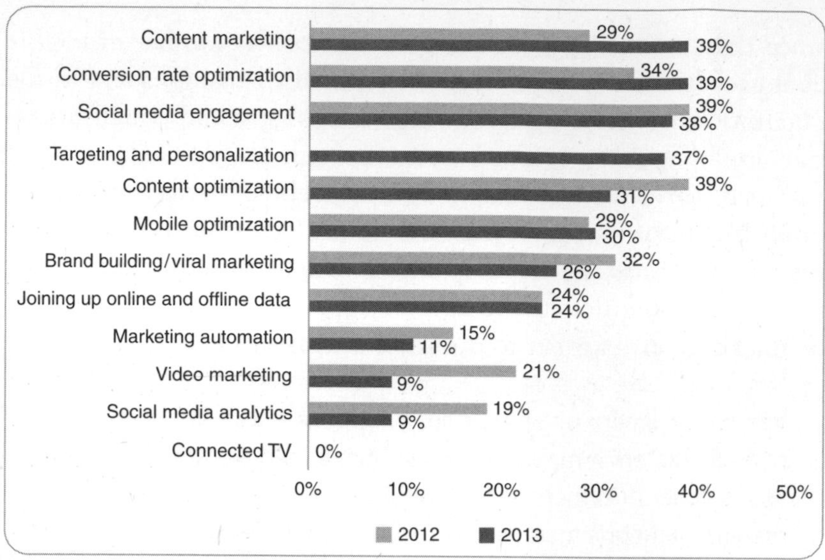

FIGURE 3.1 Content Marketing as a Priority: Content marketing topped the list of marketing initiatives in 2012 and 2013, and continues to grow in perceived importance.

professionals[6] (based mostly in Europe and the U.S.) at the beginning of 2013, asked in-house marketers to name their top priorities for the coming year. Content marketing was right at the top of the list, with the proportion of marketers naming it as a priority up from 29 percent in 2012, to 39 percent in 2013.

The Econsultancy Content Marketing Survey Report,[7] published in late 2012 and based on a survey of more than 1300 marketing professionals around the world, reiterated the fact that content marketing is increasingly seen as a discipline in its own right. Over 90 percent of respondents to that survey believed that content marketing will become more important over the next 12 months, and almost three-quarters (73 percent) agreed that "brands are becoming publishers." Despite this clear signal, the challenges inherent in an early stage, emerging disciplines were also evident. Only a minority (38 percent) of the companies in that survey reported having a defined content marketing strategy in place. Less than half (46 percent) had dedicated individuals, and even fewer (34 percent) dedicated budgets to this emerging practice.

As content marketing becomes an increasingly significant part of the wider marketing mix, it brings with it a requirement for organizations to consider not only the resourcing required to fully optimize the brand content opportunity, but also the skills and processes needed to adapt existing marketing practice. This includes incorporating more editorially driven workflows, and the understanding to develop connected and optimized distribution strategies across multiple platforms that incorporate elements of public relations, search engine optimization, social media strategy, and paid media activity. Without an approach that integrates activity seamlessly across paid, owned, and earned media channels, and one which capitalizes on the opportunity provided by the spaces in between, realizing the full potential of a content marketing strategy is impossible.

HOLISTIC LIQUID CONTENT STRATEGIES AND FRAMEWORKS

There are some useful frameworks which marketers can adopt in order to fully realize the opportunity presented by a well-rounded content strategy.

Stock and Flow

When considering the development of content strategy, one of the initial considerations for any marketer is that not all content is the same. In order to capitalize on the many different forms of content that a brand may use, and the opportunity inherent in realizing a well-rounded distribution strategy, it's useful to think of content in terms of *stock* and *flow*.

Stock and flow are concepts more readily seen and used in the fields of finance, economics, and accounting. In this context, stock may be understood to be a variable or quantity that is measured at one point in time, but that may well have accumulated value over time. Flow, on the other hand, relates to a variable which is measured over a unit or interval of time, and so often relates to the rate or speed of change in a given asset.

In 2010, technologist Robin Sloan wrote a Snarkmarket post[8] that transposed these terms to create an analogy for the characteristics inherent in modern media. In doing so, he framed a useful way for brands to consider their own content assets and strategy.

"Stock," said Sloan "…is the durable stuff. It's the content you produce that's as interesting in two months (or two years) as it is today. It's what people discover via search. It's what spreads slowly but surely, building fans over time."

Flow, however, is "…the feed. It's the posts and the tweets. It's the stream of daily and sub-daily updates that remind people that you exist."

In the context of content strategy, therefore, stock content might be considered to be the useful content assets created by an organization that can bring long-term value back to the company, often in the form of customers, lead generation, traffic to owned media assets, and visibility (in terms of ranking on search engines). Such content may include directories, guides, reports, white papers, thought-leadership pieces, or simply unique and useful content whose value doesn't degrade significantly over time. Most companies will have useful content assets or assets which can easily be turned into valuable content sitting within their organization. A key strategy for the optimization of stock content is therefore the externalization of such content assets and organizational expertise in order to bring long-term value back to the brand or company.

A secondary strategy would be to build a capability to audit stock assets periodically to incorporate them into workflows and deployment of responsibility. One could then determine their value to organizational or brand objectives, and update and refresh them with value to ensure that they continue to be optimized.

A simple example of this would be a newspaper travel editor who has, over time, built up an online repository of useful travel guides and articles relating to particular destinations in the world. Even though many of them may have been written some time ago, the guides and articles are still valuable assets to the newspaper since they still rank high on relevant search terms and bring traffic and customers back to the newspaper's website. In this instance, the newspaper editor could implement a program to regularly update the most valuable of these assets with new and relevant information. The editor might even commission new pieces that take their lead from the content that has proven to be most valuable and deploy them towards increasing the volume of useful stock assets that the travel section has.

Flow content is different from stock content in that it relates to that which might be generated rapidly or dynamically in response to changing consumer needs or competitive context—or simply to capitalize on an opportunity to achieve brand and organizational objectives. The simplest example is the regular use of content within social media channels and brand outlets on social networks. After all, content may well be considered the currency or engine of social media. It is increasingly being designed specifically with shareability or spreadability on social media channels in mind. In order to fully capitalize on the opportunity provided by flow content, marketing and organizational agility are key. Rapid sign-off procedures, established processes for team and departmental collaboration, and the smooth flow of data, information, and knowledge are all critical to making this happen.

A combination of stock and flow creates an ideal framework for a brand to consider its content strategy. What are the stock assets that we have as a brand? How can we optimize, refresh, and update them? How can we take our learning from what has worked with our existing stock assets and apply it to creating new ones? Then, how can we optimize the flow of content from our brand? What are the optimum platforms and distribution strategies for reaching our customers and prospects regularly? Who will produce the content? How can we ensure a smooth, rapid flow of information and assets from the required parts of our business? How can we empower frontline staff to be agile enough to respond to opportunity when it presents itself?

Noah Brier, the founder of the brand curation tool Percolate, has made the point that while brands have traditionally been quite good at creating stock content in the form of well-crafted advertising campaigns and experiences, this is not a complete strategy all on its own. Brier stated, "...Creating a sustained messaging strategy requires a combination of both stock and flow: longer-form, higher-quality content coupled with the quick-hit links to other interesting and relevant content on the web."[9]

The growing prevalence of always-on brand platforms and owned media assets (including websites and Facebook pages) requires marketers to consider not only short spikes of activity (such as that generated by an above-the-line campaign), but also the constant flow of content needed to engage audiences over longer periods of time. The goal is to keep them interested, keep the brand at the forefront of their minds, and ultimately to influence their behavior. Increasingly, this will be about brands finding their own balance between stock and flow content.

The Three Pillars of Content Curation

Curation is perhaps already becoming an overused word in marketing, but there can be little doubt that it is also an increasingly important concept. The way in which we discover content that we like or find useful, and how that content gets in front of us or gets our attention, is changing radically. With an explosion of choice and noise, and attention becoming the new scarcity, the methods that consumers use to choose what gets their attention is hugely important to anyone in the business of creating content. This also holds true for methods that brands use to manage and deploy content, and attempt to engage those same consumers. Since everyone is now a publisher and purveyor of content, we might argue that this applies to everyone in this digital age.

A useful beginning in this respect is to consider the three pillars of content curation that will increasingly (and already do) shape the future of content consumption and distribution:

1. **Algorithmic Curation:** Defined as the content that we discover and see because a technological process interprets, anticipates, or predicts our needs. Search engine results pages are one obvious example of this form of curation—an algorithm responding to the words that we type into the search box with links to content that it interprets as being relevant to our query. This and similar algorithmic forms of curation are becoming increasingly sophisticated as Google and other search providers increasingly personalize our search results through context. This includes the data the search engine already holds on us, what else it knows

about us, and the contextual ads it serves us. Facebook's algorithm, Edgerank, interprets which content out of that posted by our connections, is most important to us. It does this through an algorithm that weighs affinity (a measure of how much we have previously interacted with that person or brand), content type, and recency. Amazon's algorithms power a recommendation engine that dynamically generates content based on the data it already holds about our purchase history and the purchase history of thousands of others. These commonly used algorithms, which heavily impact the content that we see, have been joined by a new breed of tools that enable brands to easily curate third-party content. These tools help feed consumers' constant hunger for new and compelling content from always-on brand platforms. Comparatively new services such as Percolate in the U.S. and Idio in the U.K., offer a way for brands to easily curate content on a large scale by hooking up to and filtering relevant streams of content mapped against brand profiles, and enabling an editor to assess and publish to a brand platform. The new breed of reading aggregation apps, including Zite (the "personalised iPad magazine that gets smarter as you use it"), also utilize algorithmic curation to draw relevant content in from your connections on social networks, or to accumulate data, learn your tastes, and power content recommendations.

2. **Professional Curation:** We discover or see content because a skilled editor or content commissioner uses their insight into a particular audience to determine what might interest us. This form of curation has been around for as long as magazines and newspapers, and is one in which there remains huge value.
3. **Social Curation:** We see content because we, our friends, or a wider audience think that it's good or relevant. Social curation has long been part of digital channels; it includes content tagging and voting on social bookmarking services, ranking reviews, comments by ratings, Twitter lists, Google+ circles, and many others. Today, these applications are becoming more and more sophisticated.

> *The Guardian* newspaper in the U.K., for example, created a prototype visualization that combined social analytics (how many people shared specific pieces of content across the site or commented on that content) with web analytics (referrals, how many people have looked at it or read it) to create "a visual record of what people are currently finding interesting on guardian.co.uk at the moment."

Considering the combination of different forms of curation creates a useful framework for how companies might utilize content curation to achieve brand objectives. The aggregator app Flipboard, for example, utilizes professional curation to create content feeds on different subject areas that users can subscribe to, but then augments that with an algorithm that pulls in relevant content from users' networks on social platforms like Facebook and Twitter. American Express has used different forms of curation in its Open Forum small business content hub.[10] Content created by AMEX is combined with algorithmically curated third-party content, and the use of simple navigation tabs such as "most viewed" or "most commented" enables users to easily find socially curated and popular content on the hub.

There can be little doubt that increasingly sophisticated use of curation, and combinations of the three pillars of content curation, will give brands a significant advantage in this content-rich age.

Distributed and Destination Thinking

When thinking about getting into a digital mindset, it can be useful to consider the different approaches to content taken by traditional legacy businesses and those which have "grown-up digital." One way of framing this is to consider the differences between what might be called distributed and destination thinking.

Destination thinking employs the kind of media approaches that have been with us for many years. We create content, attract (or drive) users to that content in order to keep them there for as long as possible, serve them advertising, or make money from them in some other way. The defining characteristic of destination thinking is that the user has to be on one of our properties in order for us to be able to monetize that relationship. So, to take the example of a traditional media owner, while a newspaper publisher may have multiple channels through which it is delivering its digital content (apps, websites, and podcasts, for example), those channels are still largely owned media assets that require the user to be in situ.

Distributed thinking, on the other hand, takes the approach that the relationship might be monetized in many different places and not necessarily just on owned media assets. Google's AdSense network is a great example of classic distributed thinking. Rather than the users just coming to the Google domain, millions of sites around the world have embedded small boxes on their site that use Google algorithms to serve contextually relevant text link advertising against editorial. The relationship is one of revenue sharing, so while the publisher is deriving additional benefit from the energy and resources they have invested in creating their content, Google is also successfully monetizing access, context, and relevance. Similarly, we don't need to go to the Google domain to use Google search, since it also powers the search functionality on millions of sites around the web and has a search box within many browsers.

Distributed thinking can lead to some powerful advantages. The ability to embed YouTube videos into websites, for example, enables the platform to monetize the video content it hosts wherever it is consumed around the web. One of the big paybacks is, of course, very useful data. Twitter uses data collected from the integration of millions of Twitter *follow* buttons to recognize patterns in site and content visits that can be used to recommend other accounts to follow. Facebook *like* buttons are embedded alongside content on countless sites across the web, giving Facebook access to a huge wealth of contextual data, which it can reapply in multiple ways. Google has a beta search product (Search plus Your World) that uses data about who we are connected to on the web (via Google services including Google+ and Gmail, but also from blogs and publically available data from third-party services such as Flickr) to power enhanced search results.

The key point about distributed models are that they take value from one part of an ecosystem and use it to enhance the user experience in another part. When *The Guardian* newspaper in the U.K. launched their Open Platform initiative (a service that allowed partners to reuse *Guardian* content and data for free), Emily Bell, their director of digital content at the time, described how Open Platform would allow Guardian content "to be woven into the fabric of the Internet."[11] This is a useful way for brands to think about their own content. It's often difficult for businesses experienced primarily in legacy destination thinking to understand the value of distributed models, since they start from a completely different place and often require different styles of thinking, such as the opening up of data through Application Programming Interfaces (APIs).

The growing importance of distributed thinking does not mean that destination thinking has no place, but rather that we'll increasingly see examples of the smart combination of both types of thinking applied to all kinds of marketing and content models.

One example of such a combination is the Marketplace[12] initiative from online retailer ASOS. Marketplace was created as a platform to facilitate ASOS customers (and new young designers) selling their own clothing to other ASOS customers. It's likely that most traditional retailers would consider a functionality that enabled their customers to buy from each other on the company's site would likely cannibalize sales. ASOS, on the other hand, recognized that Marketplace creates a compelling, sticky piece of content that gives users a reason to come back to the site again and again, generating plenty of opportunity for them to also shop for new stock (i.e., it's a good piece of destination content). Doing this also provides a platform for a vibrant community whose distributed presence reaches out into many areas of the web—particularly via social platforms. ASOS Marketplace is interesting as a solution for a number of reasons: It was created by an agency as a long-term platform (rather than a short-term campaign). It also weaves the ASOS brand into the fabric of the web in a clever way. Lastly, it is very much a business solution and not simply a marketing solution.

Content-savvy brands will increasingly use smart combinations of distributed and destination thinking to power intelligent content strategies fit for our networked world.

THE 70/20/10 CONTENT PLANNING MODEL

The 70/20/10 model has appeared in a number of different contexts. In learning and development, it seeks to blend different approaches into a sum greater than its parts. Powerful learning, the theory goes, is comprised of:

- Around 70 percent from real-life and on-the-job problem solving and experiences
- Around 20 percent from feedback and working with role models
- Around 10 percent from more formal training[13]

In 2005, Eric Schmidt articulated a model for innovation at Google which advocated that employees should:

- Spend 70 percent of their time dedicated to core business tasks
- Spend 20 percent of their time on projects related to the core business
- Spend 10 percent of their time dedicated to projects unrelated to the core business[14]

When Coca-Cola announced their new strategy to shift focus from "creative excellence" to "content excellence,"[15] they talked about applying a 70/20/10 investment principle to content creation:

- 70 percent of the content should be low risk, bread-and-butter marketing
- 20 percent should innovate off what works
- 10 percent should be high risk ideas that will be tomorrow's 70 percent or 20 percent

In the same year that Schmidt was espousing the Google approach to innovation, McKinsey published a report ("Boosting Returns on Marketing Investment"[16]) in which they recommended that, in the face of declining effectiveness and trust in mass advertising, and the increasing fragmentation of media, brands spend 80 percent of their budget on banker strategies and tactics and 20 percent on learning through well-structured tests. It's a useful approach as a pragmatic way to enable greater experimentation with under-pressure budgets, but adopting an approach governed by the 70/20/10 model enables not only experimentation, but optimization of existing activity that is working well. Both optimization and experimentation are fundamental tenets of successful digital marketing. Thus, the 70/20/10 approach to budget allocation and content strategy enables an approach that is naturally suited to digital media.

But what about content planning? Could this same model have an application there as well? You could argue that in order to act like a publisher, a brand needs to not only *think* like a publisher, but *plan* like one. So let's consider the analogy of a magazine publisher and, with that comparison in mind, what a 70/20/10 content plan for a brand could look like:

- 70 percent of the content should be core content—the kind of bread-and-butter content that is central to what the brand is all about: it's positioning, proposition, and the reason to believe. For a brand community, this would equate to the purpose of that community—the reason people are there in the first place. Too many brands attempt to establish communities with no clear purpose or plan for what they're going to talk about not just over the next few weeks, but long term. These brands soon find that they can only talk about themselves for so long and they start to run out of interesting things to say. If we use our publishing analogy, the 70 percent equates to the main editorial franchises of our magazine—the key areas of our flatplan that are central to the editorial proposition and which comprise the bulk of the pagination in each issue. If our magazine is a women's monthly fashion or lifestyle title, for example, these franchises would relate to core subject areas such as fashion, food, travel, health, beauty, or celebrity.
- 20 percent should optimize and innovate off what is really working within the 70 percent. Part of this is about more responsively up-weighting core subject areas to take account of events or seasonality. In the magazine this

might be fashion in spring and autumn, summer foods, Christmas, diets in January and June, and so on. While planned content around things such as product launches and campaigns might sit in your 70 percent, maximizing the opportunity created by short-term peaks in activity focused around what you're already doing is what the 20 percent is all about. You are essentially reactively putting more resources into content that is proving particularly popular or engaging. Within the 20 percent, there is always a link to the 70 percent.

- 10 percent is completely new—the kind of content you can't possibly plan for, but which is driven either by a reactive desire to take advantage of a short-term situation (e.g., a news story or event) or a more proactive desire to experiment and test. Either way, it's new activity not directly tied to the rest of what you're doing, but something from which you can develop learnings. Following the content strategy model, this 10 percent could well become tomorrow's 20 percent or 70 percent.

The 70/20/10 model is a simple but enormously useful content-planning framework based on solid publishing principles. Combining this with our other useful frameworks creates a good template for an approach to brand content.

Content marketing is exploding. Planning in advance to enable the smart combination of content optimization, experimentation, and iteration, different forms of curation, and stock and flow content, will ensure a much higher chance of success in this digital age.

ENDNOTES

1. http://management.fortune.cnn.com/2012/02/13/nike-digital-marketing/
2. http://news.solvemedia.com/post/37787487410/native-advertising-in-context-infographic
3. http://www.sethgodin.com/purple/

4. http://www.slideshare.net/Altimeter/the-converged-media-imperative
5. http://contentmarketinginstitute.com/what-is-content-marketing/
6. http://econsultancy.com/uk/reports/quarterly-digital-intelligence-briefing-digital-trends-for–2013
7. http://econsultancy.com/uk/reports/content-marketing-survey-report
8. http://snarkmarket.com/2010/4890
9. http://adage.com/article/digitalnext/mastering-stock-flow-boost-content-strategy/230989/
10. http://www.openforum.com/
11. http://www.guardian.co.uk/media/2009/mar/10/guardian-open-platform
12. https://marketplace.asos.com/
13. http://www.amazon.com/Career-Architect-Development-Planner-Leadership/dp/0965571246
14. http://money.cnn.com/magazines/business2/business2_archive/2005/12/01/8364616/index.htm
15. http://www.youtube.com/watch?v=fiwIq–8GWA8&feature=related
16. http://www.mckinsey.com/insights/marketing_sales/boosting_returns_on_marketing_investment

PART 2

ACHIEVING SUCCESS IN DIGITAL MARKETING CHANNELS

CHAPTER 4

SEARCH MARKETING: IF THEY CAN'T FIND IT, THEY CAN'T BUY IT

—by Mike Moran

I still remember trying to explain search marketing to a dumbfounded IBM executive back in 2001. I explained how Google works, that searchers were looking for IBM, and that we could get many more visitors to our website and sell more. He looked me in the eye and asked me straight out, "So you are saying that these people are too dumb to be able to open a browser and type *ibm.com*?"

Today, few companies need convincing of the importance of search, but many still don't know how to get results from search marketing. Still fewer have kept up with the changes over the years leading to today's fusion of search and social into content marketing. People believe that search is important, but they might not know why—they just know they are supposed to believe in it. And who wants to seem clueless? But in order to get people to spend the time and resources required to beat your competition in search marketing, you probably need more.

I certainly needed more back in 2001 in front of that executive.

And it wasn't that my IBM exec wasn't a smart guy. He was actually super-smart. The problem was that I was using the wrong language—the language of search success instead of business success. I was talking about our products not being found and our pages being ranked low on the results page and—gee, why did I ever think these kinds of arguments would work? In desperation, I began reaching for some simple way to explain what was wrong and finally spluttered, "If they can't find it, they can't buy it!"

That did the trick.

Now I was talking a language that any businessperson would understand. And it is probably true for your business, too—whether you sell your products and services online with a cute little shopping cart, offline in honest-to-God stores, over the phone, through a flesh-and-blood sales force, or any other way that you make money. It even works if you aren't out to make money, because if they can't find it, they can't donate to the cause or volunteer at the shelter, or do just about anything you are trying to get them to do.

So, the point of search is to get people to do the thing your website was designed to do. In the rest of this book you'll learn about how to design your site and your messaging, how to analyze the metrics of what people are doing, and lots of other things—but in this chapter you'll learn how they *find it*.

WHY SEARCH IS IMPORTANT

No other kind of marketing offers the power of search. With other marketing, you typically are interrupting people doing something else, but searchers are literally raising their hands and begging, "Sell to me now!" With other forms of marketing, you are limited to slogans and jingles that are indiscriminately pushed at target markets, in the firm hope that those prospective customers will remember your brand at some future time when they are ready to buy. What's more, search marketing increasingly finds content personalized to the searcher, with the right content type for that particular search.

Everyone Searches

OK, maybe not absolutely everyone, but *almost* everyone. In the U.S. alone, comScore estimated that there were nearly 20 billion searches during the single month of January, 2013.[1] Worldwide, monthly searches are over 175 billion, again according to comScore.[2]

If you're a skeptic, you might debate whether your audience is really interested in social media. You can demand proof that there is a return on investment for YouTube videos or Twitter. You can argue about whether all of your outbound e-mails are getting trapped in spam filters. You can come up with all sorts of reasons why many forms of digital marketing might not work for your business. But it is increasingly hard to argue with search.

Seventy-four percent of shoppers start their product research with a search engine.[3] But it's not just shoppers: 77 percent of Americans begin their search for health-related topics with a search engine[4] and 78 percent of B2B buyers begin their journey with a search.[5] No matter what kind of business you are in, your customers are online and they are searching. The only question is: Are they finding *you*?

Searchers Buy from You

After looking at those numbers, does it surprise you that search leads to sales? Even though you don't typically know the identities or even characteristics of the searchers, you know something better: what they are looking for. If marketing is about targeting the right people with a persuasive message, search allows customers to identify themselves and reveal what they are interested in.

Not only do they tell you that they are buyers, but searchers even tell you where in the buying cycle they are at the moment. Their keywords reveal what they are thinking. In this way, search is not only the ultimate lead management tool, but it is also an unparalleled form of market research.

But market research doesn't usually command a great deal of attention. We reserve that for techniques that persuade people to actually buy—and search does that. Because you are targeting people who actually *want* your sales pitch, they are far more qualified a lead than someone who happens to see your banner ad. And, most companies find that search marketing lowers the cost they once paid for their leads.[6]

Searchers Are Checking Your Credibility

Even if you still believe that your existing advertising is driving your business, you might still need search marketing. Why? Because people increasingly use search to check you out. That TV ad or magazine article might make them aware of you, but that's a long way from a sale.

Each year, Internet hosting company GoDaddy takes out eye-catching and provocative TV ads for the Super Bowl. How do they know they worked? They see huge increases in their search volumes. Some of those searchers just want to watch the ad again, but if no one was buying, GoDaddy would find another way to spend its money.

Think about your own behavior. When you read about a new company, what is the first thing you do? Call on the phone? Ask a colleague? If you're like most people, you belly up to Google and search for that company's name. You might even search for reviews of their products. Try searching for your company's products and reviews to see what your first impression is.

HOW SEARCHERS WORK

OK, so search is important—check. But what are people actually doing when they search?

The behaviors that searchers exhibit are critical to understanding how you can persuade them to do business with you. Understanding the searcher's context—which devices they search from, what they are looking for, and how they interact with the search results—makes the difference for a persuasive offer versus a dud.

What Devices Searchers Use

Not too many years ago, searches happened on computers. Period. And that simple fact told you a lot about where searchers were located—usually in their homes or in an office, because that is where the computers were. But in the last few years, search has left the building. And that means that *local searches*, where searchers are looking for nearby businesses, are on the rise.

In 2011, U.S. local searches from computers totaled around 55 billion, compared to fewer than 20 billion local searches from mobile devices. But the growth rates of each kind of search leads to projections by BIA/Kelsey that mobile local searches will eclipse computer local searches (at around 85 billion each) by 2016.[7] It's probably time to start thinking about mobile devices.

But these numbers need to be taken with a grain (or perhaps a pillar) of salt. Just because someone is searching from a mobile device does not mean that they are out and about. The stats on mobile devices include someone using an iPad on the living room couch and exclude using your laptop on the train. So, *mobile device* means a phone or a tablet, and a *desktop device* means a desktop or laptop computer. And, while it is likely that more mobile device searches are devoted to local content because they are more likely to be used by people on the go, we need to keep in mind that these devices can be used in various ways.

What Searchers Are Looking For

You probably realize that people typing different words into search engines are looking for different things, and you likely have a few ideas of which words your potential customers might use—but you also need to consider what kinds of content they are looking for. Someone searching for "starbucks" might be looking for a map with the nearest locations, while someone searching for "quicken demo" might want to watch a video.

The old sea of blue links to web pages has given way to a colorful array of photos, videos, maps, products, news stories, blog posts, and more. What that means to you, the search marketer, is that you need to have the type of content that searchers want, not just content on the right subject. Try searching for a few words you believe your customers use and see what varieties of content are shown by the search engines. See if Google shows something different than Bing.

How Searchers Interact

If you've been following search marketing for years, none of this should be a shock, but one area has changed markedly in the last few years: the search user experience. At a high level, it seems the same—searchers enter keywords, they see a screen full of results, and then they click. But a lot has changed around that simple experience.

One big area of change is around personalization. While the search engine companies have been working on this for years, the degree to which results are now customized for each searcher is a sea change from just a few years ago. Google personalizes all results by default now. If you are logged in to your Google Account (the way Gmail users are), Google is using a raft of information about you on every search. Not to be left behind, Bing has a deal with Facebook that changes the results you see based on what your friends like. Everywhere you turn, search engines are using your location, device, interests, and even your social network to better choose what search results you see. What this means to search marketers, at least for some searches, is that there is no clear-cut answer to "Is my content ranked number one?" because there might be different top results for different people.

And being ranked number one, or at least on the first page, is more important than ever, because each year searchers spend less time deciding what to click on. Ten years ago, some searchers frequently clicked to the next page when nothing on the first page seemed right. Today, they far more frequently go back to search for something else. And it's not just the first page—it is the first item on the page. Being that number one result can yield between 10 percent and 20 percent of the total clicks.[8]

THE TYPES OF SEARCH MARKETING

Sometimes it is scary to read a heading called the "types" of anything—if it needs its own section, maybe it's very complicated. Not with search marketing. There are only two main types that you need to know: *organic search* and *paid search.*

Now, we're not going to let you off that easy, because we technical geeks like to make up new names for everything (using acronyms, if possible). We have lots of other names for organic and paid search. We sometimes refer to organic search as *search engine optimization* or *SEO* (yay, an acronym)—sometimes you might even hear it called *natural search*. Organic search is the librarian's answer to the question: What does Google or Bing really think is the best content to show when a searcher is looking for something? You can think of it as earned media, because the search engine is truly attempting to place the right answer at the top of the list, while the website that search might lead to is owned media. Now, just about every site ought to be working on organic search because it is rather inexpensive to add a few extra steps to the content creation process. But, paid media has its place in search also.

Paid search, which is also known as *Pay-Per-Click (PPC)* or *Cost-Per-Click (CPC)*, obviously has its own delicious acronyms, but it's rather simple—it's advertising. You, the search marketer, pay Google or Bing for the privilege of getting searchers to click on your ad to come to your website.

Paid search is not for everyone. If you have a clear way to profitably sell your product or service (online or offline) starting with a search, you should experiment with paid search to see whether it returns more than your investment. But if you make canned soup, you might want to stick with organic search—it might not be worth it to pay 52 cents a click for everyone who types in "cream of tomato," because you probably are going to attract a lot more people looking for recipes than would ever buy from you. But for most companies, it's worth at least testing to see if paid search pays off.

THE LANGUAGE OF SEARCH

Just as it was back in 2001, search still has its own language. And even though that isn't the way to communicate search's business value to mere mortals, you need to know it if you want to understand all the information you'll read outside of this book as you continue your journey toward becoming a search marketing guru.

We've already introduced the terminology for organic and paid search, but there are a few other words to learn, too. One important concept is what to call the text that searchers type into the search box. We'll call them *keywords*, but you'll also hear them called *key phrases*, *search words*, *search terms*, and *search queries*.

The searcher enters the keywords into the *search engine*—Google and Microsoft's Bing power the vast majority of U.S. searches—which then displays a search results page, as shown in Figure 4.1. Some folks refer to that page as a *SERP*, which is an acronym for *search engine results page*. You can see the various parts of both organic and paid search results—and Figure 4.1 shows even more words to know.

Don't be put off by all the various terms—you need to know them to read all the great advice available online about search marketing, which is the second-most important way to learn more about search. The most important way to learn is to actually try it.

SUCCEEDING AT SEARCH MARKETING

The precise tactics for organic and paid search success differ, but at a high level they are the same:

1. *Choose the right search keywords.* Your keywords are your market segments—understanding what your customers are looking for is the place you start with all search marketing. If you don't know what searchers are looking for, you can't possibly provide the content that satisfies that need.
2. *Get your content included.* For paid search, you must create ads that cover the targeted keywords. For organic search, you must ensure that your content is being discovered by the search engines. Without these steps, your content will never be found.
3. *Optimize your content.* For both paid and organic search, the text of your content is a key factor to being found by search engines. Your paid search ads and landing pages must contain the searchers' keywords and your organic search landing pages and social media content must likewise use those words (and related words) in titles and body copy. Without these steps, you won't get clicks from searchers to reach your content.

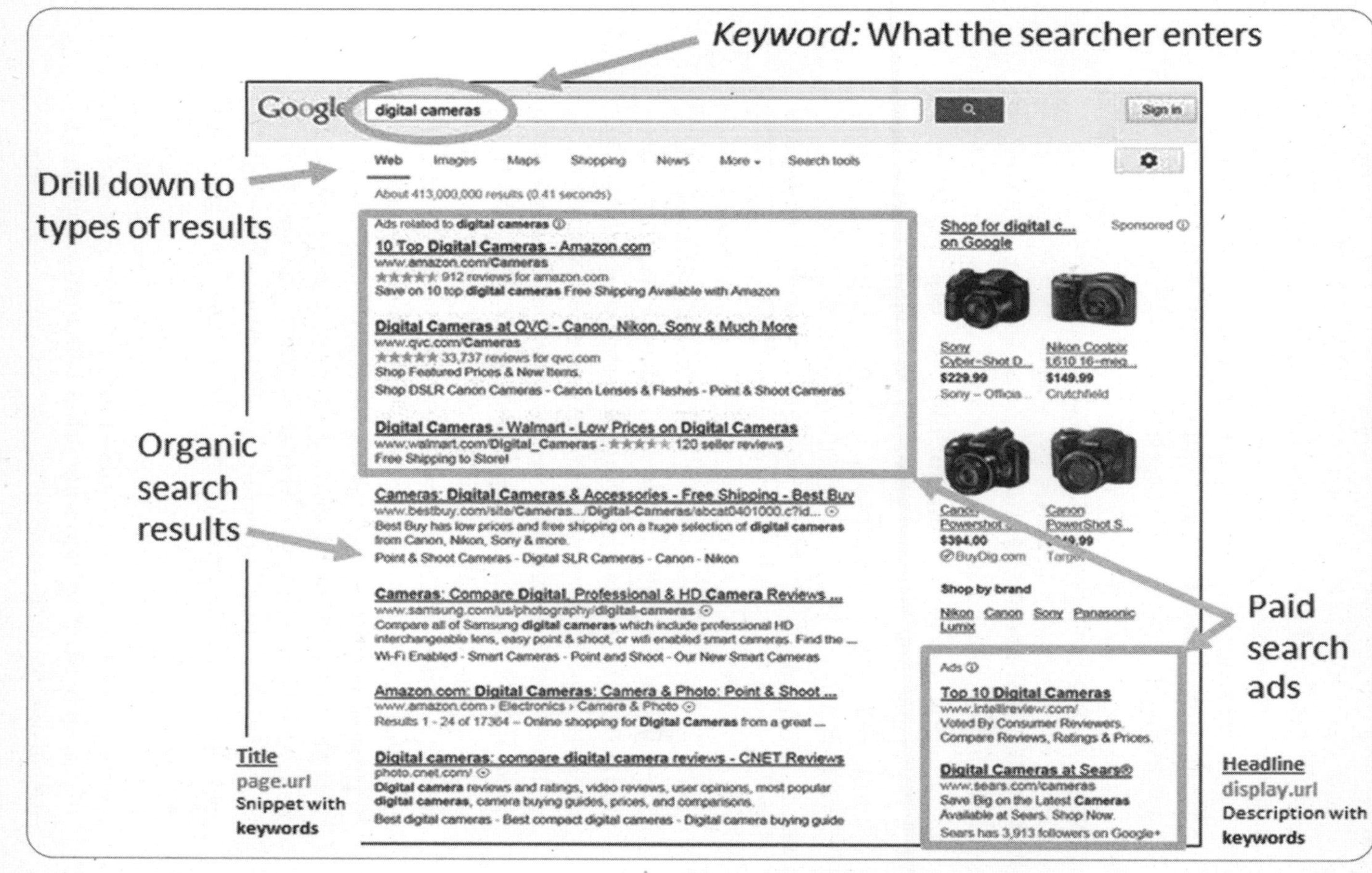

FIGURE 4.1 A Search Engine Results Page (SERP): No two search engines display results identically, but they all have a few things in common.

4. *Demonstrate your content's quality.* Both paid and organic search results depend on each search engine's estimation of the quality of your content. The high quality of your paid search ads and your organic search content allow better rankings than content your competitors provide. Combining paid and organic landing pages is an emerging technique that is proving successful.

Let's dive into strategies for achieving these four objectives.

Choose the Right Search Keywords

If you don't know what your customers are searching for, it's hard to imagine how you'll get them to find your content. If you've never performed any keyword research, you might believe that you know what your customers are looking for, but you'll probably be surprised.

So, let's get started surprising ourselves. How do you discover the best keywords?

- *Brainstorm with your team.* Try to list as many nouns as you can think of that describe your products or services. Then add nouns that describe the problem that your product or service solves. Lastly, try to add more descriptive words—adjectives, adverbs, verbs—that make the phrase more specific to your website. For example, if you are an orthodontist in Anaheim that specializes in adults, don't settle for *orthodontist*—instead focus on *anaheim orthodontist* or *orange county orthodontist* or *anaheim adult orthodontist.*
- *Check your search referrals and your site search results.* Use Google Analytics (or whatever analytics program you have) to see which search keywords people are already using to come to your site. Check your site search engine to find out what people on your site are looking for. Add these keywords to your list.
- *Watch your competitors.* If you search for these keywords and your competitors come up, they might be doing a good job of search marketing. See what other keywords they seem to include on the titles of their pages—maybe you should add some of those, too.

- "*Use a keyword research tool.* Once you have a good list of keywords, try looking them up in keyword tool provided by your favorite search engine, or a paid tool, such as WordStream or Wordtracker. They'll show you variations on your keywords that you might want to add to your list."

When you have a good list, start prioritizing. Eliminate any keywords that are not close matches to your site—or keywords where many other sites might be as good or better than yours (such as *orthodontist* from the example above, where thousands of other sites are just as good as yours). If you've got a lot of strong keywords, prioritize the most popular ones (according to the keyword tool) at the top of the list. Over time, you will develop better ways to prioritize based on traffic and conversions to your site, but you won't have that information at the start.

Keywords at the top of the list are great choices for organic search optimization, but the words lower on the list might not be worth that level of effort. You might reserve the bottom of the list for paid search only. Regardless of which keywords you go with, you'll need to take a few more steps to reach search success, starting with getting your content included in the search results.

Get Your Content Included

Yes, we all want our content to show up first in the search results, but before you can worry about where it *lands* on the list, it first has to be *on* the list.

While keyword research is very similar for both organic and paid search, getting your content included couldn't be more different, so we'll look at each one separately.

For organic search, there are three main ways to get your content included:

1. *Get found by the spider.* Search engines have a special program called a *spider* that "crawls the web" to find all the content it can.
2. *Use a sitemap.* To make it easier for the spider, you can go to sitemaps.org to find free ways to give the search engines a list of all your pages so they don't miss any.

3. *Ping the search engines.* Some kinds of content, such as blogs and product catalogs, are good candidates for alerting the search engine using RSS feeds (or other forms of web feeds) when new or changed content is available. Services such as Ping-O-Matic are free and do the job well.

Once the search engine finds your content, it stores it in a special file called the *search index.* The search engine consults the index each time a searcher conducts a search, so any pages not in the search index will never be included in the search results. You can use Google's and Bing's Webmaster Tools sites to find out how many pages from your website are in each search engine's index.

If some or all of your content is not indexed, you might be using website techniques that the spiders have trouble with, such as Flash content. It's also possible that your pages just load too slowly. You can use Google's PageSpeed Tool or YSlow to check the causes.

Worst of all, your content could be missing from the search index because your site is being penalized by the search engines because you are violating their terms of service—essentially, they feel you're spamming. Search spam is a blanket term for a host of improper techniques that tricky search marketers (known as "black hats") use to fool the search engines to show lower quality content. When search engines detect suspicious techniques, they penalize your site by lowering its content's ranking or removing it from being listed altogether. It's unusual, but it can happen, even to big brands. BMW was caught a few years ago and was banned by Google for a short period until they cleaned up their act.

But what about paid search?

It's far simpler for you to know whether your paid search ad will be included in the search results—you create your ad, associate it with keywords, and then determine yourself when it should be shown, based on a few factors:

- **Match Types:** When you choose the keyword that triggers your ad, you need to let the search engines know whether any variations of the keywords should also force the ad to be displayed. *Exact match* shows your keyword precisely as you type it (*digital camera*), while *phrase match* allows extra words (*digital camera accessories*) and *broad match* allows word variants (*digital cameras*) and words to be out of order (*camera for digital photography*).

- **Negative Match:** What if you don't want to be stuck with exact match, but there are some words that are clearly not the right ones for your ads? *Negative match* lets you specify words that must *not* appear in order for the ad to be shown, allowing you to specify broad match for *digital camera* with a negative match for *accessories* (thus avoiding showing your digital camera ad for *digital camera accessories*).
- **Geographic Location:** Local businesses might not want their ads shown all over the country. In this case, you'll want to restrict the ad to just the areas where your customers reside. You can specify zip codes or even draw on a map to set your boundaries.

Once you've gotten your organic search content and paid search ads included in the search results, the next step is to get them near the top so that searchers will click to come to your content. That's our next step.

Optimize Your Content

It's not enough to merely get your content in the list. If no one sees it, it doesn't matter—and no one sees page seven of the search results. Let's examine how to optimize your content for organic search.

Your first move in optimizing content for organic search is to test the type of content that shows up on the results page for your targeted keywords. It's not enough that your content is included—it needs to be the right content. When you search for your targeted keywords, you'll see that different kinds of content are shown for different searches. If your keywords bring back videos, or photos, or blog posts, rather than mostly web pages, you'll need to ensure that you are optimizing those content types in your search marketing. Don't focus solely on web pages if your important searches are returning something else.

Once you know which kinds of content are favored for any particular keyword, you need to choose a specific piece of content—a single YouTube video or web page, for example—that you expect to optimize for your keyword. That's your *search landing page*. Once you choose, it's time to start optimizing.

Search engines use many factors to decide which content shows up at the top of the organic search results, but you have direct control over one—using the right words in your content's title. For a web page, you need to use your chosen keyword and related words in the HTML title tag. Similarly, those words go in the headline of a blog post or YouTube video. Your content's title is the most important part of your content to optimize with keywords. Moz provides an on-page optimization tool that can help you tweak your content for organic search.

In case you think this sounds a bit esoteric and not terribly valuable, think again. If you've never paid attention to organic search optimization, you might be ignoring a gold mine. After *Entrepreneur Magazine* completed its first optimization campaign on its major pages, they improved revenue by $2 million a month.[9]

But you don't want to optimize the title to appeal merely to the search engines—it's also the single most important factor that leads a searcher to click on your content. Don't make the mistake of optimizing for the search engines alone. Unless the searcher clicks, no ranking is high enough.

Don't settle just for the keyword in your title. If you write naturally, you'll use those keywords throughout your content—and you'll use many thematically-related words, as well. The search engines look for these words, and searchers do too.

The other critical piece of information in an organic search result is the snippet. It doesn't affect the organic search ranking, but it frequently affects the click-through rate. The snippet is sometimes pulled from the HTML description tag, but is more frequently drawn from the first occurrence of the keyword on the page. If you ensure that your title and your snippet contain calls to action that entice clicks, you'll get as much traffic as you can.

Paid search is similar in some ways to organic search, in that you'll want to use keywords, related words, and strong calls to action in the headlines and descriptions of your ads. That approach will get the most clicks to your site, which we'll discuss in more detail later in this chapter.

The hardest paid search optimization work involves your bid—the amount that you pay the search engine each time a searcher clicks on your ad. Optimizing your bidding is a critical part of getting the return on investment needed for your paid search program. Each search engine provides a free *bid management system* that allows you to vary your bidding automatically. You can create detailed rules keyword by keyword, if you want, or at higher levels of organization, such as an ad group of multiple advertisements. If you want to manage your bids across multiple search engines, you'll need to use a for-fee bid management system, such as Kenshoo or Marin Software.

Although bid management seems difficult, it is worth the effort for all but the smallest paid search marketers. British Airways upgraded its paid search with a bid management system to improve its ROI by 10 percent in just one year.[10]

Despite all of your efforts thus far, you must take one more step before your content will rise to the top of the search results. The search engines won't show any content that isn't high quality—so you need to know what they look for. That's up next.

Demonstrate Your Content's Quality

Of course you want to have quality content, but search engines want it more than you do. When search engines show high-quality content in their results, searchers are happy and they use search more, which is good for any search engine's business. But how do search engines decide that any particular piece of content is high quality?

We'll examine the quality markers for organic search first:

- *Link quantity and quality.* The search engine crawlers remember which pages link to others. The content that gets the most links from the best sites ("best" means that *those* sites have lots of quality links to *them*) are considered of higher quality than the others. These links are considered votes for the content they link to—people don't create links to crappy content.
- *Social media activity.* Social media often contains links, but other kinds of social activity counts also. Bing has a deal with Facebook that tracks *likes* for content. Videos

are frequently ranked based on the number of views for each video. As social media becomes more important, social media activity is frequently used to validate the link analysis. When links indicate high quality that is confirmed by strong social media activity, the search engines are more confident in their content quality judgment.

- *Human ratings.* Google has introduced a new quality factor based on actual human ratings of search results as to whether the content is high quality. Because Google can't afford to pay people to rate every content item for every search result, Google looks at characteristics of the content and assumes that content with similar features is of similar quality. The exact features being examined change all the time, but pages loaded with ads or content that loads slowly seem like weak candidates to be rated highly.

These arbiters of quality have emerged over the years to combat the spammers' attempts to "game" the search results. Spammers began by creating *link farms*—fake sites that exist just to send links to other sites to make the linked sites seem higher quality than they are. Paid links and sham social media profiles followed, and the cat and mouse game just goes on and on.

But rather than focusing on what Google and Bing are looking for, instead you should be paying attention to what your customers want. All that the search engines are doing, in their arms race with spammers, is to find markers of quality content—usually they need help from us human beings to do that. Search engines look at how many links your content gets from those human beings running other websites, and they pay attention to social media activity (more human beings), or they finally break down and simply ask us humans to rate the content. So, stop worrying about what the search engines' latest quality detection factor is. Every tweak of the ranking algorithm adds up to the same thing: if your customers like it, the search engines will too.

Detecting quality is also important to the search engines for paid search. Google goes so far as to refer to a *Quality Score* that is used to rank the paid search ads, and Bing uses a similar formula. As we have already learned, the amount you bid—your per-click cost—is a major factor in deciding which ad is shown first. However, that bid is multiplied by the quality score so that the highest bid doesn't completely determine the order of the ads.

The reason that search engines use quality as a factor is that searchers click more on high-quality ads, which makes the search engines more money. What's more, if searchers recognize over time that the paid search ads at the top of the list are high quality, they might click on more paid search ads in general—which also brings the search engines more money. With every passing year, advertisers have more choices about how to spend their marketing budgets, so continuing pressures on search engines' revenues might lead them to focus more and more on quality.

So what kinds of factors are taken into account when paid search results are analyzed for quality?

- **Click-Through Rate:** This is the original marker of quality that Google introduced when it first launched Google AdWords, and it is still the most important factor for any paid search engine. If two ads have the same bid for their per-click cost, the one with the higher click-through rate will tend to be listed first. And that makes sense—if human beings click on your ad more than others, you probably have a better ad that is more relevant to what the searchers are looking for. Although we act as though click-through rate is just one thing, search engines sometimes use several different click-through rates: One for that exact ad, one for ads that have the same display URL, and the rate for all of your ads. Search engines weight each rate differently as part of the formula.
- **Ad Quality:** Ads that contain the keyword being searched for tend to be higher in quality. Some Google AdWords marketers use *dynamic keyword insertion* so they can use a generic ad but make sure that the exact keywords are displayed whenever the ad is shown. Regardless of how you do it, placing keywords in the calls to action of your paid search ads raises both your quality rating and your actual click-through rate.

- **Landing Page Quality.** If your landing page contains the keyword and related words, and it provides a good experience for the searcher, it will be considered to be of high quality. Some search engines use human ratings for paid search landing pages, just as Google does for organic search. In fact, using the same landing pages for organic and paid search might give you a shortcut to paid search quality, because all the optimization work that you do for your organic content will usually yield a high quality assessment of your paid search landing page.

Google AdWords advertisers can view their Quality Score to see Google's opinion. Likewise, Microsoft's Bing Ads provides a quality impact function to see how you can improve your quality. While you certainly need to know a lot about optimizing your paid search bids, with each passing year, quality becomes more important.

So, how do you get to the top of the paid search ad results? In many ways, you do the same things with your paid search ads and landing pages that you do for your organic search content—give the people what they want. Creating ads that people want to click, that highlight the words that people are looking for in the ad, and that lead to landing pages that also highlight those words are all ways to increase searcher assessment of quality.

There you have it. You've walked through a step-by-step system for search success. But you can't just assume that taking these steps will lead to better search marketing results for your business. You must measure your impact.

MEASURING SEARCH SUCCESS

Here you sit. You understand the basics of search. You know how important it is. You even know the most important things to do to succeed in both organic and paid search, along with a few tools to get you started. But you never really know you are succeeding until you can measure your success. Until you have hard numbers, you're just telling a story. So which numbers are the important numbers for search?

As you'll discover throughout this book, the most important numbers for search are the same metrics that are important for any kind of inbound marketing—actual sales. You want to count how many people buy (online or offline) from you and you need to track that they came from search. Chapter 9 on measurement and ROI will show you how to do that across all forms of digital marketing.

But what are the measurements that are purely about search and your search performance? Too often, marketers get hung up on search rankings, for both organic and paid search. Are we number one? Are we at least on the first page? That information is important, but it isn't the end of the story. First of all, as we learned earlier in the chapter, personalized search means that there is never a solid answer on who is number one for this search at any point in time—it might vary for different searchers. What's more, the search rankings for both paid and organic search are highly volatile—so you could be number one now and number three an hour from now. Don't make the mistake of focusing solely on rankings as your guide.

Rankings do matter, however, because if people don't see your content on the results page, they can't click on it. But suppose you get a high ranking in search and no one clicks on it—the rankings alone are not sufficient to drive real success in search marketing. To at least check your approximate rankings, you can use a free Firefox rank checker tool from SEO Book for organic search, while SpyFu is probably the best tool for paid search (although it's not free).

Beyond rankings, you can track clicks to your site. This is more important than rankings, because you always want to know how many searchers are visiting your site—if the visitor traffic to your site from search is good, your rankings must be OK. The simplest way to check visitors to your site is through your web analytics system. You might be using Google Analytics (which is free) or any other web metrics system—they can all count *search referrals.* Referrals can be broken down between organic and paid search—they are usually most useful when broken down by keyword, so that you can tell how many people searched for a particular keyword and then visited your site by clicking on your organic search result or your paid search ad.

It's tempting to stop there. I mean, if you are in charge of search marketing and someone searches and finds your content and comes to your site—well, job over, right? Wrong. Unless the searchers that visit your site actually buy something someday, the traffic wasn't valuable. So, you'll also want to measure your *conversions*, the thing that you are actually trying to get people to do on your website. Now, if you have a shopping cart on your site, it's rather easy—your conversion is them actually purchasing something, and your web analytics system can measure that and tell you exactly how large the volume of sales were from search.

If you sell offline, it's a bit harder. Your web conversion might be to have someone fill out a contact form or to print out a coupon to redeem at the store. Extra Space Storage, a self-service storage facility, added 100 points to its ROI by tying offline store visits to its web marketing, and you can, too.[11]

Regardless of what your conversions are, you need to track whether the search visitors you attracted gave you conversions (and if possible, whether those folks actually went ahead and completed the purchase offline). It's possible that you have a great search marketing campaign going for all the wrong keywords. Folks search and they click on your content but they are actually the wrong people to target because they won't buy your product. Only by checking conversions and actual sales can you truly find out. So, stay tuned for a continuation of that discussion later in Chapter 9.

Because you are paying for each click of paid search, you'll want to measure your click-through rate, your spending, and your conversion rate. The bid management tools we mentioned earlier can do these things. But you also want to apply the same kind of thinking to organic search. The work that you put into optimizing pages and to measure results all cost money. The fees that you pay to your agency or to the personnel running your program need to be counted, too. As you'll see in Chapter 9, you calculate return on investment when you count up all those costs against the sales that you generate.

SEARCH TRENDS

The biggest driver of search trends is the explosion of content that we've witnessed over the last few years—and there is no sign that it is stopping. According to IBM, 90 percent of the data in the world today has been created in the last two years.[12] With that kind of volume, it stands to reason that search marketing is deeply affected. So how are search engines responding?

- *Faster indexing.* Google completely redesigned its speed of adding new content to the search index so that most new content is searchable within hours of its birth.
- *More kinds of content.* Google and Bing offer blended search results that integrate more kinds of content than ever—maps, videos, photos, and more. Bing even shows results from Facebook.
- *Higher-quality content.* The more content, the harder it is to find the right stuff. As we discussed earlier, Google has introduced a human rating system to sift the wheat from the chaff and to fight spammers that try to fool them.
- *Faster results.* With this explosion of data, searchers seem less patient than ever before. Google Instant shows search results as you type your keyword.

So, what will happen next? Some trends are easy to forecast. The data explosion will not slow down anytime soon—in fact, it will probably accelerate, making it even harder for your marketing message to break through the clutter in order to be found. You can also expect that the ongoing war against spammers will only escalate. Search engines will continue to come under revenue pressure in paid search as options continue to expand for the ways that marketers can spend their time and money to spread their message.

The upshot of all of these trends puts the focus clearly on content marketing, with organic search and paid search being just two of the many ways to drive people to that content. As the amount of content skyrockets while the customers' time remains the same, the pressure to have *exactly* the information needed grows and grows.

Rather than thinking of search marketing as an end in itself, smart marketers are taking a holistic view that places their high-quality content at the center of all of their digital marketing campaigns. Yes, they will make sure that it is optimized for organic search. Sure, they will back it up with paid search ads when it makes economic sense. But your search strategy can't exist in a vacuum.

High-quality content will naturally attract links from other sites, yes, but you must promote your content with every means at your disposal. E-mail it in your newsletters. Tweet it. Share it on Facebook and LinkedIn. Promote it on YouTube. Find any possible way to make it happen.

Now, you might be asking, "If all these other means of promotion are so valuable, do I really need search at all anymore? Can I just promote using all these other methods and forget about search?"

It's a good question, but you can answer it for yourself quite easily. Think about how much effort, money, and time you need to put into a good content marketing campaign. Imagine that you've really created something high quality—that your content is extremely helpful to your customers on a specific problem that bedevils them, and now you are ready to launch the campaign in all of its glory. So, you e-mail links. You share it on Facebook, Twitter, LinkedIn, and any other place you can cram a link. You have YouTube videos that interview the experts behind your campaign. You have blog posts. You have just about anything anyone ever thought of. You blanket everything that moves with links to your content. You hit it big.

How long do you think that will last? Three days? A week, maybe? How long do you think people will pay attention to this new exciting campaign? Do you really think they will retweet something that is two months old even when you tweet it again? How about a year from now?

That's the reality of promotion of any kind. When it is new, exciting, and shiny, it's much more shareable than when it is merely high-quality evergreen information. Even though your content is just as good as it always was, it isn't trendy anymore and won't go viral on social media month after month, even if it did when it was new.

Now you are left with figuring out how to get value out of that fabulous content you put together at great effort and expense. How will people find it weeks, months, and years after you created it? (C'mon think—you'll come up with something.) Oh yeah, search!

Search marketing is becoming the long tail of content marketing. When social media and e-mail and every other event-driven news-sharing device peters out, that is when search shines. Search will still be there to direct those customers to you in their moment of need, which can be years after you created that content. And all that great promotional work you did will have driven links, social activity, and whatever new marker of quality search engines decide is important in the future.

But there is one more trend that we haven't discussed—the rise of mobile marketing. With the small form factor of cell phones, search is one of the few methods of interaction that doesn't need any modification. There's plenty of room to squeeze in a search box to type a few keywords and to show a few links. No big change to the interface. You don't even need an app.

Because it works so well on mobile devices, the volume of mobile searches rises dramatically each year—just about as fast as smartphone adoption is increasing. And the search engines are actually slightly changing the way search results appear on mobile devices. Google shows fewer ads on tablets than on computers, and frequently shows them in different places in the search results page (such as at the bottom of the page). Search engine companies are worried that people are far less likely to click on paid search ads on mobile devices—if there is even any room to display them.

The squeeze on the search engine business is being exacerbated by the switch to mobile devices. Mobile searches provide less revenue but they cost just as much to execute, placing real profit pressure on Google, Bing, and every other search engine.

While interesting, mobile search is just the tip of the iceberg. The revolutionary change to mobile-device Internet usage has huge implications for marketers. If you are curious about exactly what they are, you are in luck. Mobile Marketing is discussed next, in Chapter 5.

ENDNOTES

1. http://searchengineland.com/comscore-january-2013-search-rankings-148478
2. http://searchengineland.com/google-worlds-most-popular-search-engine-148089
3. http://www.thinkwithgoogle.com/insights/
4. http://searchengineland.com/77-percent-of-online-health-seekers-start-at-search-engines-pew-study-145105
5. http://www.slideshare.net/G3Com/2012-b2b-buyer-behavior-survey-report
6. http://www.marketingcharts.com/wp/direct/inbound-marketers-enjoy-lower-cost-per-lead-21269/
7. http://blog.kelseygroup.com/index.php/2012/04/20/when-will-mobile-local-searches-eclipse-desktop/
8. http://www.internetmarketingninjas.com/blog/search-engine-optimization/click-through-rate
9. http://www.seoinc.com/seo/case-studies/entreprenuer-mag
10. http://www.scribd.com/doc/19737533/BA-integrated-search-marketing-case-study
11. http://c.ymcdn.com/sites/www.sempo.org/resource/resmgr/Docs/case_extraspace.pdf
12. http://www-01.ibm.com/software/data/bigdata/

CHAPTER 5

MOBILE MARKETING: INNOVATION ON THE GO

—*by Alexander Kates*

Throughout the chapters of this book, woven gently into the forward-looking predictions of every media channel, you've seen references to *mobile*—the idea of marketing to your customers and clients through their phones and tablets. You've heard whispers of this revolutionary new medium on the horizon primed to change everything. You've seen it referenced in the news, shared enthusiasm for an exciting new app or device with your friends or colleagues, and watched your kids become completely swept away by the mobile revolution. In all likelihood, you own an iPhone or Android device, and are yourself the target of corporate marketing through mobile channels.

We intentionally ensured that the gravity of mobile marketing is sown throughout this book's 13 chapters. If you've been itching to confront this new (and sometimes frightening) medium head on, you've finally come to the right place.

Once upon a time, we used to wait until we got back to our desktop or laptop computers to complete common tasks that are now routinely done anywhere. Interested in looking up movie show times at the local theater for the afternoon? Needed to quickly learn how to fix your flat tire that just blew out? Wanted to respond to a time-critical e-mail for work? It just had to wait. Searching for information, responding to messages, and doing anything we might consider remotely productive, absolutely required that we be in the office or at our home PC (or Mac).

Today, whether you embrace it or not, everything is mobile. We live in a mobile world where any information we'd ever hope to stumble upon is a few mere screen touches away, on a device that we carry with us wherever we go. It goes with us on vacation. It's in our pocket or purse when we get the itch to go to the movies, when our tire goes flat, or when an important work e-mail arrives. A good majority of us don't leave our phones behind when we go to the bathroom, and most of us even keep them within arm's reach when we shower.

For me personally, it's hard to imagine not having the entire web, and the infinite repository of information it contains, at my fingertips at all times. My mobile device has become my sixth sense, and without it functioning, I feel seriously debilitated and impaired going about my life. In most cases, I would prefer if one of my original five senses had failed instead. Now, before you write me off as a hopelessly dependent technophile, I can assure you that most Americans, as well as a growing percentage of the rest of the world, feel the same way to some extent—or so the data would lead us to believe.

The explosion and rapid evolution of mobile technology has not only changed *where* we access information—it has also changed *what* we access and *how* we access it. It has completely transformed our behaviors surrounding communication and content consumption, as well as our expectations for delivery format, immediacy, and cross-platform interoperability. We are currently in the midst of a media channel revolution that is turning the world of marketing we know and love upside down, inside out, and on its technologically inept head.

Brands are just beginning to leverage mobile strategies, and there are few doing it extremely well. Done correctly, it has the ability to expand the reach and enhance the efficacy of several other digital media channels. It can also be a formidable powerhouse all on its own. Thus, in most industries, mobile represents a colossal opportunity for marketers to transform their brands and businesses, and leapfrog the competition through cleverly crafted campaigns and effective multichannel strategies. However, marketing in this arena done incorrectly (or worse yet, ignored) can cause a brand to fall behind and get left in the dust of its mobile-adept rivals.

It seems almost unfair to include only one chapter about mobile marketing in a book about digital marketing. We could easily devote an entire book, or perhaps an entire encyclopedia, to this topic alone. We've seen a feverish flurry of books, blogs, and whitepapers about mobile these last few years, as Fortune 500 companies and garage startups alike scramble to adopt effective mobile marketing strategy for their brands.

That said, I predict that within just five years from now there will no longer be content written about *mobile marketing* at all. The reason is that mobile technologies are evolving so fast, and are becoming so ubiquitous, that soon mobile marketing will just be called *marketing*. Thus, brands not embracing and planning for mobile today, will find that they are without any sort of effective marketing strategy at all tomorrow.

Does that sound farfetched? It would be silly to simply accept one mobile marketing enthusiast's word as truth. Please allow me the opportunity to convince you.

THE MOBILE WORLD WE LIVE IN

There are currently just over seven billion people on our planet. We span an immense gamut of culture, from technologically advanced postindustrial nations, to nomadic and agricultural tribal societies. We range from young children to senior citizens, and span thousands of races, religions, and spoken languages.

According to the Ericsson mobility report from November 2012,[1] there were approximately 6.4 billion active mobile subscriptions at the time of the report's publishing. That represents an approximately 91 percent saturation rate of the entire world's population, and is more than the number of TVs, home phones, and PCs in use worldwide *combined*. Since many people have more than one subscription (for work, tablets, etc.), the number of actual unique mobile subscribers—that is, the number of people with at least one mobile device with an active connection—is about 4.3 billion, or 62 percent of the entire planet. That means more than 6 out of every 10 people on earth have their own mobile device with an active subscription! When you take into account that this 62 percent necessarily excludes those physically, mentally, or geographically unable to use cell phones (including infants and the elderly), and also excludes all Wi-Fi-only tablets (e.g., those not equipped with data plans), there is no denying that the ubiquity of mobile technology is astounding. It seems mobile is quickly becoming the universal language in this globalized technological world.

Mobile devices are evolving even more quickly than they are being adopted. Of the 6.4 billion subscriptions, 22 percent worldwide include mobile broadband subscriptions (via 3G, 4G, or other broadband-based technologies). Based on smartphone sales rates in 2012, it is estimated that in developed nations, the percentage of *smart* devices hovered around 60 percent at the end of 2012. Both of these percentages are accelerating rapidly.

So, how much do we actually use our phones? Well, here are some more statistics to mull over: Usability experts estimate that the average smartphone user currently looks at his or her phone more than 150 times each day[2]—that's nearly ten times for each hour that we're awake, or every six minutes. According to the Mobile Mindset Study conducted by the mobile security company Lookout,[3] nearly 60 percent of all phone owners don't go a whole waking hour without checking their phones; 54 percent check their phones while lying in bed, and 40 percent admit to doing so while on the toilet. Of the respondents, 94 percent are seriously concerned about losing their phones, and 73 percent of those who did said they *panicked*. It seems I am in good company.

People feel lost without their phones these days because mobile phones are doing a whole lot more than just making calls. Already, in just a few years, our mobile phones have all but replaced a plethora of other devices that have existed for decades. Our phones tell time, and so watches are no longer necessary except for fashion purposes. They have built-in apps for alarm clocks, eliminating the need for those too. Our phones take pictures and videos of a quality acceptable to 99 percent of us, thus replacing cameras and camcorders in most cases. The GPS navigation on our phones is often better than those in our cars. The number of game titles available on iOS alone trumps those created for devoted portable game systems 100 to 1. Smartphones play music as well as any iPod or MP3 player, and so these dedicated music players have seen a drop in sales. Mobile devices are starting to be used for more advanced applications like medical diagnostics and monitoring. With the rise of mobile payments, even our wallets will likely soon be replaced by our smartphones. Smartphones have completely eclipsed the functionality of, for example, calculators, beepers, compasses, PDAs, personal organizers, and other measurement hardware tools. This trend is only going to continue. What devices will be replaced in the next five years?

THE MODERN MOBILE CONSUMER

Even more relevant to marketers is what these new technologies allow our customers to do now that they weren't able to do in the past. In the case of mobile, the change is rather drastic.

In the first chapter, we described a scenario where a customer uses his smartphone to compare product pricing, reviews, and social commentary on his phone to make a point-of-sale purchase decision. This example highlights the new always-connected, hyper-informed consumer that brands and businesses face today. At any given time, within a matter of seconds, the modern consumer can access more information about your brand than you ever thought possible—and it doesn't matter whether that consumer is at home, at work, driving to the store, or staring down your product in a store aisle. The point-of-sale part is particularly frightening, because for the first time in the history of retail, consumers are able to access the vast repository of ever-changing, incessantly current information contained on the web at that exact critical moment.

This information at consumers' fingertips includes pricing at every top web retailer, as well as brick-and-mortar stores within a 50-mile radius. It includes what brand advocates, critics, and personal friends have been saying and sharing on Facebook, Twitter, Pinterest, Instagram, and Vine. It includes quick comments and lengthy reviews, with tones ranging from glowingly positive to downright disparaging, from e-tailers like Amazon. It also contains videos from fans and critics around the web, mostly from YouTube. A horde of impressive mobile applications, including shopkick, ShopSavvy, and Swirl, are putting all of this data (and more) in consumers' hands wherever they go. It's all just a few swipes, voice searches, or barcode scans away!

Much of this accessible-anywhere content can be curated, influenced, and directed by you, but quite a bit comes from the community that uses or is influenced by your products or services. A bit overwhelming, isn't it?

Scarier still is that this type of activity permeates all other digital media channels, and is more prevalent than most of us ever imagined. In fact, the *mobile-first* user has become the new norm. According to Google, 27 percent of all web searches come from a mobile device,[4] and the company believes mobile will be the primary search channel by the end of 2013. At the November 2012 Open Mobile Summit conference, Google executives said that 40 percent of all YouTube views now come from mobile devices, representing a 300 percent increase over the 2011 figure.[5] Facebook also confirms a similar statistic: According to the company, more than 60 percent of its user-base accesses the service via phones and tablets.[6] The growth rate of mobile usage is simply astounding—and it's only accelerating.

Consumer expectations for content consumption have changed as well. The modern consumer expects to find *exactly* what he is looking for, at *exactly* the time that he needs the information. He expects that it will be discoverable, mobile-optimized, and accessible from wherever he is in 30 seconds or less—otherwise, it doesn't exist. He demands that if content is discovered on one device (say, a laptop), it will be equally accessible and consumable from his tablet or smartphone, and vice versa. He also expects that the content he accesses through his mobile device is interactive, and furthermore can interact with the product or service in the real world. He makes decisions quickly—usually within a matter of seconds—and the smartphone has become the engine driving those decisions. Attention spans have never been shorter, and the sheer number of choices that the modern consumer makes each day based on information passing through mobile channels is astonishing.

An eye-opening joint study between Google and Neilson in March 2013 highlights the profound efficacy of mobile marketing. According to the study, 81 percent of all mobile searches are driven by speed and convenience; 73 percent of mobile searches trigger additional actions, with two actions on average; and 28 percent of mobile searches result directly in a conversion. Furthermore, a whopping 55 percent of all conversions from mobile channels happen within the first hour. Mobile searches tend to be more decision-oriented: they result in one-third greater likelihood of a website visit or phone call, and 50 percent greater likelihood of a store visit and/or eventual purchase. Unsurprisingly, in-store searches tend to convert best, and positive outcomes were most likely for products in the beauty, auto, travel, food, and tech categories, in that order. Even mobile ads seem to add to the experience, with 59 percent of participants in the study finding them *useful*.[7]

If your business doesn't sell products in stores or online, don't be fooled into thinking you're safe from the hyper-connected customer. Whether you're a services business, or even a B2B-only business, the power of mobile allows your potential customers to access all of this information from anywhere—even during the 90-second coffee break in the middle of a sales meeting.

If you're thinking: "Wow, we're really behind the eight-ball here," you're not alone. Only one in four brands has a defined mobile strategy, and only the most innovative and technologically adept companies are making truly effective use of mobile as an integral part of their marketing mix. That said, now that you know the scale and growth of mobile, and the crucial role it will play in the future of marketing, you can begin putting a plan into place that leverages mobile to take your brand to new heights.

MOBILE UNWIRES MARKETERS FROM FORMER CONSTRAINTS

The new mobile world, rife with hyper-connected consumers that have all the world's information with them at all times, is admittedly a scary one. The attitudes, expectations, and behaviors of consumers have shifted to the "now." Few companies have effectively found ways to reach their customers with the exact information they're looking for, in a digestible way, at the exact moment they are looking for it. Most marketers underestimate the importance of this concept, and those who don't often lack the knowledge to make it a reality.

In truth, mobile may be the vector that allows this real-time serving of information to take place, but it requires the concerted effort of all other digital media channels along with it to function optimally. Mobile technology makes all of the digital channels described in this book that much more important. It acts as a *digital magnifier* of sorts, thrusting all digital strategy into the spotlight, and exponentially increasing the importance of search, social media, video, and website strategies.

Magnifying digital strategy is just the beginning of the opportunity that mobile affords. Mobile technologies, coupled with the disposition of the modern consumer, mark the end of many constraints that marketers have faced for decades.

The silver lining on this complex mobile word is that mobile marketing presents an unprecedented opportunity for brands and businesses. By utilizing a host of new capabilities afforded by mobile technologies, and tying it together with other digital strategies into cohesive and effective multichannel campaigns, mobile can be a key lever for your brand to gain a competitive advantage over the rest of the field.

Rich Media Can Be Experienced Anywhere

For the first time ever, marketers can reach consumers wherever they are with rich and interactive audio and video, extending the reach of our brands and our marketing efforts. It has been said that marketing is fundamentally about reaching "the right person, with the right message, at the right time." You'll have to use your creative acumen to reach the right person with the right message, but the advent of mobile technology makes doing so at just the right time much more feasible.

Modern smartphones and tablets are capable of streaming high-definition video from the web in real time. Through apps, they're also capable of rich interactive experiences, and with some creativity you can ensure that your brand is at the center of that experience at the right moment.

Dish Network, the satellite TV provider, leapfrogged its competitors by understanding that its customers are no longer wired to their homes, and so their content shouldn't be either. While some providers allow TV to be streamed on mobile devices while connected to the home network, Dish went one step further by allowing live TV, as well as on-demand shows and DVR recordings, to be streamed from any device, at any time, from anywhere. The move helped propel the brand to 92 percent stronger-than-expected subscriber growth for the six months following the campaign's launch. Similarly, your brand's video content can be accessed on the go too—whether consumers are searching for it, or whether it's being served to them via an interactive advertisement.[8]

Contextual Awareness Affords Targeted Ad Opportunities

Mobile devices are location-aware. Almost all modern smartphones are equipped with a GPS (Global Positioning System), allowing the phone (and its apps) to know exactly where you are at the time you are using a particular app. This includes apps like Google Maps, which are replete with local search features. Mobile devices are also time-aware, with the time standardized and set by the mobile provider. As an author of an app (and we'll get more into apps later), you have the ability to use both a user's location and the current time to serve them content or advertising that is contextually relevant to the present. This concept is often referred to as *location-based marketing*.

Take this scenario:

> A submarine sandwich enthusiast, who happens to *like* Quiznos on Facebook, is standing at East 45th Street in New York City at noon. While using his phone, he receives an advertised coupon offering $1 off a full-size sub, good only at the 42nd Street Quiznos, and only for the next hour until 1:00 p.m. How likely is this individual

to act on this advertisement? What if the mobile advertisement is served to him in the course of his doing a local Google search for lunch places around his immediate location? Quiznos partnered with mobile advertising agency Sense Networks to achieve this very thing in Austin, Texas, and saw a 20 percent increase in coupon redemptions and fantastic ROI from the campaign.[9]

Real-time mobile location data, when coupled with behavioral insights from social media like Facebook and Pinterest, gives marketers a pretty darn good idea how interested a consumer might be in a particular offering. This methodology can go several steps further: Based on collected historical data about this person's habits, such as day of the week, time of day, weather-related patterns, and consumption preferences, advertisers can utilize this individual's (and aggregated) data to serve exactly the right offers to consumers at exactly the right times. Those that are familiar with Google's forward-thinking Google Now platform have seen a glimpse of what's to come in this arena. Increased data collection and proper analysis may one day allow marketers to know and predict our consumption patterns better than we consumers know ourselves. The current and future impact of these innovations is staggering. In any case, you should certainly consider utilizing contextual awareness in your next mobile campaign as a way to provide utility to your customers or improve ad conversions.

In-Store Experiences Can Be Transformed

Contextual awareness can provide an even greater degree of engagement and customization through branded mobile applications. For instance, if a user is standing in (or walking by) your establishment's retail store, you can alert them to current promotions, demonstrate new products, or target them with discounts or offers for that store. If the retail establishment has done its job collecting and utilizing customer data across platforms, it could even demonstrate new or on-sale products that match a customer's shopping history or preferences. The absolute best mobile apps for retail combine this contextual relevancy with rich media and interactivity within the store, and even tie them into Customer

Relationship Management (CRM) and loyalty systems to maximize impact.

One company doing this particularly well is Sephora, the U.S.-based makeup and fragrance retailer. Sephora's apps target its most loyal customers, who can sync their mobile devices with their store accounts, allowing them to access their wish lists and recommended products within the store or anywhere else. The iPhone app allows these customers to scan product barcodes within the store to view ratings, reviews, and additional product information. It also alerts users to special promotions, stores Sephora gift cards within Apple's Passbook application, and allows extremely simple purchasing and shipping of scanned products as gifts for others. Sephora has seen more than 1.1 million app downloads, 75 percent increased mobile traffic, and a 167 percent increase in mobile orders.[10] The results truly speak for themselves. Other retailers have found success in partnering with mobile loyalty and reward platforms. Macy's partners with shopkick's mobile platform, which recognizes automatically that a user has entered a Macy's store, and allows shoppers to earn points through store visits and product interactions.

If your brand sells a physical product but doesn't have a retail store, you can still utilize apps that interact with your brand's products to create value for your customers. Service-based businesses too can utilize mobile technologies to enhance the service experience or to make wait times more tolerable or interesting. Can you think of a way that your brand can utilize mobile technologies to improve customer experiences with your product, service, or store?

Mobile Transactions Let Us Glimpse the Future of Commerce

Mobile technology's place in commerce (or mCommerce) has manifested itself in three main ways over the last few years. Mobile devices can be used to: (1) make Internet purchases from home or on the go; (2) pay for items in-store, as an alternative to cash or credit cards; and, (3) receive payments, mostly for small or highly-mobile businesses.

The magnitude of mobile purchasing is nothing to sneeze at. Mobile commerce purchases totaled $25 billion in 2012, accounting for 11 percent of total purchases nationwide. They are expected to top $85 million by 2016, or 27 percent of total purchases in that year.[11] Furthermore, according to Google, 85 percent of smartphone owners shop for a product on one device, and then make the purchase on another device,[12] highlighting the need for multichannel interoperability to create a seamless experience for customers. The total dollar value of transactions that are taking place in particular through tablets is accelerating very rapidly, and as of this writing tops the smartphone total by about 50 percent.

For these reasons, it is essential that marketers provide mobile channels to allow product purchases. Unsurprisingly, Amazon and eBay are leading the way in this department. Both companies have created iPad applications that, in my sole opinion, best the experience they provide from a traditional computer. New technologies from companies like Google, PayPal, and Square allow businesses to accept payments from mobile devices anywhere, and also allow consumers to purchase products using nothing but their mobile phones.

Starbucks implemented a mobile payments system last year around a *virtual card*. Coffee lovers can load money onto a virtual Starbucks card via the web or their phones, and the balance appears within the Starbucks mobile app. Customers can then pay for coffee using only their mobile devices by allowing baristas to scan a unique barcode on the their smartphones' screens. As of November 2012, Starbucks processes over two million mobile payments each week using this creative marketing technique.[13] The Starbucks mobile app also includes a rewards system, gift-giving options, and a location-aware store locator that guides users to the nearest open Starbucks.

A few U.S. retail banks have also done a fantastic job of utilizing mobile transactions to improve experiences for their customers. JPMorgan Chase has its QuickDeposit app, which allows customers, at any time of day or night, to deposit checks directly into their checking or savings accounts by simply snapping pictures of the front and back of the checks within the app. Bank of America has a similar app, which in addition to check cashing, also allows customers to view transaction histories, pay bills, and locate the nearest BofA branch or ATM. If banks, the granddaddies of all security worrywarts, have found ways to utilize mobile commerce to improve their customer experience, shouldn't your brand be able to as well?

Games On the Go Engage and Expand Product Offerings

Everybody loves games. The gaming industry has exploded over the last decade, with mobile gaming showing the strongest growth of all. Innovative brands are beginning to borrow this concept to engage customers on a deep level and increase the reach and virility of their marketing campaigns.

Companies can do this by awarding achievements or *badges* to consumers for completing milestones related to their brand, such as visiting a certain number of stores, or interacting with their brand in various ways using digital media. The most successful gamified apps are inherently social at their core, and often allow for competitive or friendly rivalry. Gamified apps that cleverly and tastefully utilize mobile hardware features (such as the camera, GPS, or accelerometer) to improve the experience also tend to fare better.

Nike is one brand paving the way for others in this exciting area. The company's incredibly popular Nike+ app tracks your total number of steps, calories burned, and workout statistics each day using compatible wristbands and shoe accessories. From your mobile phone or tablet, you can see how your fitness metrics are progressing according to your goals, and how your activity stacks up against your friends' activity. The app allowed Nike to extend its brand image from a products company to a complete fitness solutions company. Nike has seen incredible growth from its gamified fitness endeavors.

Some other successful gamified mobile applications utilize the collection of virtual items, coupons, or barcodes, and reward customers with real or virtual rewards. For companies looking for a more turnkey gamified solution, there are third-party platforms like Bunchball and Badgeville that can be leveraged to easily incorporate game elements into a brand app.

Gamification can produce impactful results for brands of all types. Even if a brand's image isn't typically associated with youthfulness and fun, the utility and sense of satisfaction brought by gamification can be a boon for even a traditionally forthright brand. It is the job of marketers and their agency partners to do gamification tastefully, and in a manner that does not conflict with a brand's image.

Mobile essentially turns what was previously impossible into possibilities for innovation. The opportunity is colossal—the likes of which we have never seen in the history of marketing. Let's drill down into specific mobile technologies, and explore tips, best practices, and opportunities for their use.

MOBILE WEBSITE CONSIDERATIONS

People often refer to the *mobile web* as if it were its own unique world, completely separate from the Internet. In truth, there is really only one web. The mobile web is simply the regular web viewed through the lens of a mobile device. That said, given the rise and impending dominance of mobile, you might have already guessed that the mobile web is extremely important to your digital marketing effort. If more than one-quarter of total search traffic is from mobile, you can bet that they're coming to your website via mobile devices. Additionally, customers are likely visiting your site at even more critical times when visiting from a mobile device—often just before a decision of some sort is made. Check your own brand's website now from your mobile phone. How does it look? Is it readable? Is it easy to navigate? Are the important site components and action points readily accessible? Is this the experience you want your customers to have when they stumble upon your website?

Web-enabled mobile devices range in screen sizes from three to ten inches, and span more than a dozen common sets of dimensions (called resolutions). Thus, creating a single website that looks and works great on all of them isn't easy. The one near-universal truth is that websites designed for desktop and laptop PCs/Macs almost never look and feel right on any mobile device. After all, a four-inch touchscreen necessitates a very different interface than a fifteen-inch screen utilizing a mouse or touchpad as inputs. Thus, special attention to mobile websites is an absolute must.

Fortunately, at the exact moment that someone visits your website, you're able to tell exactly what browser and type of device they are using, and serve them the appropriate experience accordingly. You really have two viable options for mobile website strategy:

1. *Build one or more separate mobile sites alongside your main website.* These mobile sites must be developed and maintained separately, but can be designed from the ground up to provide the exact experience you intend for each device type. For instance, the entire interface can be touch-centric, and the entire contents of the site can be shifted and streamlined for a better user experience. You can even bring certain site elements that make sense for mobile, such as store-locators or time-sensitive information, to the forefront of the experience. Large brands that have the resources to do so often segment mobile markets into smartphones and tablets, creating two completely separate mobile websites with the experience optimized for each type of device. For instance, Google uses this tactic with great success for its Gmail web interfaces, creating great experiences across all types of devices. Including mobile apps, Gmail can be accessed in a total of at least six completely different interfaces! We wouldn't expect your brand to utilize mobile as effectively as Google, but it gives us a picture of what best-in-class looks like, and provides us with something to shoot for.
2. *Utilize fully responsive web design.* In recent years, some savvy web developers have been creating single websites that essentially automatically adjust to any screen size or display resolution. This allows the development team to manage a single repository of code that spans all devices. I'd purport that for simpler, information-based sites, responsive web design (RWD) can be cheaper and more manageable in the long run. However, for more complicated and interactive sites, responsive design can create colossal headaches for the development team, as testing and refining complicated features across all device

types, screen sizes, and browsers, can be frustrating. When you're speaking with your internal development team (or an external agency) about your mobile website, be sure to include responsive design as a part of the discussion, and together come up with the best strategy for your brand. The only truly wrong choice is ignoring mobile website strategy altogether!

SMS AND MMS CAMPAIGNS

SMS (Simple Message Service), commonly known as *text messaging*, has been around almost as long as mobile phones themselves. Despite a move toward real-time chat communications among smartphone users, SMS is still the most widely used data application in the world, with 3.6 billion users, or 78 percent of all mobile subscribers.[14] It is also an incredibly powerful (and often neglected) mobile marketing channel. MMS (Multimedia Message Service), the high-tech variant of SMS that allows rich media (like images and video) to be sent over this channel, can also be utilized for marketing purposes.

SMS is as close to a surefire method to reach customers as any marketing method available. It is estimated that 95 percent of all users who opt-in to a brand's SMS communications will open and read the messages they receive.[15] No other marketing channel in existence can reproduce a number like that! It's also relatively cheap to run and administer.

That said, SMS is highly regulated by its governing bodies, in much the way telemarketing phone services are. In the United States, subscribers must always opt into your communications and must be able to opt out at any time by texting the word "stop." There are also strict rules for contact expiry and list management. You should not let these regulations alone deter you, however. I suggest reading the rules, and considering if SMS marketing might be of use to your brand.

If you do engage in SMS marketing, I also suggest being extremely tasteful with the messages you send—choosing only the most important and impactful communications—and doing so infrequently. A high opening rate comes at a cost: The messages are indeed very obtrusive. Even though many of the SMS recipients won't bother to opt out, some may still perceive your messages as spam. Furthermore, SMS marketing is socially accepted in Europe and Asia, but less so in North America. Be wary!

MOBILE APPLICATIONS: THE LOW-DOWN

Apps—you've certainly heard of them. Your kids, nieces, nephews, and young cousins use them incessantly. You probably use them yourself on a daily basis for a variety of purposes. It's time to learn their good qualities, and how marketers can use them to engage current and prospective customers in ways you may have never thought possible.

With the advent of smartphones, mobile applications have become the dominant feature of mobile interfaces over the last several years. Their rise to dominance grew out of the need for simplified interactions on small screens, and was perpetuated by the arrival of touchscreens, which are now a staple of modern devices. The term *app* became truly ubiquitous following Apple's immensely successful "There's an app for that" campaign. This phrase highlights an incredibly important fact about apps: They seem to nearly infinitely extend the uses of smartphones to do what required an entire backpack of gadgets before.

I'm often asked by marketers: "Why should our strategy include a mobile app? What can an app do that a mobile website can't?" The short answer is that apps provide a laundry list of advantages and opportunities that no other media type can match. Here are the three big ones:

1. *Apps utilize mobile hardware.* With the user's permission, apps can make use of the many hardware innovations in today's mobile devices. These include the GPS (for contextually relevant content and advertising), camera (for photo and video integration, barcode scanning, and eye sensing), accelerometer/gyroscope (for tilt controls

and rotations), internal storage (to save information), vibration controls, near-field communication technologies (also known as NFC, for device-to-device communications), and fingerprint scanners (for security).

2. *Apps can access core software.* With the user's permission, apps can access a user's personal contacts, utilize user accounts (such as Apple ID or Google Account), and integrate with the phone's notification system to display relevant alerts and messages. These collectively give marketers the ability to personalize the user's experience to a large degree. Notifications increase the amount of engagement users have with an app by reminding users that it exists and reaching users in a timelier manner.
3. *Apps offer better user experiences.* Apps afford many interface advantages over alternatives. They are more accessible than mobile sites, being just one screen touch away. They can offer a great deal of flexibility in how their interfaces are developed, allowing for more advanced user interactions and better touch-optimized controls. Thus, user interfaces (UI) for apps are more visually appealing and afford a more pleasurable navigation experience than other mobile media. Apps can also store most of their content locally (in the phone's storage), dramatically improving load times, and reducing dependency on network access and data speed. Lastly, they manage user sessions better, allowing people to stay logged in much longer and more easily without the need to reload and login. Despite many advances in mobile website development, these advantages net to a rich user experience that no mobile website can match.

So if your brand doesn't have a mobile app, you should acquire the resources and build one immediately, right? Well, not necessarily.

Not long ago, a brand manager at a well-known Fortune 500 clothing retailer asked me to diagnose the poor usage of his brand's newly released mobile app, which had ample marketing dollars behind it. The app was essentially a portal to its (poor) mobile website, with a few useless features tied in. The conversation started something like this:

Me: "What's the actual purpose of the app?"
Brand Manager: "To improve brand engagement of course."
Me: "What value does it provide to your customers? Why should any customer use this app?"
Brand Manager: (5 seconds of silence) ... "Well, it provides one-click access to our website. Our loyal shoppers use mobile phones, and we want to be everywhere they are."

He's not wrong in any respect, but he's also missing the point of making an investment in a mobile app. Unlike a mobile-optimized website, you don't need to have an app just to demonstrate your presence. For the most part, customers and prospects are not actively seeking out your app as they might with your mobile website. With the exception of apps that go viral, brand apps are primarily sought out and used by the customers already loyal to the brand. Furthermore, app store dynamics demonstrate strong network effects, meaning that unpopular (and poorly rated) apps get pushed into obscurity very rapidly, making them practically undiscoverable unless someone is searching for them specifically.

For this reason, building a mobile app without a clear purpose is generally a waste of marketing budget and human capital. Far too many brands, large and small, fall into this trap of creating apps with no (or insufficient) value proposition. Be sure that your mobile app clearly demonstrates at least one of the following (and preferably more than one) to avoid this pitfall:

1. *Improved experience with product or service.* This condition can be satisfied in any number of ways, but should very clearly provide some value to the app users. If your brand is a physical product, the app could interface with the product in the real world in some way—as a companion, tracking mechanism, or organizer. For example, Johnson & Johnson's Care4Today app reminds users to take their pills at specific times, and keeps a record of pills taken

that can be shared with a person's healthcare provider to improve adherence for prescription drugs.[16] Your app could also permit quicker access to customer service, or allow easy product reordering or modification. For service-based brands, the app might provide core features that utilize mobile hardware like location-based tools. It could even provide quick access to streamlined versions of commonly used core product features, helpful information, or easy access to user accounts and settings.

2. *Entertainment.* For an app to be classified as fun, it can provide gamified interactions, literally be a game, or incorporate clever humor in some other way. Using gamification—essentially adding game elements to a user experience—is a great way to keep users engaged with your app. Fun apps often have an increased chance of going viral, but are often more costly and difficult to do correctly. If your app includes (or is) a game, be sure that it keeps consistent with your brand's image and overarching marketing goals.
3. *Provide tangible rewards.* Everybody loves deals and free stuff. Apps that can earn users discounts, free products, or swag, have a better chance of making an impact for your brand. This might take the form of mobile couponing or loyalty-based rewards for using the app in various ways, such as completing tasks, consuming media, or sharing via social channels. Tie-ins to CRM systems are a great way to make tangible rewards work in your favor by helping to identify and target brand evangelists.

Apps can be a fantastic opportunity to improve brand engagement when done correctly, but they are not for every brand or organization, and should not be pushed out the door without the proper strategic and creative planning. It's okay to experiment here, as it is with all digital channels, but be warned that app store critics can be rather brutal in their reviews, thinking little of giving their otherwise favorite brands one-star ratings for a single sub-par mobile experience. Many negative reviews upon an app's release can be damaging to the future success of an app and can represent a deep hole for your brand to crawl out of.

Also, since apps remain on the app store and on users' devices, they generally represent an ongoing investment, and one that plays into a brand's holistic long-term marketing strategy. Only large brands have the luxury of using apps for one-off campaigns and one-time events, but these are often well worth the investment when done correctly.

Apps should not be the first piece of mobile strategy brands dive into. We recommend brands start by optimizing mobile websites, utilizing mobile search and advertising channels, and perhaps dabbling in basic SMS campaigns when first approaching mobile strategy. That said, apps have the potential to be a brand's most impactful use of mobile technology and represent a great opportunity for your brand to deeply engage customers on the go and in different and unique ways.

Mobile App Development Considerations

When developing a mobile app, the first decision you'll have to make is what mobile operating system(s) your app is going to reside on. There are really only two mobile OS platforms that you should care about: Android (open source, by Google) and iOS (proprietary, by Apple). Android runs on a variety of manufacturers' handsets, including Samsung, HTC, Motorola, and Sony, while iOS only runs on Apple-branded hardware. As of the end of 2012, Android had an approximately 70 percent global smartphone market share, while iOS had about 20 percent. In the United States, the race is a bit closer, at 52 percent and 38 percent, respectively.[17] Additionally, iOS and Android just about split the tablet market equally, and on average, iOS users consume more data and are more active with apps by a slim margin. iOS is also more prevalent for business.[18] All in all, Android growth rates are a bit higher, but as of this writing the race is about tied.

If a brand wants to reach both Android and iOS device owners, they must develop apps for both of them. Unfortunately, each platform must be developed for independently, and doing so nearly doubles the amount of time and resources necessary to complete your app. iOS must be coded in a language known as Objective C and utilizes Apple's software development kit (SDK). On the other hand, Android is generally coded in Java and utilizes

Google's SDK. To make matters worse, while large agencies generally have developers that can do both, small development shops often specialize in either just one or the other. So where does a brand start?

On the whole, I can't really recommend that marketers focus on one operating system versus the other. It really depends upon the individual demographics of your app's intended audience and your long-term goals. My general advice would be to pick just one of the two platforms, and launch that one first. If your app is gamified, intensely social, and/or targets the bleeding-edge early adopters of new software, perhaps start with iOS. Over the last two years, iOS has tended to be the first-choice platform for brands outside of the IT space. If your goal is the widest possible audience, and your app is best-suited for mainstream smartphone users, consider starting with Android. This is not to say that the two audiences differ in this way universally—I'm nitpicking to provide you with a useful starting point. I suggest doing thorough market research, and speaking with your agency about how your campaign's specific goals can utilize each platform to maximize reach and impact.

After successfully launching your iOS or Android app, continue testing, learning, and incorporating user feedback to begin improving upon the app. At this point, you can begin development on the other platform if prudent, taking lessons learned from the initial launch into consideration. For very large brands with ample marketing budget behind them, a simultaneous launch on Android and iOS might make the most sense to create the biggest initial splash for your campaign at launch.

Budgeting and Partnership Considerations

Depending upon the complexity of the app, and the scale of the integration necessary with other company resources, the cost of an iOS or Android app can range from $5,000 to many millions of dollars. In general, partners will quote you a price for the requirements you specify, and changes or additions to those requirements will be tacked on by mutual agreement. Development could take anywhere from a few weeks to a year, depending upon a number of factors and on your budget. Some companies acquire talent to develop and maintain their apps internally, while others rely on long-term agency relationships. When choosing a partner for app development, be sure to look for a proven track record of creating clean, functional apps with great user experiences. App store reviews of previously developed apps can be useful as well to determine how the developers dealt with bugs and ongoing issues, as long as you take the reviews with a grain of salt (as the brand influences these activities as well). I personally tend to place additional emphasis on development partners hell-bent on creating fantastic user interfaces (UI) and user experiences (UX), those with strong functional computer science backgrounds, and those who are communicative and easy to work with. As is the case with other digital strategies, it will require the concerted creative and planning efforts of marketers, in conjunction with great development talent, to achieve success.

I'd also caution brands to be extremely methodical and understanding during the development process. Do as much planning, sketching, and designing as possible prior to even starting development so that your partners have a very clear idea of your requirements. Be sure to let the developers use their creativity and mobile-specific acumen to augment the product at times, but feel free to push back at other times. Be flexible and open-minded, but simultaneously maintain devotion to your vision and campaign goals. Far too many brands are hellish partners for agencies, often changing requirements mid-project, or failing to incorporate useful advice out of stubbornness. At times, we must recognize that highly technical marketing products (like mobile apps and websites) require some specialized knowledge to implement effectively, and that not all marketers possess this knowledge.

MOBILE TECHNOLOGIES TO WATCH: SNACKS FOR THOUGHT

By leveraging mobile technologies and tying in other digital channels, mobile affords a plethora of unique and innovative marketing strategies that can be utilized by today's brands. Each of the following new technologies can be leveraged to help create impactful mobile strategies, and are intended to inspire you to dream up creative mobile app ideas for your own brand. These technologies are not ubiquitous just yet, but keep an eye on them; they will each play a colossal role in the future of marketing!

QR Codes

Do you recall hand-scanners used at supermarkets—the ones that flash a red light onto a product barcode to identify its item number and price? Well, our smartphones, using their built-in cameras, can also scan barcodes and identify products in much the same way. In fact, mobile devices can even scan and recognize two-dimensional barcodes that carry a lot more information than the one-dimensional ones found on store products. One such type of two-dimensional barcode often used in marketing is the *QR code* (see Figure 5.1). The information contained in QR codes, when scanned, can instruct a mobile device to take any number of actions, including:

- Launch any website, including a social network page.
- Play a video.
- Play an audio file.
- Download a file from the web.
- Download a mobile app from an app store.
- Open an existing mobile app and navigate to appropriate content.
- Take actions within an app, like earning points, discounts, etc.

FIGURE 5.1 Advertisement with a QR Code: The QR code on this 2011 circular from Peapod can be scanned with a mobile device, allowing recipients to easily download the Peapod mobile apps.

These are just a sampling of things you can do with QR codes. They are often useful in marketing because they push users down the conversion funnel, improving the probability of taking some desired action. QR codes can appear on advertisements like banners, posters, and t-shirts. They can appear on product tags, signs, business cards, or just about anywhere. QR codes can even be dynamic when using intermediary software, allowing the actions they take to be updated at any time, or to take different actions for different users. They have been used by dozen of brands in brilliantly creative ways.

Macy's department stores have begun putting QR codes on product tags that, when scanned, display the clothes on models and provide fashion tips about what to pair the garment with. Spotify, the social music company, allows users to scan a friend's QR code to acquire their music playlist, effectively creating the modern-day version of the mix tape.

Tesco supermarkets used QR codes in a truly creative way. The company placed lifelike billboards in subways in Korea that depicted stocked supermarket shelves. Busy citizens could scan the QR codes on the shelves with their phones, checkout, and have the products delivered to their houses, saving them the need to physically do the shopping or carry heavy bags. In the United States, Peapod implemented a similar concept in Philadelphia and saw 50 percent growth in orders from mobile devices, which now accounts for 30 percent of the company's of total revenue.[19] The company is planning to roll out the concept in more than 100 major U.S. cities. One thing to keep in mind, however, is that QR codes require an active data connection to work properly, so underground subways without data access (such as those in New York City) could not use this type of strategy effectively. Plan carefully!

Augmented Reality

Augmented reality, or *AR* for short, is the use of mobile technology to overlay information or imagery onto the physical world. By holding the phone up in front of you, the mobile device's rear-facing camera displays what's directly behind it, creating the illusion of a completely transparent mobile device. However, instead of showing the real world exactly as it is, AR technology overlays additional information, for a variety of purposes, that doesn't actually exist in the real world.

For instance, holding a mobile device up in a city may point out the actual locations of various points of interest, such as ATMs, restaurants, bars, and entertainment, replete with reviews and real-time information from the web (see Figure 5.2). Nokia did just this with its City Lens app, which displays virtual signs to recommended places to eat, drink, shop, and sightsee in major cities around the world.[20] The city of Hong Kong did something similar, improving the tourism experience for visitors by eliminating the need for maps, books, and hired guides.

Several auto manufacturers have used AR to improve engagement during live events. Kia Motors created a companion to the U.S. Open, which allowed viewers to enhance their experience with tennis- and car-based content. The brand saw a 58 percent increase in searches for the Kia Optima, and beat sales estimates by 57 percent that month, much in part to the app's success. Volvo created an AR-based racing game that worked in conjunction with a YouTube video and saw nearly 200,000 clicks on the masthead ad and nearly 300 percent increased traffic to volvocars.com. Volkswagen's take on AR manifested itself using interactivity with Volkswagen billboards, allowing them to become interactive and three-dimensional.[21]

Augmented reality has even been used to create virtual games in the real world. AR company Ingress recently created a massively multiplayer game out of the concept, for which the beta seems to be very well-received.[22] I'm personally excited to see what comes of the concept, which perhaps gives us a small glimpse into the future of game-based entertainment.

The downside of augmented reality is that it often requires your own custom app alongside the AR-enabled content, necessitating a sort of confluence of circumstance that may reduce the potential impact of the investment. This stands in stark contrast to QR codes, which are universally recognized by any barcode scanner across all mobile operating systems. Companies like Layar and blippar are trying to create the best of both worlds by utilizing a single, universal AR app. Other companies can partner with these

FIGURE 5.2 Augmented Reality: Augmented reality apps appear to overlay objects and information onto the real world to enhance the experience for users.

companies to have their AR-enabled content viewed through the Layar or blippar app, thus eliminating the need to develop and market a self-branded AR app. Luxury watch brand Omega partnered with blippar to create an interactive AR print ad that lets readers view the advertised Planet Ocean watch in 3-D, and even try it on their own wrists virtually to see how it looks.[23]

While some brands are making clever and successful use of augmented reality, most that have dabbled in this technology have failed to create truly useful or memorable experiences that perpetuate their brand's image. Geico's BroStache app, which overlays a virtual mustache on one's face using AR, is a prime culprit of this. Conversely, Band-Aid created a similar Magic Vision app that displays dancing Muppet characters, which won several awards for creativity and garnered more than 115 million earned media impressions.[24]

The truth is that AR has yet to hit mainstream marketing due to its technical drawbacks and companies not taking this technology seriously. However, there are ample opportunities for brands to utilize AR today, and considering the use of AR in your next campaign could be just the thing to draw attention to your brand. I predict that when the mobile paradigm shifts away from handsets and into wearable devices, AR will become the dominant driving force behind mobile innovation. Keep an eye on this technology!

Near-Field Communication (NFC)

Near-field communication technology, or NFC for short, is a new mobile technology that's starting to have a big impact on marketing. This technology allows two devices in close proximity to share or exchange information with one another. This exchange could take place between two mobile phones, allowing them to share photos, music, or in-app collectibles. It could also be between one mobile phone and a stationary object in the environment—like a sales kiosk, or even a printed poster equipped with a paper-thin microchip tag.

NFC is incredibly powerful because it combines the universal nature of QR-codes with two-way device communications, all rolled into an even simpler method of data exchange. NFC technologies, combined with fingerprint-sensing technologies, will together power the future of mobile commerce. With the release of the next generation iPhone that is expected to utilize these technologies, coupled with continued upgrades to NFC-equipped Android phones, I predict 2014 will be the year that mCommerce finally gets thrust into the mainstream. I expect that in just three years from this writing, we'll all be leaving our wallets at home and utilizing our mobile devices exclusively for transactions at points-of-sale, and everywhere else. Google's Wallet app already allows payments, complete with stored loyalty-card information, with just a single swipe of the phone. The future is already here!

Like AR, I expect that NFC will also play a colossal role in the future of marketing. However, NFC and AR are only the start of mobile innovation. Hardware manufacturers are constantly dreaming up new technologies that can make mobile technology even better. In early 2013, manufacturers are already releasing devices with 8-core processors, flexible displays, eye-tracking and facial recognition technologies, and fingerprint-reading security features. As these technologies become reality, new opportunities will arise for forward-thinking marketers to exploit to gain leverage over the competition.

MEASURING MOBILE MARKETING SUCCESS

Measurement is absolutely critical for all digital strategies, and mobile is no exception. We strive to impart to all of our clients a culture of incessant testing, measurement, and refinement—one that relies on data-driven insights above all others.

Measurement and analytics methodologies for mobile strategies are not terribly different from those used for other digital strategies. The exceptions are that the incoming data can be forked between tablets and smartphones, and that there are a few key measurement variables that mobile affords that are not available elsewhere. Notable among these variables is pinpointed location-based data, which can be very valuable to your marketing efforts. The three main categories of mobile opportunities each have specific tools and methods for collecting, analyzing, and drawing conclusions from data.

Mobile App Analytics

Analytics can (and absolutely should) be built into the design of any mobile app you release. When your customers use the app, various pieces of data can be collected about your app users and about your app's usage. These include granular analyses about your user demographics, as well as specific conversion statistics. Various platforms, such as Google Analytics (which includes mobile app analytics), make tracking easier and provide a flexible dashboard for your convenience. You can also collect the data yourself and build your own dashboards, budget permitting. Some of the data that you can track using these dashboards includes:

- **User Reports:** Discover who is downloading and using your app, and where the usage traffic is coming from by geography, device, OS version, etc. Understanding your app's audience is critical to your ongoing marketing effort, and may help to identify opportunities or oversights.
- **Usage Reports:** Track how much and how frequently users open and use your app, as well as which features they are interacting with. You can even track what typical usage flow looks like, from page to page, or feature to feature. You should be able to gain insights into the stickiness of your app and its constituent features, giving you a great picture of user behavior along its entire spectrum. For instance, Google Analytics generates complete behavior reports that assess loyalty, frequency, and engagement. Usage reports will also help to diagnose bugs and usability problems within your app.
- **Conversions:** Effective mobile analytics tracks whether or not users are taking the desired actions within an app, such as sharing something, making an in-app purchase, or clicking on a particular ad or link. These statistics above all others demonstrate whether your app is achieving its intermediary goals and, via additional analysis, its ultimate goal of campaign ROI. For example, popular free analytics platform Flurry (flurry.com) offers its own unique mix of big data insights, customer acquisition analytics, and in-depth conversion analysis.

- **App-Store Insights:** There are a handful of platforms, both free and paid, that provide in-depth app-store analytics. These platforms should be used in conjunction with your in-app analytics to provide a complete picture of your app's success. One of the most popular tools is App Annie (appannie.com), which touts itself as "one dashboard to rule them all," and is compatible with both the iOS App Store and Google's Play app store. It breaks down revenue and download statistics by apps, countries, and purchase methods, allowing great visual flexibility and fantastic insights. It also aggregates app-store user ratings and comments, and notifies you when your app has been featured in one of the stores.

Mobile Websites

Measuring mobile website traffic and success is almost identical in methodology to measuring your brand's main website. The aforementioned Google Analytics, as well as a host of other web analytics tools and dashboards, can provide this valuable data in neat and easily digestible formats. In addition to being able to see how your mobile website is performing using statistics like *bounce rate* and *visit duration*, you can ascertain which sources the traffic comes from, and which devices, operating systems, and apps your users are using to access your site. Of particular interest for mobile websites, you can also see exactly where, geographically, your site is being accessed from on a world map. For more granular information about website analytics, see Chapter 9, Measurement and ROI of Digital Strategies.

Mobile Advertising and Paid Search

As with mobile websites, tracking the success of mobile advertising and paid search campaigns shares a lot in common with its desktop counterparts. Marketers can measure click-through rates (CTR) and other metrics in much the same way, using many of the same tools. One major difference is that mobile conversions sometimes take the form of a phone call from the mobile device, or even an in-store purchase, as opposed to the purely web-based conversion typically tracked by analytics platforms. This makes it slightly more difficult to track if these ads are achieving their intended goals. One tactic is to utilize a popular format like click-to-call to give an idea of how a particular click led to the next step in the conversion funnel. Knowing that a click led to a phone call, you can utilize your typical conversion rate for phone-based transactions, in conjunction with your estimated revenue-per-transaction, to estimate revenue-per-click. To help get a handle on in-store purchase conversions, clickable ads that lead to traceable incentives (such as in-store coupons or rewards) often help determine if the click led to an actual purchase.

Lastly, as we recommend with all digital strategies, marketers should endeavor to estimate ROI for any mobile campaign components using any and all data available to them. Internal company data (from mobile and other digital channels), coupled with publically available industry usage data, can be used collectively to make sense of the actions your users are taking in mobile channels. Furthermore, the impact that a given mobile strategy has on other digital media channels should be estimated, rather than simply viewing mobile in a vacuum. In doing so, the overall impact mobile strategies have on the brand's overall marketing mix becomes apparent, and the ROI of a given campaign can be compared to other investments on equal footing.

I personally find this type of analysis to be exciting and enjoyable, but if you're scared by the thought of this, at least be sure that your brand's actuaries and analysts are incorporating all of these concepts into their predictions. Data-driven approaches will lead to better decision making, and ultimately, better marketing ROI for your brand.

DEVICE CONVERGENCE AND THE FUTURE MOBILE LANDSCAPE

Via trend extrapolation, the Ericsson mobile data report estimates that there will be 9.3 billion mobile subscriptions by 2018, and that 6.5 billion will be broadband enabled.[25] Although the number of subscriptions will undoubtedly continue to grow as developing nations adopt mobile technologies, I believe this number is a bit aggressive (excluding machine to machine connections*) due to a phenomenon known as *device convergence* that will first affect developed nations.

As I mentioned earlier, mobile devices have already replaced so many other devices like watches, alarm clocks, home phones, and others that were staple technologies of the last decade. However, the number of mobile devices (and hence subscriptions) is on the upswing as we adopt tablets, broadband-enabled notebooks, mobile hotspot devices, and second cell phones. However, we're starting to notice that for certain mainstream users, certain devices (e.g., laptops) are no longer necessary. For these individuals, their tablet (or smartphone) has become powerful enough to do the vast majority of work- and pleasure-related tasks, rendering the larger and clunkier device obsolete. Strong sales of *phablets* (a tweener device between the size of a normal smartphone and full-sized tablet) are already proving the convergence theory correct.

Despite convergence accelerating, as of this writing the majority of us still require the additional power or larger interface for particular tasks. I might argue that as our mobile devices improve, more and more of us will become *convergists* until we all rely on only one device. Don't think you'll ever ditch your desktop or laptop computer? I boldly conjecture that you're mistaken. Thinner, lighter, and more powerful devices are certainly on the horizon that make today's ultrabooks and smartphones look like dinosaurs—but that represents only a myopic view of the very near future. We'll very quickly witness a paradigm change that takes mobile—and computing in general—to new heights. If Google's Glass concept is any indication, these devices of tomorrow will likely be wearable, and allow us to interact with them in ways we haven't yet dreamed. I foresee a world where we all have our one device, and everything else we interact with is simply an accessory. Even further down the road, the device may be integrated so deeply with our persons that they'll literally become a part of us.

Indulge me for a second. Imagine a device from the future that's worn on your wrist, or perhaps on your head like spectacles. It has the power of today's best mainframe computer, and is no

*If machine to machine connections are included, I believe Ericsson's estimates are actually an underestimation of mobile growth in the future.

larger than the common wristwatch. It projects, in three-dimensions, in 360 degrees around you, interactive full-color imagery, with deep surround sound and even tactile texture sensations. You interact with it using gestures with both hands, eye-tracking controls, and perhaps even your brainwaves directly. It goes with you everywhere, and can be used to interact intimately with your surroundings. It's also perpetually connected to the vast information repository of the web, and every human being you know, in real time. Is a wristwatch or spectacles too indiscreet for you? Researchers are currently working on contact lenses that serve this same purpose.[26] Most of this technology isn't as far off as you'd think.

For the entire millennium leading up to about the year 1900, there was very little technological innovation. The next 100 years, up to the year 2000, saw more innovation than the entire millennium that preceded it. The next ten years, up to 2010, saw more innovation than the preceding century. We utilize today's technology to build tomorrow's, resulting in exponential change that shows no signs of deceleration. This phenomenon will soon make it difficult for even the most diligent technophiles to keep pace with our changing world. We'll look back on the 2010s and laugh about how we used to carry different devices for different tasks. Today's science fiction will undoubtedly become tomorrow's reality. Still adamant that clamshell-style laptops and candy-bar smartphones are in your future?

Most of us mobile enthusiasts like to talk about machine to machine (M2M) communications and their implication of an impending *Internet of Things* (IOT): a world where all inanimate objects are connected to the web—and to each other. Using sensors and current information from the web, machines talk to one another, and collectively form a network that represents the infrastructure for a smarter world. With the prerequisite technologies already in use today, I have no doubt that this future is fast-approaching.

Mobile and other emerging technologies are going to have a colossal impact on the way we consume information and how we interact with our world. The implications for marketing are staggering, and keeping up with this change is going to be increasingly important for brand survival. That said, I've already delved too far into the future for a one-chapter overview of mobile. If you're interested in the future of mobile technology and the IOT, follow me on twitter (@ajkates) for the latest in these developing concepts.

I believe that marketers and senior executives at Fortune 500 companies are just beginning to understand the importance of mobile. Investments in mobile marketing budgets and human capital will accelerate as mobile becomes even more ubiquitous, and forward-thinking campaigns that many companies currently scoff at will become a staple in brands' marketing activities. Commerce through mobile devices will continue to accelerate at least as rapidly as most models predict, resulting in mobile-aided purchases ultimately surpassing the total for regular in-store and desktop purchases combined. Lastly, mobile integration with all other digital channels will tighten in the coming years as companies finally wrap their heads around effective holistic and multichannel digital marketing strategies.

CLOSING THOUGHTS

I hope this chapter has inspired you to utilize mobile in your forthcoming marketing efforts, and convinced you that it must be taken very seriously while planning your brand's future. At the very least, I hope I've moved you to familiarize yourself with the world of mobile.

If you're an aspiring or current marketer (and wish to stay one), I hope you own a modern smartphone and explore its features and uses yourself. If you don't, please do yourself a colossal favor: Take a drive to your local wireless carrier, trade in that old flip-phone, and join the rest of society in the present. I promise you'll thank me later!

At the outset of this chapter, I made the bold claim that all marketing will soon revolve around mobile—and brands that fail to act will be unable to compete in the world of tomorrow. I did not mean to threaten you (or maybe I did, but just a little), but as a marketer, you'd do well to remember how quickly our world is evolving and what that means for the future of your brand. Mobile is not an *emerging* technology. It has already emerged—and it's here to stay.

For those of you who are thoroughly convinced, proceed boldly—and cautiously—into the world of mobile marketing. Learn as much as you possibly can about mobile and its evolution. Test the waters, measure constantly, and be creative. Opportunities abound for you and your brand. The only action you cannot afford to take, is inaction.

ENDNOTES

1. http://www.ericsson.com/res/docs/2012/ericsson-mobility-report-november–2012.pdf
2. http://www.techcentral.co.za/the-next–10-years-in-mobile/27622/
3. https://www.lookout.com/resources/reports/mobile-mindset
4. http://www.marketingcharts.com/wp/direct/27-of-google-searches-estimated-to-be-mobile-in-q4–26361/
5. http://www.businessinsider.com/a-majority-of-googles-business-will-be-mobile-in–2013–2012–11
6. http://socialmouths.com/blog/2012/09/17/facebook-mobile-growth/
7. Google/Nielsen Life360 Mobile Search Moments Q4 2012.
8. http://www.fiercecable.com/story/dish-network-subscriber-growth-slows–14000-q4–2012/2013–02–20
9. http://www.qsrweb.com/article/209529/Quiznos-touts-mobile-ad-campaign-at-SXSW
10. http://www.mobilecommercedaily.com/sephora-exec-mobile-orders-up–167pc-year-over-year
11. http://www.emarketer.com/newsroom/index.php/emarketer-tablets-smartphones-drive-mobile-commerce-record-heights/
12. http://www.digiday.com/brands/inside-sephoras-mobile-strategy/
13. http://www.mobilemarketer.com/cms/resources/mobilegends-awards/14499.html

14. http://communities-dominate.blogs.com/brands/2011/01/time-to-confirm-some-mobile-user-numbers-sms-mms-mobile-internet-m-news.html
15. http://www.forbes.com/sites/marketshare/2013/03/04/pulling-back-the-curtain-on-text-message-mobile-marketing/
16. http://mobihealthnews.com/18061/janssen-launches-mobile-medication-reminder-system-care4today/
17. http://www.cultofmac.com/218619/apple-is-top-u-s-smartphone-maker-to-start–2013-as-android-loses-marketshare-to-ios/
18. http://www.tech-thoughts.net/2013/02/android-tablets-overtake-ipad-market-share.html#.UUH3LjBFtkg
19. http://www.runtri.com/2013/03/mobile-commerce-results–30-of-total.html
20. http://conversations.nokia.com/2012/09/10/nokia-city-lens-comes-out-of-beta/
21. http://econsultancy.com/us/blog/9842-seven-awesome-augmented-reality-campaigns
22. http://www.theverge.com/2012/11/15/3649668/google-ingress-augmented-reality-game-beta
23. http://econsultancy.com/us/blog/8063-blippar-a-qr-code-killer
24. http://www.google.com/think/campaigns/band-aid-brand-adhesive-bandages-johnson-johnson-band-aid-magic-vision.html
25. http://http://www.ericsson.com/res/docs/2012/ericsson-mobility-report-november–2012.pdf
26. http://www.technologyreview.com/news/515666/contact-lens-computer-like-google-glass-without-the-glasses/

CHAPTER 6

VIDEO MARKETING

—by Greg Jarboe

I got a crash course in video marketing back in the early days of YouTube.

Here's the backstory: Jill Carroll was kidnapped in Baghdad on Jan. 7, 2006, while reporting in Iraq for *The Christian Science Monitor*. She was freed on March 30, 2006.

On Monday, August 7, 2006, Robin Antonick, the *Monitor*'s chief web officer, asked me to provide some guidance. Carroll was going to tell the story of her 82 days as a hostage in Iraq in an 11-part series.

She was writing about her experience for the first time since her release in Baghdad, and she was going to share detailed information about her time as a hostage, the daily activities of her captors, and how she struggled to stay alive. Part One of "Hostage: The Jill Carroll Story" was scheduled to appear on CSMonitor.com on Sunday, August 13, at 6:00 p.m. The *Monitor* had already negotiated a broadcast deal with ABC News, but that story wouldn't air until Monday evening, August 14. Antonick asked if there were other, measurable ways to help promote "Hostage: The Jill Carroll Story."

I recommended using an approach that combined media relations, blogger outreach, and press release optimization. Antonick hired my agency to work on the project.

On Tuesday, August 8, we used Google News and Technorati to identify the top journalists and bloggers who had written about "Jill Carroll" or "*Christian Science Monitor*" back in January through March when she became an international cause célèbre. We assumed—correctly—that they were the most likely ones to be interested in writing about "Hostage: The Jill Carroll Story."

We asked the *Monitor* for a 150-word excerpt and a graphic to offer journalists and bloggers, under embargo, in order to persuade them to prepare their stories in advance. We also asked journalists and bloggers to add a link in their stories to the complete 11-part series on the *Monitor*'s website.

However, when we started pitching "Hostage: The Jill Carroll Story," we kept getting asked, "Do you have any video?" We didn't ... yet. Video marketing hadn't been part of our initial plan.

So, on Wednesday, August 9, we created a short video clip using a narrator's voice over some still photos. We used the Ken Burns effect—a type of panning and zooming effect used in video production from still imagery. Then we uploaded it to YouTube (see Figure 6.1).

On Thursday, August 10, we recontacted influential news sites and blogs and provided a link to our new YouTube video. That helped us to persuade CNN.com, MSNBC.com, Yahoo News, AOL News, The Huffington Post, and Boing Boing to prepare stories to be published on Sunday, August 13, at 6:00 p.m.

On Friday, August 11, we included our video clip with our press release, increasing the likelihood of journalists, bloggers, and consumers clicking our headline. We also optimized the release for the terms "Jill Carroll" and "*Christian Science Monitor*," increasing the chances that it would be found in news search engines.

Our campaign worked. There were 247 news stories and 1,014 blog posts about "Jill Carroll" within the first 24 hours after *Part One* of the series went live. More than 450,000 unique visitors flooded CSMonitor.com within the first 24 hours—seven times the site's daily average in July. Page views broke through the 1 million mark, a massive increase from the site's July average of 121,247 page views per day.

While credit for the quality of the story belongs to Carroll and the editors of the *Monitor*, Antonick gave our agency virtually all of the credit for generating publicity and increasing website traffic. Why? From August 13–28, 2006, CNN.com, MSNBC.com, Yahoo News, AOL News, The Huffington Post, and Boing

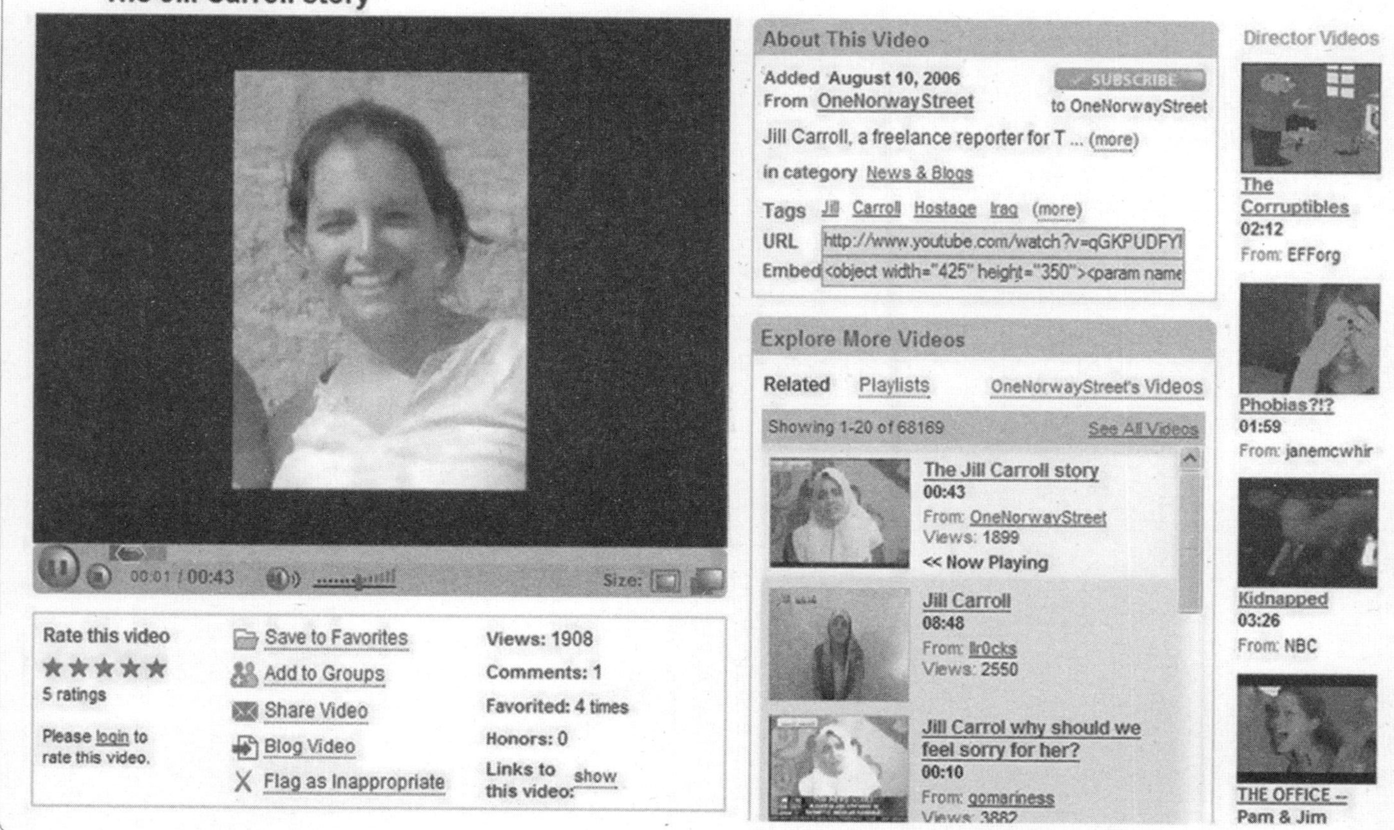

FIGURE 6.1 The Jill Carol Story: The YouTube video we created about the story, seen here clad in YouTube's early user interface.

Boing generated almost 291 times more visitors to CSMonitor.com than the ABC News site.

My crash course convinced me that YouTube and video marketing "had legs." So, I did what any journalist or blogger would do to gather more information about this video-sharing website: I asked Who, What, Where, When, Why, and How. The "Five Ws and one H" constitute a formula for getting the complete story on a new subject.

To help you prepare for your crash course in video marketing, here are the questions that you'll want to ask and answer:

- **Who** are the most-likely people to discover, watch, and share your YouTube videos?
- **What** steps should you take to plan, shoot, edit, and publish your videos to YouTube?
- **Where** should you optimize your videos and channel so more people discover them?
- **When** does viewing experience and programming encourage more people to watch them?
- **Why** should you build community and promote your videos so more people share them?
- **How** do you find out who watched your videos, get insights, and improve your results?

WHO DISCOVERS AND WATCHES VIDEOS?

More than 1 billion people from all over the world visit YouTube each month. In just the United States, YouTube.com had 161.6 million unique visitors in June 2013, according to tracking platform Compete. This is a very large potential audience, but people rarely watch the same video at the same time. Among the exceptions are big events on YouTube Live like the Royal Wedding, which was live-streamed 72 million times around the world to 188 countries. Other exceptions are YouTube Homepage Roadblocks, which gives advertisers 100 percent share of the homepage for 24 hours. The YouTube homepage averages 205 million global impressions and over 70 million unique visitors per day.

But generally, some people are more likely to discover, watch, and share your YouTube videos sooner than others. Everett M. Rogers, the author of *Diffusion of Innovations*, called individuals who are able to informally influence other individuals' attitudes or overt behavior with relative frequency "opinion leaders."

Research published March 20, 2013, by Google called these opinion leaders "Generation C" or Gen C. On the AdWords Agency Blog, Gunnard Johnson, Google's Advertising Research Director, said, "The way people consume content is changing. For the first time, an entire generation has grown up watching content on their own terms. This generation is defined by the Internet, mobile, and social – consuming content when and where they want. Nielsen calls this group Generation C because they are not just defined by their age group, but by their connected behavior."

Gen C is not an age group; it's an attitude and mindset. However, 80 percent of the Millennial Generation has Gen C characteristics. According to The Millennial Generation Research Review by the U.S. Chamber of Commerce Foundation, Gen C is a powerful demographic—not only are they cultural tastemakers, they influence $500 billion of spending a year in the U.S. Yet they can be a hard to reach audience for brands. According to GfK MRI Fall 2012 data, members of Gen C are 45 percent more likely to be light TV viewers, choosing instead to consume many forms of content across many screens.

For example, the Nielsen Mobile Insights Survey, Q4 2012, found that that the number of Gen C viewers who regularly watch YouTube on smartphones caught up to the number of viewers tuning in on their PCs. And 67 percent of Gen C watches YouTube on two devices or more, compared to 53 percent of the general population.

The survey also found that Gen C tunes in to YouTube throughout every part of their day. YouTube usage by Gen C on smartphones mirrors usage on PCs and peaks during prime time hours. Gen C watches YouTube on their smartphones as a complementary activity to their lives. For example, 41 percent tune in to YouTube on their smartphone while waiting for something/someone, 18 percent while commuting from work or school, and 15 percent tune in while commercials are running on TV.

Finally, the survey found that most members of Gen C engage with YouTube as a destination by actively searching for videos on

YouTube (47 percent on a smartphone and 57 percent on a desktop) and through a search engine (10 percent on a smartphone and 7 percent on a desktop). Viewers are also discovering videos socially—18 percent watched a video on their smartphone because it was shared on a social network (compared to 13 percent on a desktop), while 9 percent of respondents said they watched a video on their smartphone because it was shared by friends in an email (compared to 7 percent on a desktop).

Of course, with more than 1 billion people worldwide visiting YouTube every month, many are men and women 35–65+. But when targeting the audience you want to reach, it makes more sense to target the opinion leaders who have adopted Gen C behaviors.

YouTube has also learned this lesson. On October 7, 2012, Claire Cain Miller of *The New York Times* interviewed Robert Kyncl, global head of content at YouTube, when he announced that YouTube was adding 50 original channels to the 100 it had introduced the previous year. Kyncl said that YouTube had learned that viewers who have spent decades in front of their televisions are not about to throw them out in favor of YouTube, so it was going after younger people who have grown up online.

"The thing we learned is it's certainly best to fish where the fish are," Kyncl told Miller. "In terms of making investment decisions and putting dollars at risk, **we're going to focus on audiences of 35 and below**, who are already on YouTube."

That's a demographic description of YouTube's target audience. But I don't think YouTube would be publishing a psychographic profile of Generation C unless this research provided an even better description of the people who are more likely to discover, watch, and share your YouTube videos.

STEPS TO PLAN, SHOOT, EDIT, AND PUBLISH

As this was written, global sensation PSY and his wildly popular "Gangnam Style" music video had surpassed Justin Bieber's

"Baby" as the most viewed video of all time on YouTube. As of July 14, 2013, the view counts stood at 1.7 billion for "PSY – Gangnam Style (강남스타일) M/V" to 872.4 million for "Justin Bieber – Baby ft. Ludacris."

And music videos aren't the only types of video that are going viral. "Kony 2012" topped the 2012 Unruly Global Viral Video Ads Chart,[1] the annual ranking of the year's most shared video ads. Unruly Media measures "shares" rather than "views" because it's a better metric for an ad's "virality" and the strength of the emotion it triggers in viewers.

"Kony 2012" was created and released by the not-for-profit *Invisible Children*. The 30-minute-long video had been shared 10.1 million times across Facebook, Twitter, and blogs from March 5, when it was launched, to December 9, 2012. That's 10.7 percent of the video's 94.3 million views.

"Emotive content and bottom-up sharing stole the show this year," remarked Unruly Media cofounder and COO Sarah Wood. "The world's biggest brands can learn from Invisible Children: it's not about a 30-second commercial anymore when a 30-minute video gets 10 million global shares."[2]

In second place on the 2012 Unruly Global Viral Video Ads Chart was "A Dramatic Surprise On A Quiet Square." Created by Duval Quillaume Modem for TNT Benulux, the 1-minute-and-46-second long video ad had 4.4 million shares, which was 10.4 percent of the video's 42.3 million views as of December 9, 2012.[3] So, even though the length of this video ad was significantly different, the ratio of shares to views was remarkably similar.

If you go to YouTube Trends at youtube-trends.blogspot.com, you'll see that the latest trending videos and video trends on YouTube fall into 16 categories: Advertising, Community, Culture, Gaming, Holidays, Local, Movies, Music, Newsroom, Politics, Search, Sports, Technology, Viral, Weather, and World. Given this list, you could create popular videos on a wide variety of topics.

What matters more is the strength of the *emotion* that your content triggers. According to an Unruly White Paper "The Science of Sharing," published in July 2013,[4] "The most shared ads in our study evoked intense emotional responses, including *warmth, happiness, awe* and *pride*. These ads also successfully leveraged key social motivations, such as *attention grabbing*, *shared emotional response* and *zeitgeist*"

B2B videos can also have emotional or cultural triggers. Just watch "A Day Made of Glass… Made Possible by Corning." As of December 9, 2012, it had 1.8 million shares, 8.7 percent of 20.6 million views.

Make a Plan

When it comes to creating your video, a little planning goes a long way. It helps everything go more smoothly and can save you time in the long run.

With a plan you'll know what you need to shoot, what you're going to say, and how your video will fit together when it's time to edit. You might want a creative strategy, a script, or a storyboard—whatever creative approach works for you.

There are a variety of creative approaches. You could create informational videos like customer testimonials or product demonstrations, educational videos like how-to videos or presentations, or sales videos. How you choose to showcase your company or products depends on your audience and their needs as well as your goals.

Shoot Your Video

Once you've chosen a creative approach, you're ready to start shooting. Don't feel like you need the fanciest camera, microphone, or lighting equipment, though. The fact is you'll be able to get quality audio and video from almost any camera—including your mobile phone—so just use the best camera you can get your hands on.

Here's an equipment checklist to make sure you have everything you need before starting to shoot your video:

- Must have
  - Camera
  - External microphone
  - Computer (to upload video from your camera)
- Good to have
  - Tripod
  - Lights
  - Extension cables

- Optional
    - Light reflector
    - Camera charger

Edit Your Video

With digital video, editing is easier than ever. Now you can drag and drop your favorite takes, add music, and arrange your videos however you want.

The best way to put your video together is to use editing software. Almost every new computer comes with a free video editor, like Apple's iMovie and Windows' Movie Maker. There are plenty of other web-based programs, like the YouTube Video Editor, which lets you piece together videos right in your web browser. The YouTube Video Editor is a free tool available through your YouTube account that allows you to edit various clips and produce an entirely new video. In the Video Editor, you can:

- Combine multiple clips you've uploaded to create a new, longer video.
- Trim the beginning and end of your clips.
- Add a soundtrack from the YouTube Video Editor's AudioSwap library.
- Create new videos without worrying about file formats, and publish the new videos to YouTube with one click (no new upload is required).

To get started, go to youtube.com/editor and login to your YouTube account.

Publish to YouTube

Follow these three simple steps to publish to YouTube:

1. Create or login to your free YouTube account. Just go to www.youtube.com/signup, enter your information, and click Next Step. When you're done, click Back to YouTube.
2. Create your free YouTube user name. If you're logged into your YouTube account, click Upload in the top right corner of the homepage and choose a YouTube user name. This

will be associated with your YouTube account, so pick a name that reflects your business, top-selling product, or area of expertise. User names are limited to 20 characters or less.

3. Upload your video to YouTube. Now that you have a YouTube user name, upload your video at www.youtube.com/upload or click Upload from the homepage. The upload page offers a range of options, from simple single uploads to multiple file and instant webcam uploads. Drag and drop videos onto the page, or click Select Files to get started. While your video is uploading, you can add your description and other information, which is covered in the next section of this chapter.

BUILDING VIDEO CHANNEL STRATEGY

Your video is creative, insightful, and spot on for your YouTube audience. Now, it's time to sit back and watch the view count rise, right? Not quite.

A ton of great content already lives on YouTube and 100 hours of new video were being uploaded to YouTube every minute as this was written. Creating a stellar video is crucial, but it's only half of the battle.

You should ensure that your videos reach the widest possible audience. To give your videos and channel the best potential for success on the platform, you've got to optimize them. This means developing an intimate understanding of both the way discovery and audience engagement on YouTube work and the tools available to take advantage of these key insights.

Optimize Your Metadata

Metadata is the information that surrounds your video: title, tags, and description. YouTube is the world's second largest search engine; optimize your video to take advantage of this fact. This set of data informs the YouTube algorithm of a video's content, indexing it for search, promotion, related videos, and ad serving. It also provides viewers context for a video before, during, and after they watch.

Use one or more of the keyword-generating tools below to help you find relevant and compelling keywords for your metadata.

- **YouTube Search Suggestions:** Start to type keywords in the YouTube search box, and see what suggested searches come up.
- **YouTube Keyword Suggestion Tool:** Go to ads.youtube.com/keyword_tool and use the free tool to get new keyword ideas. Either enter a few description words or phrases, or type in a YouTube video's ID (or watch page URL).
- **YouTube Trending Topics:** Go to www.youtube.com/videos and identify trending topics in your category.
- **Google Trends**: Go to www.google.com/trends and type in one or more terms to explore their search volumes.

Create Custom Thumbnails

Thumbnails, along with your video title, act as mini marketing posters for your content on YouTube. You should always create custom thumbnails to be uploaded along with the video file. There are a few general guidelines to follow, but the right thumbnail depends on what the video is about.

The thumbnails you create for your videos, along with title and description, show up in many different sizes and formats across various pages of the platform. Many of the thumbnail and metadata placements that can drive significant traffic for your videos will be small. Being strategic about the limitations of and opportunities for various placements will help you create the most effective metadata and thumbnail for each video you publish.

Add Annotations

Annotations are text overlays that you can place on YouTube videos. There are numerous uses for annotations. Producers are consistently finding new, creative, and strategic ways to apply them to their videos. And YouTube is constantly unveiling new capability.

For example, YouTube unveiled Associated Website annotations on November 29, 2012. According to YouTube Help, these annotations provide verified members of YouTube's partner program who are in good standing with a way to put links to their associated websites directly from annotations in their videos.

According to Chris Atkinson of ReelSEO, "The opportunities presented by these annotations are huge, as your calls to action can lead viewers to your website, where you can sell your own stuff, offer exclusive content, and not be inhibited by the rules of YouTube."[5]

Use Captions

YouTube is a global platform and your audience can be watching from anywhere in the world. Take extra steps to optimize your content to help your videos reach broader audiences, including foreign language speakers and viewers who are hard-of-hearing.

For example, you can provide your own captions and transcripts, or YouTube has several features to help you create and translate transcriptions of the audio in your content. A transcript is a text version of the audio in your video that you can upload to YouTube along with your video. This can be used to create captions for the current language of the video or to create subtitles in other languages.

Optimize Your Channel

According to the YouTube Glossary, "A channel is the public page for a user account on YouTube containing uploaded videos, playlists, 'liked' videos, 'favorited' videos, channel comments, and general activity." YouTube channel pages can be optimized in a number of ways to help make your channel a discoverable destination that offers consistent, current content. When setting up and optimizing your channel page, you should be thinking about visual branding, channel metadata, and channel organization.

For example, the first 45 characters of the description appear in the channel browser and across the site where viewers discover your channel. This text is essential for optimizing your channel for the guide.

Maintain Your Channel Feed

Your channel's activity is summed up by your channel feed, your main line of communication with your subscribers. A powerful communication tool, your feed should promote the content important to you, stay updated, and never overwhelm your subscribers with too much content.

For creators who don't upload on a weekly schedule, the feed allows an easy way to appear active by curating other content. By simply commenting, "liking," "playlisting," and "favoriting" videos from other channels, your channel can become a destination as a tastemaker for other great content.

VIEWING EXPERIENCE AND PROGRAMMING

Your next step is to build a cohesive viewing experience and channel strategy. Gone are the days when YouTube was exclusively a place for one hit, viral videos. If you're a creator interested in building a successful channel on YouTube, you've got to consider your channel's long-term plan. What does this mean, and how do you do it? The answer largely lies in developing a viable programming strategy.

Programming means creating a cohesive viewing experience across videos on your channel, where each video fits into the larger channel vision. It encapsulates both preproduction and production activities—what type of content to produce, as well as when to publish.

As of December 9, 2012, YouTube Charts at youtube.com/charts, showed that the two most popular channels were Ray William Johnson, who had 343 videos and 6.3 million subscribers, and Ryan Higa (Nigahiga), who had 135 videos and 6.2 million subscribers. As Johnson and Higa's popularity shows, funny videos still work—although creating videos that are funny week after week is hard work.

But it's worth it. According to an article in *The Wall Street Journal* by Emily Glazer, published on February 12, 2012,[6] Johnson earns an estimated annual income of around $1 million, partly by participating in YouTube's Partner Program, which gives him a cut of the ad revenue generated by his video commentaries. In addition, he sells merchandise like Ray William Johnson bobble heads and mobile applications for the iPhone like his Pimp Hand Strong app.

Other published reports[7] say Higa is also earning around $1 million a year. And Google's senior vice president and chief business officer, Nikesh Arora, said during the company's Q2 2012 earnings call that thousands of YouTube partners are making six figures a year on YouTube.

Captivate Your Audience

Captivating and retaining viewers for the entire length of a video is achieved both by making creative content and by ensuring that the video's production maintains interest levels throughout. You must hook viewers early, and you must craft a video that keeps their attention.

Many viewers decide whether they are going to keep watching your video within the first few seconds. Attention spans can be short, and viewers are just one click away from abandoning your video. The video's content should be made perfectly clear in the first few moments to give them a reason to stick around. Then, follow your video's catchy opening with compelling and engaging content. Whether you create short- or long-form videos, the right length for a video on YouTube is exactly as long as the content remains compelling to its audience.

According to David Waterhouse, the head of content for Unruly Media, t**he average length of the top 10 most shared video ads of all time is 4 minutes and 11 seconds**.[8] Four **of the top 10 are more than** 4 minutes 57 seconds long. And two, including the highly successful "Gymkhana 4," created by DC Shoes, are more than nine minutes long.

And this list does not include "Kony 2012." If it did, then the average length of the top 10 most shared video ads of all time would increase to 6 minutes 12 seconds.

Include Calls to Action

Watching content online is an interactive and social experience and content creators rely on the actions of their audience to help them succeed—but many viewers won't act unless you prompt them. Videos you produce and publish should have specific calls to action (CTAs). Depending on the message, you can use the beginning, middle, or end of the video to direct the actions of your viewers.

CTAs should be minimal and simple. Too many prompts can cause confusion. The goal is to make it as easy as possible for viewers to perform an action.

There are many ways to communicate with your audience and include calls to action in your videos. In many cases, talking to the audience can be the most powerful, but there are other effective ways to prompt your viewers to take some action. For example, create a video "end card" to appear at the end of your video. Use it to direct viewers to more content, encourage them to subscribe, or lead them to visit your channel page. You can create a template that builds consistency into the end of your videos by directing the audience to take specific actions.

Feed Your Channel's Feed

Regular activity on your channel's feed is one way to keep your audience engaged. The value of your subscriber base is strongest when they are notified of your upload activities and engage with them. In other words, "feed" your channel's feed!

Some of the same trends and viewer interests that drive television viewership are applicable to the web. Regular release schedules, programming, and timely publishing are all important for online video. For example, release videos on a set day of the week, if possible. Releasing videos on a recurring schedule helps build a structure for your channel that an audience can rely on and know when to return.

Create Playlists

You can create playlists using your own content, other channels' videos, or a combination of both. Playlists can be used as an organizational tool and creators can create playlists as a linear viewing experience for their audience. Playlists can be featured on your channel, linked-to via annotations, and appear in search results and suggested videos.

Playlists should be an essential part of your channel strategy to increase watch time and develop a programmed experience for your viewer. Best-of playlists, for example, help pitch your channel to potential subscribers and keep your channel's content organized. Playlists also have some new and powerful features that allow channels to create the best playlist experience. Channels can use the new interstitial creator tool or the new start-and-end-time settings to create hosted-style playlists.

Create Tent-Pole Programming

Why does the Discovery channel have Shark Week every year? Why do scary movies get released near Halloween? Why do talk shows have relationship experts on the week before Valentine's Day? The answer to these questions is tent-pole programming.

Tent-pole events are the cultural events that promotion, sponsors/advertisers, and viewing trends orbit around throughout the year. Big movie releases, sports, holidays, and niche events should act as guides for the content you produce. This strategy can apply to all partners. Any channel can create or participate in tent-poles relevant to their specific audience.

Focus on Your Channel Strategy

Making great videos is where you begin your strategy as a YouTube creator. However, building an effective channel strategy across your videos will help you turn video viewers into a channel audience that will support long-term success on the platform.

Creating an effective channel experience and promoting your channel to the audience will help retain viewers across multiple videos and increase watch time for your channel. Just as you produce videos that you hope will retain viewers' interest for the duration, you will also want to create an experience that drives viewers' completion of a video to their watching more content from your channel.

Start by using InVideo Programming, a new suite of features available to partners, to promote your channel and content using your entire video library. This new product allows you to add a dynamic module to all existing videos that features an image linking to your channel, videos, and more.

BUILDING COMMUNITY AND PROMOTING YOUR VIDEOS

You should engage with and build a genuine community around your channel and what it stands for.

YouTube provides a unique experience for both creators and audience alike, one that is social and interactive. As a creator, you have the ability not only to foster authentic engagement around your channel, but also the opportunity to interact with these viewers.

Building a community on YouTube will transform your fans into an engaged and loyal audience. They, in turn, can serve as a social army to promote your content.

In addition, you can jumpstart your traffic with video ads. For example, Google AdWords for video enables you to get your video in front of the right audience at the right time.

Build Your Community

Online video is social; it is a two-way dialogue. People are drawn to online video and web series because they can interact with the channel in ways that they can't with television. The ability of creators to interact with their viewers is one of the keys to the medium. So, speak to your audience, and listen to what they say.

If you actively engage with your audience through your channel, it will pay off in the long run. An engaged community of viewers often leads to a loyal following. Your fans will become your social army—empower them to grow your brand and they will be your best promoters.

Your viewers want to be part of a community. They want to engage with your channel and interact through comments, messages, and more. Make sure you are a part of that conversation and representing your brand well. If your videos attract a large viewership, a community will emerge with or without you.

It's good practice, whenever possible, to respond to comments in the first few hours after you publish a video. These first commenters are your core audience, and keeping them engaged builds loyalty.

Identify Cross-Promotion and Collaboration Opportunities

Think holistically about your YouTube community. Sure, it includes your most avid fans and followers, but it also includes other YouTube creators. It's important to identify similar or relevant channels and invest in these relationships.

Cross-promotion across channels and collaboration with other online creators are some of the most effective methods in terms of building audience and subscribers. Accessing new audiences on

YouTube begins with finding the channels where those audiences are already engaged.

No matter what kind of channel you have—blogger, branded, comedy, music—make it a priority to identify similar or relevant channels with whom to work on cross-promotion and collaboration, in a mutually beneficial manner. You must do the initial work to build your content, your channel, and your audience into something that other channels will want to support or partner with.

For example, check out the music video, "OK Go – Needing/Getting – Official Video." It was made by OK Go, an American alternative rock band, in partnership with Chevrolet. OK Go set up over 1,000 instruments over two miles of desert outside Los Angeles. A Chevy Sonic was outfitted with retractable pneumatic arms designed to play the instruments, and the band recorded this version of Needing/Getting, singing as they played the instrument array with the car (see Figure 6.2).

The video took four months of preparation and four days to shoot and record. Published on February 5, 2012, the video had 1.1 million shares in Unruly's Viral Video Chart and 23.8 million views on YouTube by December 9, 2012.

Leverage Social Media

Social media can also be leveraged to build viewership on your channel and engage with your audience in new ways. For example, you should have a Facebook presence for your YouTube channel. Facebook is a great tool to interact with your fans in different ways and can drive viewership to your YouTube channel. Remember, both your activity and your fans' on Facebook get multiplied out to their groups of friends. Rely on your fans to help increase your reach and introduce your show to new viewers.

Twitter is another tool to that can be used to interact with your fans in a conversational way. It's also a great way to identify your peers, contribute to the conversations that are relevant to you and your audience, and spot what's trending on the web. According to the YouTube Creator Playbook, 700 YouTube videos are shared on Twitter every minute.[9]

You should also set up a Google+ page or profile to engage with fans and other YouTube creators. Google+ allows you to organize people into different "circles" to help you guide your interactions and

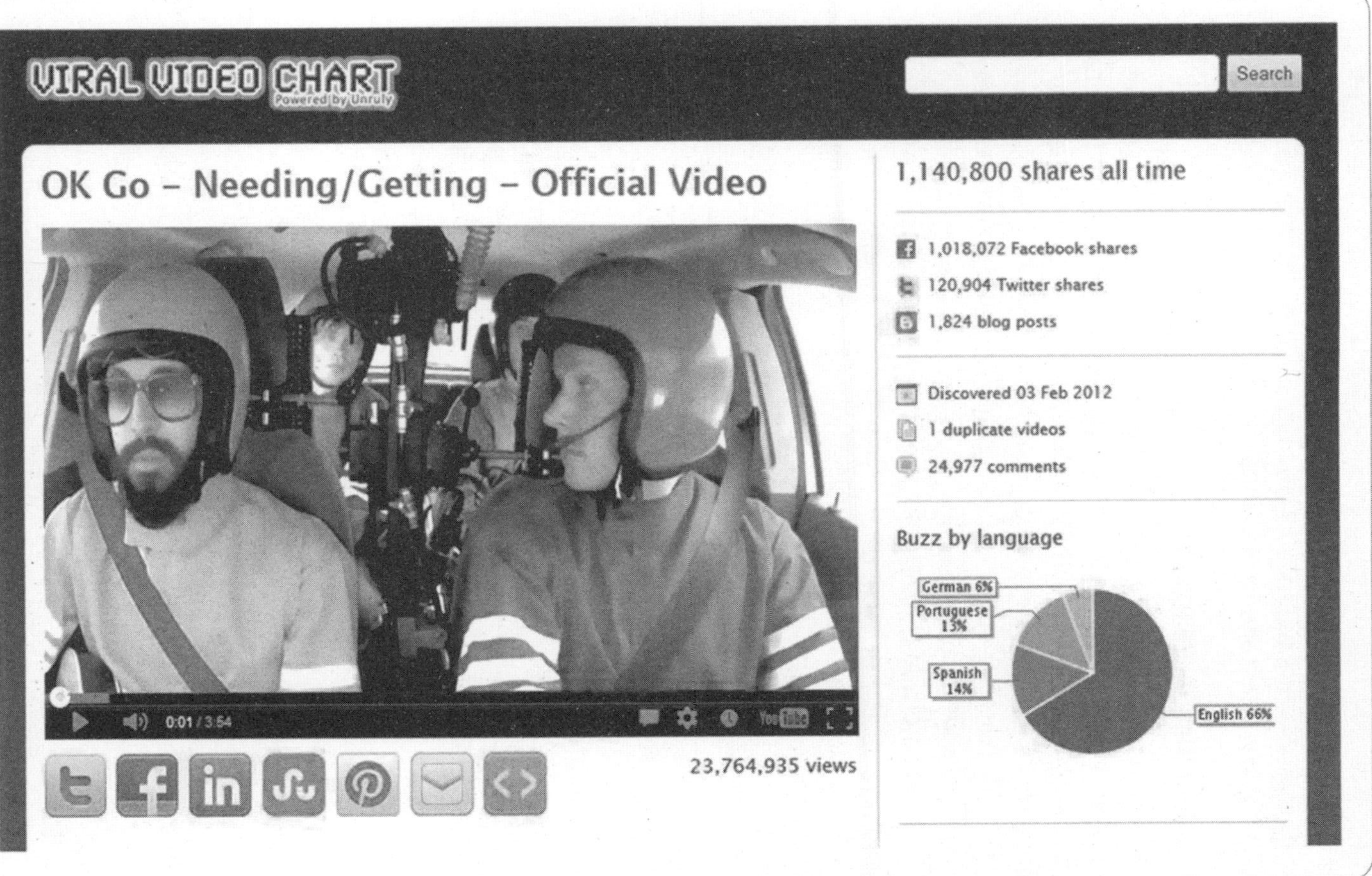

FIGURE 6.2 OK Go—Needing/Getting Video: The band's creativity propelled it to "go viral."

tailor your engagement to a circle's specific interests or needs. Not only can you share videos and other media, you can engage directly with your audience in Google Hangouts and broadcast live hangouts on your YouTube channel via Google+ Hangouts on Air (HOA).

Conduct Blog Outreach

Don't limit your purview to YouTube. A lot of viewers find content on YouTube through other sites on the Internet. There are tons of sites and blogs that are always looking for great content to write about or to feature. Make it easy for these people to promote your videos by reaching out to them with high quality, tailored content that is relevant to their audience.

For example, keep track of which blogs and sites are featuring your videos and driving views. Identify the key drivers of views and consider sharing content with those places first, letting them know they are getting the inside scoop.

JUMPSTART YOUR TRAFFIC WITH AN AD CAMPAIGN

You can promote your video to potential customers on YouTube and across the web at the exact moment they're thinking about your product or service. How? It's easy with AdWords for video.

Creating your first video ad campaign is a five-step process:

1. *Create your AdWords for video account.* Sign in at adwords.google.com/video.
2. *Choose your budget.* You decide how much you want to pay per view and per day, so you're always in control of your costs. And with YouTube's TrueView Video Ads, you only pay when someone watches your video ad.
3. *Create your video ad.* You can create a new video ad or simply choose an existing video that you wish to promote. Then you need to write a few sentences to grab your audience's attention.
4. *Choose from a variety of targeting options.* AdWords for video provides you with a range of options to reach the right audience. For example, you can pick the perfect audience by demographics, like women over 35. Or, go geographic

and show your video ad in your own zip code. You can target by language and show your video ad to only Spanish speakers. You can try interest categories to reach people who watch videos about golf, food, or video games. Or, you can remarket to people who have visited your site before. You can select keywords to put your video ad in the right YouTube search results and related videos, or you can simply pick the YouTube videos and channels that suit your needs.

5. *Measure the effectiveness of ad spending.* On average, YouTube has found that video ads drive a 20 percent increase in traffic to a company's website and a 5 percent increase in searches for their business.[10] With AdWords for video, you can see how many viewers watched your entire video, visited your website, stayed on your channel to watch another video, or subscribed to your channel after viewing your ad.

You also have the option of creating a call-to-action overlay to drive traffic from your video ad to an off-YouTube web page at no extra charge. I strongly recommend that you take advantage of this opportunity.

In 2009, YouTube featured a video from charity: water on the YouTube home page to commemorate World Water Day. The video included a call-to-action overlay that encouraged YouTube users to donate money to help build wells and provide clean, safe drinking water for those who don't have it. The response from the YouTube community was overwhelming. In fact, charity: water was able to raise over $10,000 in one day from the video. That was enough to build two brand-new wells in the Central African Republic and give over 150 people clean drinking water for 20 years!

WHO'S WATCHING YOUR VIDEOS?

All the views, shares, and subscriptions you generate represent a wealth of information about your audience and your videos. With just a few clicks, you can explore this data, learn about your viewers, and take steps to more effectively market your business with YouTube.

It's a powerful cycle of testing, learning, and improvement that can help your business grow.

You can get basic insights into your video's performance from its dedicated viewing page, also known as its *watch page*. Just click the bar graph icon underneath your view count to see views and key discovery events, engagement, and audience demographics.

Tools of the Trade

To get a deeper look into what your audience likes (and doesn't), you need to learn the tools of the trade. You can discover who watched your videos by using YouTube Analytics, AdWords for video, and other tools that give you detailed information about your audiences and videos.

YouTube Analytics is a robust tool that provides informative data and insights about your content, your audience, and your programming. What you learn by using YouTube Analytics can help inform programming and production decisions for your channel. The information has the potential to help you be smarter and more strategic with the videos you produce.

Introduced on November 30, 2011, YouTube Analytics replaced YouTube Insight. What does YouTube Analytics offer that Insight didn't? YouTube Analytics includes a number of new features:

- A new overview that displays key information quickly, while also enabling you to easily access more detailed information
- More detailed statistics so that you can get a more precise understanding of your content and audiences
- The ability to discover which videos are driving the most views and subscriptions
- The ability to see how far viewers are watching through your video in a new audience retention report[11]

On October 11, 2012, YouTube announced some improvements to YouTube Analytics. First, YouTube enhanced the Views report to show more time-watched data to give you additional insight into engagement for your videos. You can now see "Estimated minutes watched" from the Views report or choose other data options from the Compare metric drop-down menu. Second, YouTube introduced a beta version of an Annotations report to view data on the performance of your video annotations, with insights on viewer click and close rates. As I mentioned earlier, annotations are one of the most-used features to drive audience engagement in YouTube.

AdWords for video gives you valuable insights into your audience and how they respond to your video ads. You can use it to see how your video ad is performing, learn from your progress, and find new targeting opportunities. Just click on a campaign to enter the campaign report. Campaign reports are made up of four clickable tabs:

- The Ads tab lets you see how your ads are performing by True View format, network, and targeting group.
- The Videos tab shows you how much of your ad your viewers watched, as well as the performance of your call-to-action overlay.
- The Targets tab shows your campaign performance by targeting group. Just select a targeting option from this tab to compare how viewers responded across demographics, interests, and keywords.
- The Setting tab lets you adjust your daily budget, change the regions where your campaign is targeted, and make other adjustments that may help you reach your audience.

Among the other tools that give you detailed information about your audiences and videos is the Viral Video Chart powered by Unruly Media and available at viralvideochart.unrulymedia.com/all, as well as the Mashable Global Ads Chart from the same site.

Read YouTube Success Stories

Summing up, it is clear that video marketing holds great opportunities. It also holds pitfalls. As Woody Allen once said, "The trick will be to avoid the pitfalls, seize the opportunities, and get back home by six o'clock."[12]

To accomplish all that, I also recommend that you read about how other marketers have found success on YouTube. You are much more likely to get back home by six o'clock if you can learn how they were able to avoid the pitfalls and seize the opportunities. For example, ReelSEO published a YouTube case study in

December 2011 entitled, "Rokenbok Toy Company Using YouTube to Transform into Online Business."[13] I often use this case study when teaching the YouTube Marketing Strategies and Secrets session in the Rutgers Mini-MBA program on Digital Marketing.

Here's the backstory: The world of children's toys has evolved from wooden blocks to high-end construction sets which stimulate young brains. And the toy industry has changed dramatically as well.

In 1995, Paul Eichen left his corporate gig as an executive at an international data projector company to start the Rokenbok Toy Company. Eichen says, "The concept of uniting robotics with a construction system and creating a classic toy system really interested me." Until three years ago, his marketing strategy was simple. He reports, "About 80 percent of customers came through specialty toy stores, 20 percent through word-of-mouth, and zero via the Internet."

When the economy shifted, specialty toy stores began shutting their doors, and Eichen and his team needed to find a new platform to connect with customers and demonstrate how the Rokenbok toy operated. Eichen admits, "It's not obvious to folks from static images what our toy system is or how you play with it. The construction vehicles are very sophisticated robots within a very sophisticated construction system, but you can't tell unless you can witness a demonstration of Rokenbok."

Eichen continues by saying, "As the opportunity to demonstrate in toy stores was disappearing, we needed to be creative with new ways which we could demonstrate our toy system. We thought of everything—from renting kiosks in malls during Christmas time to attending events like maker fairs and robotics conferences. Ultimately as we tested different methodologies, we found that creating videos—that not only demonstrated our products, but are really fun and show kids how they can play with Rokenbok—was what really took off for us."

It also took off for their customers. Rokenbok users also upload videos of themselves playing with their Rokenbok construction systems. Eichen reveals, "There are a lot of teenagers creating YouTube videos. Some of these kids have been playing with

Rokenbok for 10 years." Eichen and the team have tapped into this YouTube community of Rokenbokers.

One of Eichen's favorite customer videos is Tim and Charlie's Summer Rokenbok Build, which features the combined Rokenbok sets of these two Rokenbok fans.

Eichen says, "We started experimenting with uploading to YouTube in 2006, but we just started building up the Mr. Rokenbok channel over the past couple years. Really just this year, we discovered it could be such an important vehicle for communications for us, and that really has to do with the new interface and the ability for us to be able to target so easily."

Rokenbok shoots all of their videos in-house. They write their own scripts, record the voice-overs, and shoot and edit all the content, which ranges from product demo videos for their "Rokenbok Product Demonstrations" playlist to educational videos for their "School of ROK" playlist. Production value depends on the series. For quick product videos, sometimes Eichen will quickly shoot, edit, and post a product video all from his iPad. Check out the X2 Elevators video, which was completely produced and posted via iPad.

In fact, Eichen and his team have found that some of the "lower production value" videos that are shot while just playing around actually perform as well as the scripted "higher production value" videos.

The Rokenbok team began using YouTube Promoted Video ads in 2010, and they began using TrueView in-stream ads in 2011. Eichen says, "TrueView has allowed us to refine our campaigns and make sure we are targeting the right customers."

Eichen reveals, "What we have learned through our exit survey is that children who like to watch videos of construction equipment or machines were discovering our videos." The Rokenbok team implements keyword motifs like *bulldozer*, *cement truck*, *trash truck*, and *airplane*—words they anticipate kids and families are searching for on YouTube—with their videos ad campaigns.

A set of ROK blocks is $50, and a complete action set is at least a $100 investment. Eichen says, "We don't expect anyone to buy the product the first time they encounter us, so we need to build a relationship. Our ultimate goal with YouTube is to get families to watch our videos. Rokenbok is not an impulse item. We need to have a relationship with the family before they make an investment to start a collection of our educational toys."

Eichen adds, "YouTube is becoming our most important vehicle for advertising. We are transforming ourselves from a classic toy system that was sold in specialty toy stores into a direct marketing company. We only sell online now." YouTube is the number one source of traffic to the Rokenbok site. Today, half of the people that are being introduced to Rokenbok first hear about it through YouTube videos.

Eichen adds, "Half of our business happens in the last couple months of the year." As the company dives into its most important sales season of the year, Eichen and his team are gearing up with banner ads on the Mr. Rokenbok channel that promote their holiday bundles and a new series of Rokenbok Adventures. He concludes, "Rokenbok is Santa's big gift. It is a crazy time for us, helping families getting ready for the holidays."

Stay Up-To-Date

The six questions covered in this chapter are probably the right ones to continue asking for the foreseeable future:

- **Who** are the most-likely people to discover, watch, and share your YouTube videos?
- **What** steps should you take to plan, shoot, edit, and publish your videos to YouTube?
- **Where** should you optimize your videos and channel so more people discover them?
- **When** does viewing experience and programming encourage more people to watch them?
- **Why** should you build community and promote your videos so more people share them?
- **How** do you find out who watched your videos, get insights, and improve your results?

And hopefully these current answers will help you prepare for your crash course in video marketing. But remember: The only constant on YouTube is change. So, I also recommend that you read the YouTube Blog at youtube-global.blogspot.com daily. You should also read the YouTube Creator Blog at youtubecreator.blogspot.com weekly. Why? The latest answers to the six questions you'll want to ask are changing from day to day and week to week.

ENDNOTES

1. http://viralvideochart.unrulymedia.com/all
2. http://viralvideochart.unrulymedia.com/youtube?id=Y4MnpzG5Sqc
3. http://viralvideochart.unrulymedia.com/youtube?id=316AzLYfAzw
4. http://www.unrulymedia.com/unruly-whitepapers
5. http://www.reelseo.com/youtube-associated-website-link-annotations/
6. http://online.wsj.com/article/SB10001424052970204624204577179073123148432.html
7. http://myona.com/2011/08/10/raywilliamjohnson-nigahiga-earning-more-than–1m/
   http://idealtechblog.com/top–10-youtube-earners-income-over–100k/
8. http://www.reelseo.com/how-long-video-should-be/
9. http://www.youtube.com/yt/playbook/social-media.html
10. http://youtube-global.blogspot.com/2012/04/helping-every-business-play-big-on.html
11. http://searchenginewatch.com/article/2129127/YouTube-Analytics-Replaces-YouTube-Insight
12. http://www.famousquotes.com/author/woody-allen/5
13. http://www.reelseo.com/rokenbok-toy-company-youtube-transform-online-business/

CHAPTER 7

SOCIAL MEDIA MARKETING

—by Stan Smith

It started with my Internet connection speed sputtering to a crawl. The effects of the slow down rippled across the household. First my son, then his two brothers started yelling as their online gaming flickered and ended. Next my wife started shouting, the reality show she watched religiously every week, pixelated and vanished. Our cable TV and Internet connection was down.

I knew what to do. I picked up my iPhone, opened my Twitter app, and visited the @comcastcares. Immediately I saw that others had congregated around the digital town square screaming bloody murder.

"Comcast Bill" calmly fielded the irate tweets. Within 15 minutes, Comcast Bill confirmed a problem in my area and gave me an ETA of when my content digitally soaked life would be back on track.

Thirty minutes later all was well in the world. I tweeted a relieved thanks to Comcast Bill that was shared with over 20,000 people in moments.

You and I have unprecedented economic power. We no longer are confined to islands, cut off from the world. The days of calling customer care lines and waiting on hold, are over. Now we can rant and praise to the world. We have the power to start viral thunderstorms that can cripple the holiday sales of retailers or catapult an unknown Korean rapper to international fame—all from the monitor-lit coziness of our home office.

Things have changed. Business isn't leading the charge, consumers are, and executives across the world are only just learning to cope with the new economic landscape.

WHAT IS SOCIAL MEDIA?

This might seem like a basic question, but it isn't. In fact, not understanding the true definition of social media could cripple your organization's marketing efforts for years to come. Here's why: About 5 years ago, a new class of marketing consultant, the social media expert, finally received a fair hearing. They stressed that Facebook, Twitter, and LinkedIn were growing at incredible rates. More importantly a growing percentage of customers were holding "brand conversations" on these platforms.

The takeaway was clear: jump on board or lose respect in the *new town square*.

But this time, cagey CMOs and CEOs, veterans of the dot-com bust, weren't biting. Sure social media was "interesting," but is it really a strategic marketing tool?

The social media crew had a ready response: "Is targeted media a strategic marketing tool?" Match point.

For years, marketing teams had watched their old standbys—TV, newspaper, and banner ads—flounder and drown in the digital tidal wave. Customers were tuning out TV commercials or fast-forwarding through them. Newspapers were dying. Radio only worked in isolated cases, and banner ads were quickly succumbing to subpar response rates.

The reality was that broadcast media tools weren't getting the job done. But maybe, social media could.

Propelled by eye-popping membership stats from Facebook and others, social media quickly gained legitimacy.

Normally, this kind of rapid rise would be followed by an equally ignominious fall. Not this time.

This time, the technology and the companies behind it were swimming in a sea of honest-to-goodness revenues. More importantly, consumers loved the new social tools and were happy to welcome any brand that could add value to the experience.

THE REAL DEFINITION OF SOCIAL MEDIA

Social media now describes a new approach to marketing—an approach that relies on dialogue, storytelling, and long-term relationship building. It's an approach that has a healthy respect for the power of citizen influencers who can make or break a brand with a keystroke.

Some precocious startups have embraced social media as a strategic response to their deep-pocketed competitors. AirBnB can compete against Hilton by leveraging the conversations, goodwill, and referrals from satisfied customers. Fab.com can wield massive media power by simply asking visitors to share their favorite products with Facebook friends. A presidential candidate can marshal hundreds of thousands of citizen volunteers and get out the vote with a few tweets.

Be warned... It's easy to mistake social media as just another media purchasing option. Yes, you can purchase access to millions of eyeballs on Facebook, LinkedIn, Twitter, and others. Yes, you can use display banner ads to shout for attention from the page margin. And yes, you can track and optimize Facebook ad responses.

But these tactics aren't as effective as actually participating in the daily lives of customers. It doesn't take long for a business to discover that simply throwing budget at ads is a game of trying to outpace banner burnout and attention decay. Again, you can use social media to shout at targeted groups of friends, but you might not like being labeled as the awkward guy at the party who can't stop talking about the latest network marketing "opportunity."

Social media is new. It's not an evolutionary extension of broadcast TV. It's a revolutionary step forward that displaces competing mediums. Before you can truly embrace the power of strategic digital marketing, you must master the tools of social dialogue and persuasion. That's what we'll spend the rest of this chapter exploring.

THE NEW DIGITAL EXPERIENCE

It's helpful to divide social media into three customer-focused social experiences. Each of these experiences offer customers new ways to critique, question, and promote brands. Businesses must understand and adapt their marketing and cultural paradigms to the new reality.

Social Experience #1: Peer Branding

It's fascinating to watch someone using Facebook for the first time. They fiddle with the interface, randomly clicking on tabs. They soon gravitate to the newsfeed where they notice rapid-fire updates from their friends. They click through to a friend's profile page and browse their photos. They find their way back to their profile page and then—in a flash—it happens.

They quickly hunt down a new photo for their profile. They upload photos into their album. In an hour they are cruising their newsfeed like a pro.

Zoom in on their conversations and you see a nuanced peer-branding system at play. Two moms discuss Elf on a Shelf and trade photos of elf poses. A guy mentions he's running the Warrior Dash and 10 of his friends volunteer to run it with him. Grandparents ask for webcam recommendations that are answered by their grandchildren's friends.

Traditional advertising loses in this arena. Brands get respect if they are recommended by a friend, family member, or trusted influencer. Sophisticated psychographics and copywriting techniques yield to photos, *likes*, and shares.

We call this peer branding because the brand is built one authentic experience at a time. A product that earns peer respect is rewarded with a vibrant and resilient brand supported by the crowd. A brand that squanders peer-branding credibility gets down-voted to obscurity.

For many businesses, peer branding feels arbitrary, unpredictable, and dangerous. Some businesses have chosen to not play, studiously avoiding the peer-branding social experience. Ultimately, taking your toys and going home is a losing strategy for two reasons:

1. *Your competitors are playing, learning, and mastering the peer-branding experience.* It's a safe bet that tomorrow, another business will step into the social media space and compete for attention, respect, and peer-branding "street cred." They will unearth insights about their brand. They will wrestle with customer service issues. Their PR team will cope with social-media-fueled publicity firestorms. Their marketing teams will master the nuanced communication needed to discreetly imprint a brand's values on a social group.

   Within months, they will secure the respect of their fans and begin attracting new prospects. Those prospects will be stolen, from you. If you aren't on social media, you can't respond. There's a Chinese proverb that advises: "The best time to plan to plant a tree is 20 years ago. The next best time is today." Take heed and start planting your social media tree today.
2. *You are getting judged even if you don't participate.* The only option your business has is to opt-in. You can't opt-out. Dads, aunts, acquaintances, high-school sweethearts, and more are already discussing your brand. The crowd is vetting your brand promise, customer experience, value, and "coolness" without your input. Yes, your marketing campaign might be establishing your brand promise with a carefully vetted demographic segment. But this same segment will quickly forget your unique selling point (USP) if they hear a different opinion from someone they trust. You need to move in—if only to closely observe how your brand is being described. All social platforms offer formal measures such as *likes*, retweets, followers, shares, Klout scores, and *pins*. Use these measures as directional clues to prompt deeper investigation. As you get more comfortable with the space, begin to plot the key aspects the social media community uses to evaluate your brand. There are golden insights here, but like all gold, it must be mined.

Social Experience #2: Crowd-Based Customer Service

In the introduction to this chapter, I discussed my ultimately successful customer service interaction with my cable company. Similar scenarios are played out every day on Twitter, TripAdvisor, Facebook, and any other social platform with a "submit" button. Unlike peer branding, businesses are guilty until proven innocent.

The last few years have been filled with customer snafus that have gone viral. A United Airlines passenger films his guitar, mangled by United's baggage handlers, and posts the video on YouTube. The video goes viral on YouTube, garnering over 12 million views and earning the passenger a few new guitars and a book deal.

A tired and stressed dad races to get a few groceries before he goes home. Unfortunately, he arrives 15 minutes after the Publix closes. As he turns back to his car, he hears the door open, and sees the lights flicker on, turning around he's shocked to see an employee wave him back to the store. The grateful customer posts his experience on Facebook getting over 119,000 *likes*, and 7,000 comments.

If your employees interact with the public, pay close attention. Bad customer service isn't a private, one-on-one situation anymore. You now have an audience numbering in the hundreds of millions. Good customer service is equally infectious. Social media participants love responding to customer service stories. Influencers race to be the first one to share it with their audience. Good or bad, your customers and their community can generate enough "media impressions" to rival a TV commercial. To survive, you need guts and a plan.

Your plan is simple. It follows the same rules you follow (and sometimes bend) in your relationships. When you upset a friend, by forgetting a lunch appointment or birthday, what do you do?

First: Make it right. Find another time for lunch. Buy a (big) birthday present.

Second: Get face-to-face. Pick up the phone, race to their house, whatever it takes to deliver.

Third: Apologize. Sometimes it's prudent to apologize, even when you've done nothing wrong.

Fourth: Follow up. Make sure that your apology sticks. Double down on humility, attention, and focus.

Here's a quick example from Apple. The iPhone 5 came with a brand new maps application. Apple tossed the trusty Google Maps application in favor of their homegrown Apple Maps solution. Within days, irate customers were filling blog comment sections, forums, and Twitter with horror stories of bad directions and shoddy performance.

Apple had learned from its last customer service dilemma (dubbed Antenna-gate), when the iPhone's cellular signal strength depended on how you held the phone.

This time, here's what Apple did:

1. *First, they made it right.* Tim Cook, Apple's CEO, assembled his team to figure out the problem, come up with alternatives, and decide how to explain the lack of quality to their customers.
2. *Second, they got face to face.* Tim Cook did the best thing a company can do to reach as many customers as possible—he took out an ad in the *Wall Street Journal.*
3. *Third, they apologized.* Cook apologized to the Apple legions, telling them to use Google Maps until Apple had figured out the problem.
4. *And, fourth, they followed up.* Cook fired Scott Forestall, the senior vice president responsible for rushing the malfunctioning and unfinished app to market.

The tumult around Apple subsided. The powerful social media community applauded Cook's frank "we screwed up" approach and the iPhone 5 went on to be one of Apple's most successful product launches.

Don't be the business that ignores the problem, sends a boilerplate, legally-vetted, form letter (three weeks after the fact), refuses to apologize or recognize the inconvenience, and forgets the situation. This doesn't work and it's the best way to create a social backlash that will land your executive team on CNN with egg on their face.

Social Experience #3: Shared Discovery

The last social experience—shared discovery—taps into a seemingly hard-coded behavior. On Friday evening, you'll see office workers begin polling each other about their weekend plans. Look closely and you'll see one or two people who have the best suggestions. Their knowledge about the best clubs, shows, and off-the-beaten path hangouts has earned them credibility. Their social currency is based on their ability to discover new entertainment options and share them with others.

Companies have recognized the power of these mavens and actively seek them out by browsing blogs, lurking in forums, and using tools like Klout to quantitatively evaluate someone's influence score.

Other organizations have tapped into larger communities of influencers and provide them with innovative ways to spend real dollars along with social currency. Kickstarter, an online crowd-funded micro-financing site, gives anyone the ability to pitch an idea to the Kickstarter community. This community chooses to fund an idea by preordering the product. The most innovative ideas often get shared by influencers at online publications and popular blogs, often raising hundreds of thousands of dollars within days.

AirBnB is another example of social discovery being used to create real, very profitable, and insanely disruptive organizations. AirBnB's founders, Joe Gebbia and Brian Chesky, were looking for a way to make a little extra cash. The pair looked for a problem to solve. They discovered that people attending a local design conference couldn't find places to stay, since all the local hotel rooms were booked. They got online and offered to rent their San Francisco loft for the weekend. Their idea was a hit and a few days later they had a few thousand dollars in their pocket and an idea for a new company.

AirBnB has grown to be a popular option for travelers looking for a genuine bed and breakfast (B&B) experience without paying outrageous B&B prices. At the core of AirBnB is the ability to discover new and unique places to stay in any city in the world. AirBnB visitors often share their discoveries with their social audience on Facebook and Twitter. AirBnb gets free advertising, penny-pinching travelers get new options, and social discovery mavens get the reputation as a go-to person.

Nimble marketing teams are learning that creating unique experiences and allowing their customers to discover and share them is much more effective than screaming with traditional ad units. Social discovery works because every participant gets to do what they enjoy. The business offers the solution. Social mavens share the discovery. The public gets to find and experience something to talk about at the water cooler on Monday morning. This is the future of marketing.

You might be skeptical. The idea of entrusting your marketing to prospects, customers, and faceless third-parties seems a little farfetched until you realize that social marketing has been around for longer than you think.

WHY SOCIAL MEDIA IS IMPORTANT

A healthy capacity for cynicism is an essential trait for top marketers, and especially for online marketers. The dot-com bubble and bust demonstrated that hubris and dreams cost real money. As the tech world recovered in the early 2000s, dot-com refugees turned to metrics to tie lead anklets to digital dreamers. "Show me the numbers" became a popular chorus heard during many marketing meetings.

When social media began appearing in PowerPoint presentations, battle-hardened cynics often dismissed the tools as novelties. "Why do I care about a some person's lunch-time menu?" they crowed.

But as Facebook, Twitter, and LinkedIn became a fixture in the lives of nonmarketing types, CMOs began to take notice. The key, as you probably already know, is that you can't market by shouting in an empty room. You have to find your audience, and in 2012, over one billion people were having a hell of a good time on Facebook. Millions are happily sharing their favorite brands on Pinterest and Twitter. Now, social media cynicism seems like dangerous naiveté.

Social media is important because your customers prefer to gather, review, and share information about your company with people they trust. This has been the case for millennia, but now we can track and monetize this behavior. Zynga, the creator of Farmville, leveraged the attention of millions of addicted Facebook users into a multi-billion-dollar valuation. Red Bull, the prolific energy drink purveyor, is an astute social media tactician, managing a community of over 34 million fans. These fans are already on Facebook, and Red Bull makes sure it provides them with a lot of cool stuff to talk about. These are just two examples pulled from a pool of thousands. The ubiquity of social commerce and media is so breathtaking that many believe that social media *is* the Internet.

This isn't so farfetched.

On June 29, 2011, Google, the world's largest search engine, launched the Google+ project. For weeks social media pundits panned the entry. It seemed a pale imitator of Facebook and just slightly better than Twitter. But within a year, many realized that Google was playing chess, not checkers. Google realized what we now know—social media is the eyes, ears, and hands of the Internet. If you want to be the number one search engine, you have to make it easy for Google users to identify great content via their social network. Today search engine listings come complete with author photos and are selected based on their social relevancy.

If this turn of events is news to you, then it's likely your business is already behind the curve.

Facebook hasn't let Google innovate without a fight. Facebook's Open Graph is a simple power-play—a sucker punch designed to daze Google long enough for "Zuck's" team to steal the fight. The Open Graph is a utility that allows any 3rd party website to login members using their Facebook credentials. This is a win-win because the site visitor can login with one click and the website owner get's access to incredibly rich user data. The transaction is straight-forward: Hand over user data and get access to the deepest treasure trove of consumer data in history. While Facebook battles privacy concerns, companies are quietly using its data to create rich and sticky experiences for their users.

This isn't about *tweets* and *likes*. Social media is a revolutionary shift in how you view customers, their behavior, and your product. Dragging your feet means ceding your customers' social network to your competitors. It's like showing up at your prom date's home to discover that she has gone to the dance with your rival.

Liquid marketers understand how to pick the right social elements that make the most strategic sense. They adapt their marketing to leverage the data, access, and social networks to discreetly sponsor the experiences that mean the most to their customers. This isn't a left-brained game of numbers; it's a right-brained seduction based on relationships.

If you want to play, you need to start with a clear-eyed appraisal of your channel strategy.

SOCIAL MEDIA CHANNEL STRATEGY

Social media is essentially the strategy of telling a compelling story, engaging a receptive community on the most effective channel. Each element of the strategy must be finely tuned to move the participant from ambivalence to advocacy. We'll walk through each element and discuss the key success drivers for each.

Creating the Story

We are storytelling creatures. We love to gather around a central place and swap our perspectives. We use stories to make sense of the world, understand our purpose, and refine our values. The simple words "Let me tell you a story" immediately capture the attention of the listener. We all gravitate to the person or brand that has mastered the timeless ritual of storytelling.

Storytelling is social media's secret handshake. The brands that understand that customers are heroes on a problem-solving journey to capture followers and fans. Marketing teams that understand how to advise and mentor their customers effortlessly distribute their message and often cash in on the elusive viral message.

Job number one for your organization is to create your organizational, cultural, historical, brand story. This story is enriched with everyday anecdotes mined from customer service interactions, brainstorming meetings, crises, founders, and employees. All of these mini-plots must be fused together into a narrative and then distributed to the appropriate communities and platforms.

This is hard work. It isn't easy to switch from a cultural monologue to a dialogue. Telling your story on a new social platform feels a lot like your first high-school dance. But, the rewards of telling a compelling story are astounding.

Remember this simple rule: You can't sell until you can tell. Telling isn't a 30 second commercial, it's an ongoing dialogue with strangers. Embrace the shift in perspective and you'll arm your organization with the most important ingredient for social media success: a story worth telling.

Selecting a Channel

The most curious attribute of social media is that it is locked into a symbiotic relationship with our senses. YouTube excites with motion, sound, and rich imagery. Pinterest and Flickr excel at still-life photography. Twitter taps into communal white noise that organically surfaces the latest crowdsourced sensation. Facebook is the first social utility that combines photography, video, and rapid-fire dialogue.

Understanding the role of each channel in your customer's life is essential for using it to maximize your story's appeal. From a high level:

- Twitter excels at real-time updates. It's the nervous system of plugged-in content curators and influential sharers. Twitter's structure prevents long-form storytelling. Instead, Twitter is best used to rapidly share valuable resources and deliver personality-revealing oneliners.
- Facebook is a vast digital cafeteria filled with millions of cliques. Facebook rewards influence and engagement. A high-school teenager often has more influence than their city's mayor. Your story must have enough appeal to attract a crowd, and enough variety to keep the community returning for more.
- Blogs represent the premier long-form storytelling social platform. They favor persistent, methodical delivery of high-quality information. The best social media strategies position their blogs at the hub of their social program. The blog assumes the role of narrator for the organizational story. Blogs are favored by Google and other search engines because they often are focused on a single subject and are frequently updated.

- Pinterest, Youtube, and Flickr are the artistic and expressive soul of social media. These platforms are talented community aggregators and can capture the attention of users for hours. The trio also presents the largest challenge for businesses. Video and photos are devilishly hard to create, edit, and present. Even so, the best stories have the best pictures and video. As a result, smart businesses are assembling the multidisciplinary teams needed to translate their brand story into compelling short videos and photos.
- LinkedIn is perhaps the most misunderstood and underestimated social channel of the bunch. LinkedIn's roots were sunk deep into the professional community. Early users valued LinkedIn's ability to collect and categorize business contact information. The HR and recruiting crowd immediately saw the potential of the platform and fought a largely successful campaign to turn it into a job-hunting tool. However, LinkedIn has revamped the user experience to offer powerful tools for organizing and communicating with hard-to-target B2B audiences. Nimble professional services, business services, and niche-oriented businesses are mastering how to tell their story to the LinkedIn community.

Successful channel selection is built on shrewdly selecting the platform best suited to host the businesses' story. This often means abandoning channels that force the organization out of character and overly taxes its resources. Many B2B businesses are trying to make Facebook strategies work and burning time, people, and money in the process. B2C companies commit the same channel selection errors with LinkedIn. Like most successful strategies, the ability to say "no" is often the key to positive results.

Mastering Channel Fundamentals

Now that you understand how these channels can strengthen your communications and branding, let's turn our attention to mastering the success drivers for select channels. We'll do this with a simple "Dos and Don'ts" list that can be used as a checklist. For brevity, we'll focus on the top three social platforms—Twitter, Facebook, and LinkedIn.

Twitter

Dos

- **Brand Your Twitter Page:** Twitter gives you a profile page where you can showcase your brand's creativity, along with the web addresses of your online properties. Customize this page to communicate your brand look and voice.
- **Follow Influencers:** Use Twitter's search tool to find people who are actively sharing information on Twitter. Follow these influencers to get their tweets delivered to your Twitter stream.
- **Retweet (a lot):** The core principle of social marketing is "Giver's Get." Take every opportunity to retweet anyone that offers quality information on Twitter. Your willingness to share the stage will be noticed and reciprocated by other savvy social marketers.
- **Promote Your Content:** You might have heard that it's unprofessional to promote your own content on Twitter. Pay these folks no mind, they are wrong. Tweet your content to your audience on a regular basis. I recommend scheduling promotional tweets in the morning (8 a.m.), around the lunch hour, and in the evening between 8 and 10 p.m. This will insure your tweet doesn't get lost
- **Be Polite:** Make a point to thank people for retweets and mentions. Your positive reinforcement will get more retweets and shares from people following your Twitter feed.
- **Add A Twitter *Follow* and *Retweet* Button:** Twitter's *retweets* button allows readers to share your content with their Twitter audience with one click. The Twitter *follow* button makes it easy for visitors to follow your account. Place both of these buttons in prominent positions near your content.

Don'ts

- **Over Tweet:** Your Twitter stream should be a drinking fountain not a fire hose. I recommend a pace of about one tweet per hour during your audience's working day. You can up the tempo to two to three posts per hour if you cater to an audience that actively uses Twitter to find and curate information.
- **Hero Worship:** People tend to retweet popular influencers and ignore smaller publications or rising stars. This isn't a good strategy. It takes a concerted and time-intensive strategy to get top influencers to notice and retweet your content. You'll find that the smaller players are the most likely to retweet your content. Every retweet counts.
- **Share Links Only:** Your audience wants your opinion about the links you retweet. Simply hitting the *retweets* button offers little value to your audience. Make it a practice to include a few words of endorsement or editorial to the majority of retweeted links.

Facebook

Dos

- **Relax:** Facebook users are having fun and using Facebook to relax and catch up with people they care about. Let your hair down and talk about funny employees, unusual events, interesting photos, and videos shared around the audience. Give your audience a glimpse into the culture of your organization.
- **Personalize:** Facebook's timeline and header areas are excellent for creating a distinctive feel and experience for your audience. Create a timeline photo that is attention-getting and illustrative of your organization's core values.
- **Mix it Up:** Update your timeline with a variety of different content types. Photos and videos are very popular on Facebook and are more likely to get spread by your audience.

- **Build Your E-mail List:** Use a tab to build your list by giving away valuable content, trial products, or services in exchange for an e-mail address.
- **Add the Facebook Widget and Button to Your Blog/ Website:** Adding Facebook's share icon lets readers spread your content on their timeline. The Facebook *like* widget can be placed in your blog's sidebar, making it easy for visitors to *like* and follow you in their newsfeed.

Don'ts

- **Sell:** Direct pitches for your product on your timeline will not do well. Facebook users aren't in a buying mindset; they are looking for information and connections. The hard sell will turn off visitors and hurt your brand.
- **Be "Corporate":** Save the industry lingo and insider-jargon. Facebook users want to *like* people, not logos and jargon.
- **Rely on Off-Facebook Links:** People using Facebook want to stay on Facebook. They are extremely resistant to linking to a site that isn't on Facebook. It isn't always practical, but try to handle the majority of your transactions on Facebook. For example, companies use Facebook tabs and custom-built applications to sell merchandise or collect leads for consultations.

LinkedIn

Dos

- **Create a Company Page:** LinkedIn is aggressively adding new ways to drive prospects to your company page. Take the time to complete your company page profile with services and at least one offer for a free trial or consultation.
- **Encourage Employees to Sign-Up:** Ask your employees to sign-up for LinkedIn and reference your company in the "Experience" section of their profiles. Next, ask these employees to follow your profile on LinkedIn. The follow feature is similar to Twitter's follow. Your follow count is listed next to your company profile information, adding a bit of social credibility to your profile.

- **Join Groups:** Join every group that is relevant to your organization's core product or service. These groups are excellent resources for getting access to potential influencers, employees, and industry contacts. Participate in group discussions where appropriate, and look for opportunities to answer questions from fellow group members.
- **Add a LinkedIn Share Button on Your Blog/Website:** LinkedIn offers a share icon that enables people to share your content on their LinkedIn update list. Content that generates a high number of shares is often featured on LinkedIn Today. LinkedIn Today is a homepage customized for each LinkedIn user based on their interests. Getting features on this page can attract hundreds of visitors to your website.

Don'ts

- **Mass E-mail Group Participants:** LinkedIn frowns on mass e-mailing group participants with offers. Doing so will get you kicked out of groups and reported to the LinkedIn staff—not a good move.
- **Neglect Your Profile and Company Pages:** Review your LinkedIn profile on a monthly basis and update any information. Start with your company's service pages and regularly rotate in new offers.
- **Ignore Invitations and Notifications:** Other LinkedIn members will e-mail questions and notify you about important events and information. Responding to these communications shows that you are an active member and a potentially useful resource.

Converting Participants into Customers and Advocates

In the end, conversations started on social platforms need to evolve into transactions. Even though the social media intelligentsia would love to banish selling from the social sphere, it's a naïve and self-defeating goal. The best marketing organizations know that customers love to buy. They just hate being sold. Customers love to be entertained. Customers love stories. Customers love connecting with companies with world-changing ambition. Your task is to audition for the role of a trusted, respected, and valued brand.

Before we move forward, it's important that we clarify something. Social media platforms are terrible places to engage in direct selling. Trying to use social media as a replacement for face-to-face selling is a waste of time and can be damaging. On the other hand, social media is especially skilled at "warming up" prospects and framing the benefits of a future relationship.

For example, Dell's social media efforts demonstrate the company's dedication to unparalleled customer service. Dell's social media team's responsiveness sets the buying criteria for the industry. Future customers select Dell because they know that they are responsive and diligent.

Your social media program needs to hit similar notes. Your goal is to show the benefits of engaging with your brand. Once you've established rapport with your audience, begin the process of moving them toward a transaction.

E-mail Isn't Dead

Every year, someone climbs on the table and shouts, "E-mail is Dead!" Dire statistics about spam, deliverability, and plummeting open rates adorn the diatribe. But, every year, e-mail continues to outpunch its weight compared to other marketing channels. E-mail works and it will continue to work for a long time.

That's why precocious social marketers like Groupon, AirBnB, Fab.com, UPS, and others make it a priority to capture the e-mail addresses of their social audience. They know that trying to direct sell on Facebook is a fool's errand, while sending offers to their social audience via e-mail is a winner. Spend five minutes on any large social media player's channel and you'll observe a strategic effort to collect e-mail addresses.

You must do the same.

It's safe to up the ante and say that social media's goal is to turn participants into e-mail subscribers. Of course, this focus can be overdone. But delivering an e-mail subscription incentive to your social audience is the first best step to seeing ROI from your social media program.

Broadcast Media's New Gig

Broadcast media stalwarts—TV, radio, and print—are gaining new life as social media invitation platforms. While TV's effectiveness has been on the decline, you still can't match TV's ability to speak to millions of people at a relatively low cost. Using this ability to invite potential customers to *like* and tweet via hashtags is a powerful way to jumpstart a social campaign.

Reality show producers are taking the lead by suggesting hashtags for their reality show. In the recent Biker Build-Off featuring Jesse James and Orange County Chopper's Paul Sr. and Paul Jr., viewers were encouraged to tweet using their favorite teams hashtag. Viewer tweets were often mentioned on the reality show. The entertainment worked both ways, with show participants creating spoof content that was fed back to the Twitterverse.

Other popular shows like The Voice and X Factor leveraged their massive viewing audiences to create equally compelling and popular Facebook and Twitter followings. Corporate advertisers use the same tactics, often giving their social media addresses more visibility in advertising than their website addresses.

This strategy works by exposing social audiences to a well-structured menu of content optimized for easy pass-along. Toyota's Sienna minivan campaign was supported by an incredibly effective social media campaign anchored by utterly ordinary middle-class parents who rapped about their extraordinary parenting skills.[1]

Broadcast media's changing role allows marketing teams to integrate social messaging across a variety of platforms. Social media isn't displacing broadcast media. In fact, the opposite is happening. Broadcast media is providing the media efficiency that platforms like Twitter, LinkedIn, and Google+ lack. The strategic marketing approach uses the strengths of one channel to compensate for the weaknesses of another. Together, the entire campaign works to provide a cost-effective media campaign that reaches a targeted audience.

Now that we understand the potential of a socially equipped strategic marketing campaign, let's take a closer look at the tools needed to plan, launch, and evaluate the campaign.

TOOLS OF THE TRADE

The strategic marketing approach requires accurate data that can be mined for practical insights. Social media is blessed with a growing community of analytics tool builders who are scrambling to provide the best real-time data available. The challenge is sifting the useful tools from the "me-too" eye-candy proliferating the market.

While this section can't hope to comprehensively cover all analytic tool options, it will focus on the most effective. We'll highlight the top-level analytics tools and then discuss some platform-specific standouts.

Top-Level Social Analytics Tools

Google Analytics[2]

Google Analytics is Google's free analytics offering. It is incredibly powerful and is routinely updated to keep pace with enterprise demands. The program is web-based and is installed with a basic script addition to your pages. From there, Google's powerful algorithm matches up social channels with visits, providing you with an excellent view of which social platforms are contributing visitors and driving engagement.

In mid-2011, Google enhanced Google Analytics' social measurement capabilities. The new measurements allow businesses to directly evaluate social media's impact on their conversion goals (i.e., subscriptions, leads, and sales). Initially this service worked best with Google's social offering Google+, but Google has steadily added full functionality for social platforms like Twitter, LinkedIn, and Facebook. This added capability makes Google Analytics a must-have in any liquid marketer's toolkit.

Sysomos[3]

Sysomos is a full-featured social media listening and evaluation tool. Sysomos excels at "listening," or reviewing all data from a social platform and highlighting engagement around specific keywords. The program is web-based and fairly easy to use, with excellent training provided by the Sysomos team. Sysomos was one of the first tools to tackle Facebook monitoring, and has successfully added this feature to its offering.

Sysomos works well for an organization seeking a meta-view of its social presence across all social platforms. The ability to evaluate sentiment and mentions, while identifying influencers, makes Sysomos a powerful partner for CMOs and social media managers.

Argyle Social[4]

Argyle Social combines impressive social analytics capabilities with social platform management. The combination makes it the Swiss army knife of social analytics tools. The software also adds team collaboration options to spread social monitoring and audience management duties among the entire marketing department, rather than just one overworked intern. It's important to consider that Argyle Social's value proposition targets small and mid-size businesses. Their feature set is standardized, allowing for reasonable customization but not the full-customization offered by other platforms.

Argyle Social works best for organizations that have outgrown basic social media management tools and need to streamline their process, while getting excellent analytics data. It's also important to consider that, unlike Sysomos or Radian6, Argyle Social isn't a social monitoring platform, meaning that it doesn't mine public social data. Instead, Argyle monitors the users' owned platforms. This data can be used to guide team members' use of the software's social management tools.

Salesforce Radian6[5]

Radian6, recently acquired by Salesforce, is considered a leader in the social listening space. Radian6 offers comprehensive analysis of all the social conversations happening across the Internet. It's a tall order, but Radian6's acquisition by Salesforce gives it the technical infrastructure to deliver on its proposition. Radian6 is a full-featured enterprise tool designed for Fortune 500 firms requiring real-time measurement and listening capabilities.

Radian6 suits large organizations that see social media and social business as a critical competitive advantage for their market space. C-level executives can use Radian6 to assemble an in-depth picture of how their market is discussing and engaging with brand assets in the social space. Managers and directors will find the dashboards helpful for monitoring activity and adjusting day-to-day social initiatives based on real-time data. Of course, Salesforce has integrated its powerful CRM platform with Radian6 to show sales teams which social platforms are contributing leads and sales.

Blogging Tools

WordPress[6]

WordPress is the core software used to power CMS-driven sites like blogs. CMS or Content Management Systems make it easy for nontechnical users to create web pages with text, photos, and videos. As of mid 2012, WordPress was used on 48 percent of the top 100 blogs, including UPS, CNN, and GM, and was the preferred software for 72.4 million sites worldwide. When a business decides to start a blog, they often turn to WordPress first.[7]

WordPress is free to use and is offered in two varieties:

1. **Hosted:** New users can host their blogs on WordPress.com. This option is easy, free, and requires just an e-mail address to get started. While options are limited for business and enterprise users who need direct control over their content, the hosted option is very popular, with 50 percent of WordPress users selecting the hosted version.
2. **Self-Hosted:** The WordPress CMS software is free and open-source. It can be downloaded from WordPress.org and installed on a private web host. This option is often used by businesses and professionals who want creative, programming, and security flexibility. The WordPress CMS is updated frequently and users can update their software version with built-in update tools.

Tumblr[8]

Tumblr is a streamlined blogging platform that combines the best of blogging, Twitter, YouTube, and Flickr into one platform. The platform is often used by creative professionals who want attention focused on their visual work. Like WordPress.com, users register and set up their Tumblr sites on Tumblr servers.

Tumblr is an excellent option for organizations that have visual content and require a quick way to frequently publish it. Tumblr's templates can be modified extensively from an intuitive interface offered in the user's administrative dashboard. In addition to the simple interface, Tumblr promotes member blogs in its growing community of Tumblr users.

Twitter Tools

Twitter is a popular social media platform that enables quick 140 character messages (tweets) between individuals or groups of users. The service has over 100 million active users who follow each others' Twitter feeds. Blog publishers place Twitter buttons on their blog posts to encourage users to tweet their posts, hoping to attract readers from the user's following. Twitter users can also retweet other tweets to their followers, exponentially increasing the reach of a single message.

Businesses build Twitter followings to enhance the reach of their marketing messages while keeping track of social conversations about their brand. Many businesses maintain multiple Twitter accounts, each associated with a different business function such as marketing, specific product lines, and customer service.

HootSuite[9]

HootSuite users can manage single or multiple Twitter accounts from a single interface. Users can also create and send tweets, respond to other Twitter users, and send direct messages. HootSuite presents information in a column format, allowing for a single dashboard populated with separate accounts or columns configured to follow Twitter keywords, lists, or even specific users.

HootSuite is best used for keeping track of all Twitter activity from one screen. HootSuite also makes it simple for multiple team members to monitor accounts and respond to specific issues.

Crowdbooster[10]

Crowdbooster helps Twitter users identify popular influencers who are interacting with their Twitter account. The software can identify people with high follower and retweet activity and send an e-mail alert when one of these people follows the user's account or retweets a message. The software also offers impressive analytics features that analyze follower demographics, message reach, and overall Twitter account growth.

Use Crowdbooster to evaluate your Twitter account performance and keep track of potentially influential users who follow your account. This information is valuable for refining your social media messaging and overall marketing strategy.

Facebook's Insight Tool

Facebook raced past one billion visitors in 2012. The most astonishing statistic, however, is that over 50 percent of Facebook users log in and use the social utility every day—which is more people than the population of the United States. Facebook's gargantuan audience and unprecedented reach makes it a key consideration for any business's social media program.

Facebook offers its own analytics tool—Facebook Insights. The tool analyzes account reach, the popularity of specific messages, and an increasing number of demographic data points. Insights can also provide information on how many active users engage with your account and detail how many views your Facebook page receives. While the tool isn't perfect, it's the only tool that can accurately track Facebook statistics, since other tools can't get past Facebook's login requirement. Facebook is slowly opening new analytics options to third-party tools. However many tools can only evaluate publicly accessible Facebook data, restricting their usefulness.

BEST-IN-CLASS EXAMPLES

Everyone is waking up to the latent but explosive power of social marketing. One of the biggest challenges, however, is understanding how to marshal your business's resources to take advantage of social media's benefits. It's often helpful to review how other organizations have met the challenge. We've highlighted the efforts of three organizations in this section. This by no means is a complete or comprehensive exposition, but it does point to a common aspect of successful social campaigns, namely, the best campaigns understand the power of a great story told by real people with authentic insights.

Pure Michigan[11]

There are many noteworthy examples of businesses doing well with social media but what about government organizations? Travel Michigan, the team behind the Pure Michigan campaign, has done an incredible job using social media to spur tourism.

Creating the Story:

From the start, Travel Michigan wanted to enlist the "locals" to tell Michigan's story. They understood that Michigan is filled with amazing sights, events, and landmarks, and the most credible ambassadors where Michigan residents. Michigan grew its Facebook fan base by posting breathtaking photos, inspiring video, and a steady stream of fun events and festival information. Michigan residents responded by spreading the information to their network and actively answering questions from people seeking information about Michigan. Over time, the Travel Michigan team was able to take a step back and let users support the Facebook community.

Michigan used the same strategy to build its Pure Michigan blog community and Twitter following. The Travel Michigan team has brought all communication stakeholders to the table and encouraged everyone to provide ideas and content for the social media channels. Michigan's efforts and success provide a salient example of social media's ability to deliver results.

Red Bull[12]

Red Bull, the leading energy drink maker, has mastered the art of building socially-enabled stories around its brand. While many brands just sprinkle their logo on social properties, Red Bull works to create high-production value video, text, and photos, and actively build a fan base around its content. This approach allows Red Bull to generate media reach that rivals cable TV, and even network TV, on many occasions.

Creating the Story:

One notable example is Red Bull's sponsorship of the highest skydive in history. Actually, it was a space dive. The jumper, Felix Baumgartner, jumped from his hot air balloon, parked 23 miles over the surface of the earth. From his balloon, he could see the clear curvature of the earth and the separation between blue skies and the inky blackness of space. Red Bull's social media team supported their sponsorship with a Facebook event and Twitter hashtags. At one point, Red Bull-driven social conversation represented 1 percent of all the conversations on the web, an unprecedented accomplishment. Facebook followers were treated to exclusive photos and content. Twitter followers received real-time updates of the space jump by following the #livejump hashtag. The event was also supported with a popular Instagram feed populated with breathtaking imagery.

Researchers believe the event drew over 2.6 million social mentions on the day it occurred, along with plenty of mentions for the days surrounding the event. This was clearly a home run for a brand that understands how to leverage free social media platforms for extraordinary media reach.

Nike's Olympic Campaign[13]

Nike is a brilliant guerrilla marketer. Every four years, marketing professionals are treated to another example of Nike stealing the limelight from official Olympic sponsors. In 2012's London Summer Games, Adidas, the official sponsor, was beat (again) by Nike's offline and social campaign.

Adidas took an orthodox approach. They spent millions of pounds to be the London Games' official sponsor. They built an inspiring campaign around U.K. athletes. They obtained the hashtag #takethestage and began tweeting up a storm. The results were impressive, with 9,295 Adidas-related tweets between July 27 and August 2.

Nike did something different. It ran an "everyday athlete" social campaign that was supported by purchasing billboards around the Olympic Village. The billboards featured ordinary athletes who were celebrated using Nike's Twitter hashtag #findthegreatness. The clever campaign resonated with an audience gripped by the thought that anyone who works hard can achieve an Olympic gold medal. The billboards' egalitarian appeal prompted people to share the #findthegreatness hashtag. As a result, Nike generated over 16,000 Twitter mentions of its hashtag. They added salt to Adidas's wound by attracting over 166,000 new Facebook fans, doubling Adidas's gains of just 80,000 fans.[14]

Nike's campaign shows that it's not good enough to simply create a Twitter hashtag. Successful social media starts with a compelling social story supported by smart media execution.

SOCIAL MEDIA ROI

Gary Vaynerchuk, a respected social media thinker and incredibly popular wine taster, was cornered. He was giving an interview, and he was being asked to explain the business efficacy of social media. The question was simple, "What is social media's ROI?" Gary danced around the answer, opting to explain the power of conversations and engagement. The interviewer didn't bite, he tried again: "What is the business case, the ROI of social media?" Gary paused, and then parried, "What is the ROI of your mom?"

No, it wasn't a "mom joke." It actually elegantly summed up Gary's central argument. Social media is built on relationships and the conversations between friends. This conversation has incredible potential value, considering that I wouldn't think twice about buying a movie ticket, a book, or another gadget based on my best friend's recommendation. But how can you put a number or value on that conversation? My mom telling me to eat my vegetables or purchase Robitussin for my cold has value because it's my mom's advice. A television commercial may have the same message but hold zero value. Hence, Gary nailed it—"What is the ROI of your mom?" Pretty darn high, but I can't quantify it beyond that.

Many social media thinkers wish that we could stop there, pat Gary on the back, and go back to writing content. But that won't work.

Social media requires investment in people, software, and equipment. You can't get the CFO to approve a budget request with the *mom argument*. So we're going to have to tackle the ROI question a different way.

The Traditional Approach

Social media is being used to encourage people to purchase a product or service. Google Analytics and other tools are getting better at attributing a sale to a source. Simply, if a person arrives from Facebook and purchases a widget, then Facebook gets credit (or partial credit) for the sale. At the end of the reporting period, tally up your sales and determine how many of those sales could be reasonably attributed to a social channel.

Your table looks something like this:

Monthly Unit Sales: 100
Twitter: 2
Facebook: 18
LinkedIn: 10
Pinterest: 5
Total Social Media Related Sales: 35

Take this one step further by adding the cost of social activities and the value of the sales. These costs can describe personnel payroll for managing social channels and/or the cost of advertising on specific platforms:

Social Media Related Revenue
Twitter: $20
Facebook: $180
LinkedIn: $100
Pinterest: $50
Total Social Media Revenue: $350

Social Media Costs
Twitter: $100
Facebook: $150
Linkedin: $50
Pinterest: $20
Total Social Media Costs: $220

In this simplified example, social media contributed $1.59 for every $1.00 invested. Using the standard financial ROI calculation, ROI = (Investment Gain – Investment Cost)/Investment Cost, we get a return on investment of .59.

We can dig deeper and calculate the ROI of each channel. ROI itself can simply be calculated using the above formula, but it requires the business to accurately track where each sale came from—social media, traditional media, or another means. For the most part, many analytics tools are based on this basic math: How much revenue did social media customers create and how much did it cost to do it? The drawback to this ROI calculation is attribution. Does social media get 100 percent of the credit or just 25 percent, understanding that the customer could have been persuaded by a TV ad, a magazine ad, and a billboard on their commute. While attribution is difficult to determine, it isn't just a social media problem. Every media channel must contend with it. However we are much closer to giving the correct weight to social media and accurately getting a helpful ROI number.

Social Media as Profit Builder

Let's shake things up a bit. Most CFOs chuckle at the notion that marketing is an investment. They will say (correctly) that a true investment is an asset. This asset is correctly accounted for on a balance sheet along with buildings, a fleet of vehicles, or computer systems. Basically an asset can be sold when it's not needed anymore. Assets can also be written off (depreciation) as their value declines.

Marketing isn't an investment in this regard. You can't sell off your Facebook *likes*. However, marketing *is* an expense. You purchase ad space. You hire social media specialists. Marketing as an expense is put on the profit and loss statement. You manage your marketing expense to insure that it doesn't eat up all your profit. This fact is easy for financial types to understand, but a rude slap in the face for marketers. You can't buy a marketing package and place it on your balance sheet as an asset. Instead you invest in marketing hoping that it builds revenues at a good cost. Another way of thinking about it is that a great marketing plan boosts revenue while shaving marketing costs or great marketing contributes to profit.

This approach asserts that to estimate the value of a brand's social media, your primary concern should be determining the *contribution to profit.* This involves not only generated sales, but also potential costs saved by forgoing other activities. For instance, without social media, the marketing team would need to purchase advertising to reach enough people to build a given volume of sales. Advertising is much more expensive than social media. However, as the business gets better at social media, traditional advertising expenses decline. As a result, the social media specialist can effectively reach more people with a combination of tweets, blog content, and Facebook updates than spending several times the amount of his salary on TV ads.

At the quarterly meeting, the marketing director stands up and says "Our social media effort has lowered marketing costs by 20 percent while boosting revenue by 30 percent." Combining these two together, we can actually determine the value of our social media investment.

At the end of the day, these two approaches have the same goal. It's up to you whether the traditional ROI methodology or the social media as profit builder concept makes more sense for your business. Strategic marketers are often best served using ROI as a basis for comparison, but it's interesting to note that top performers such as Apple, Southwest Airlines, Virgin Atlantic, and Coca-Cola embrace the fact that marketing is the cost of doing business rather than a quasi-asset that must be squeezed for a return.

THE FUTURE OF SOCIAL MEDIA

The maddening part about social media is that much of it didn't exist five years ago. When I try to imagine what the future holds, I have to plausibly accept the notion that the current players—Facebook, Twitter, LinkedIn, Pinterest, and legions of others—may not exist in their current form. In 2006, no one would have predicted that Google would be fighting for social media credibility, MySpace would barely survive, and Microsoft would be a "non factor" as a social media technology powerhouse. We definitely couldn't have foreseen Facebook's billion-person membership base.

So it doesn't make sense to extrapolate the future based on the current players. Instead, I'm going to back into the future of social media based on the real power players—customers.

Marketing Is Replaced by Social Storytelling

Marketing as an advertising-based discipline will cease to be useful. Instead the science and art of social interactions will absorb and marginalize traditional marketing. Just like direct mail seems quaint in today's technological age, marketing will barely hold intellectual and practical legitimacy. Instead, a new breed of social storytelling will become the dominant form of commercial persuasion. Social storytellers will draw on the science of statistical modeling, psychology, sociology, and anthropology to discreetly smuggle branded names into customer networks. Customers will care less about brand aesthetics and assign more value to a company's ability to be practically relevant in their lives.

In five years it's easy to imagine the networks abandoning 30-second commercials and inviting brands to contribute to screenplays and scripts on a deeper level. The best brands will shape the look and feel of our entertainment on a subconscious level, reinforcing the core story. I'm not talking about putting a Coke bottle on a table, but integrating Coke's value of nostalgia and classic taste into the story itself. Other messaging via Twitter, mobile messaging, and Facebook will be timed to create a 360 degree experience that invokes the thought "I love Coke."

Customers as Rock Stars

We are already seeing the rise of customers as key marketing players.

Much of the past marketing orthodoxy was based on the customer as an individual actor. You show the customer an advertisement and wait for them to make a purchase. The customer didn't have all the information they needed to make a decision. Advertisements acted as the invitation to visit a showroom, store, or website to gather information and start the purchasing process. We assumed that the customer relied on their own information and made an independent decision to make a purchase.

This isn't the case today and it will never be that way again.

Social media has equipped customers with the tools to influence millions of fellow customers. Customer social networks are used to gather information, read customer reviews, and in some cases, make a transaction directly from their social platform of choice. In the future, companies will focus exclusively on reaching and compensating individual customers who can influence their networks. Companies will create a partnership with these customer rock stars, giving them unprecedented access to the product ideation, manufacturing, and distribution process. Customers will become the new corporate shareholder, investing time and attention into their brand of choice.

In this scenario, simply viewing customers as an audience is a mistake. Instead, socially adept companies will listen closely to social channels, identify customer – partners, and recruit them as ambassadors. Companies that use a monologue to control their message will find themselves outflanked by their competitors' customers.

Trust and Credibility Become Real Currency

In the future, every customer will be able to quickly evaluate the trustworthiness and credibility of brands and brand representatives. Imagine someone using a pair of Google Glasses, an augmented-reality device, to see a person's trust score. This score, along with other critical factors, would be displayed as a floating icon above their head. For example, a woman buying a pair of shoes will be able to see a crowdsourced "usefulness" rating of the salesperson. The rating would be an aggregates score calculated from the real-time advice of her social network. The same type of trust and credibility information could be displayed above individual products. Customers would rove the shopping markets getting real-time reviews from their networks, even messaging brand champions for specific advice.

In this scenario, the marketing will be built into the product. A poorly built product will be flagged based on the experience of actual customers. Advertising and PR will not be able to obfuscate the data gathered from social networks. Customer service will become the first and last line of defense for brands needing to establish high trust scores for their product. Social platforms like Facebook, Twitter, and Google+ will be the new battleground for customer attention where brands compete ruthlessly for influence.

Many aspects of social media's future role are visible today. Coca-Cola has publicly embraced the roles of social media and content marketing as growth drivers for their company. Customers are being courted to accelerate the launch of new products. Today, anyone can join Klout and receive a score reflecting their influence, reach, and trust. Google Glasses, a pair of eyeglasses that displays wireless information are moving closer to public launch.

The social engineers (not marketers) of the future will assemble these items into a seamless conversation with key customers. The future will be here much sooner than we think.

ENDNOTES

1. You can see the addictive video Swagger Van here: http://bit.ly/TspwdA.
2. http://www.google.com/analytics
3. http://www.sysomos.com/
4. http://argylesocial.com/
5. http://www.radian6.com/what-we-sell/marketingcloud/social-enterprise/
6. http://wordpress.com
7. http://visual.ly/wordpress-usage
   http://yoast.com/wordpress-stats/
   http://en.wordpress.com/stats
8. http://tumblr.com/
9. http://www.hootsuite.com
10. http://www.crowdbooster.com
11. http://www.Michigan.org
12. http://www.redbull.com
13. http://www.Nike.com
14. http://econsultancy.com/us/blog/11244–10-of-the-best-social-media-campaigns-from–2012

CHAPTER 8

BUILDING A WEBSITE WITH PURPOSE THAT GENERATES RESULTS

—by Jeremy Floyd

INTRODUCTION

Despite the influx of digital media, one thing remains true: an effective website is the critical link to a company's overall online success. From Facebook pages to corporate Pinterest boards, you can spend all of your time creating and claiming all of your digital assets. So you may ask: Why in the world do companies still even need a website? As we will discuss, your website is the central hub (see Figure 8.1) and foundation of all of your brand's online activity. Thanks to the maturity of a few web technologies, creating a website with purpose has become much easier and cheaper.

No company should bypass a website. To start with, a well-designed website with expert content allows your customers to find you whenever they are trying to satisfy a need—regardless of the time of day. Creating great content on your website allows your clients to find you through search engines. In turn, your website will be one of the first touchpoints that potential clients will have with your company to build trust and credibility. Finally, you can

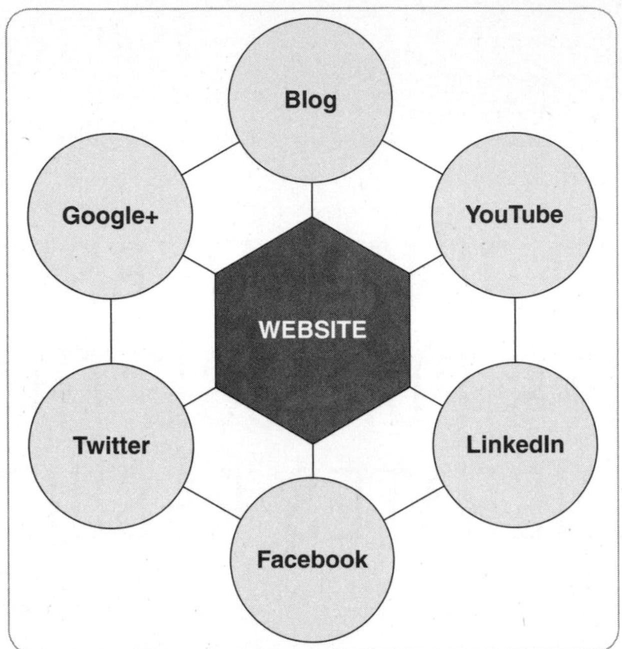

FIGURE 8.1 Websites are the Hub: While the peripheral networks may change, the construct allows a free flow of information and traffic between the networks and the website.

gain interesting insight into your clients' interactions by measuring their activity and interaction with your website.

Any website worth having has a clear purpose. Unfortunately, many websites are not much more than electronic brochures with useless information placed in key areas of the page. When viewed as one tool in the overall digital toolkit, the website should have a very specific purpose with directed goals. From the purpose, clear measurable goals can be established, which define success on the website. With that purpose in mind, the other tools such as Twitter, Facebook, and e-mail marketing will play a supporting role in the overall digital objectives.

In the modern technological world, websites should be intensely personal, using collected data to create customized experiences for visitors. They should also have seamless and user-friendly experiences across platforms and device types, including mobile devices. Modern technologies and tools allow our websites to be more personal and more dynamic than ever before—whether the user is visiting from a laptop, tablet, or smartphone.

Finally, all websites must include goal-based reporting that measures performance and provides the necessary data to make continuous improvements to the site.

BEGIN WITH PURPOSE

> A young woman was preparing a ham dinner. After she cut off the end of the ham, she placed it in a pan for baking.
>
> Her husband asked her, "Why did you cut off the end of the ham?"
>
> And she replied, "I really don't know, but my mother always did, so I thought you were supposed to."
>
> Later when talking to her mother, she asked her why she cut off the end of the ham before baking it, and her mother replied, "I really don't know, but that's the way my mom always did it."
>
> A few weeks later while visiting her grandmother, the young woman asked, "Grandma, why is it that you cut off the end of a ham before you bake it?"
>
> Her grandmother replied, "Well dear, otherwise it would never fit into that oven that we used to have."
>
> **—One of a thousand similar e-mails we've all been forwarded**

In other words, the end of the ham is cut off because that's the way that it has always been done. Many organizations go about the process of building or rebuilding their website by varying and improving the way it has always been done. Rarely does someone, from the inside, stop and ask "Why do we have a website in the first place?"

Why have a website? Elementary question, right? There are a variety of answers to this question, but most often it's answered with a stuttering, "Um...because everybody who's anybody has a website?!" When I hear that answer, it always makes me think of the ham story.

Contrary to the approach that most companies take to their website planning, the approach taken in this chapter does not start with the design and features of a website. This approach is divided into three sections (hat tip to Simon Sinek's golden circle): (1) Why have a website? (2) How to get there? (3) What is success?

So, what are a few common purposes of brand websites?

1. **Inform Your Audience / Establish Expertise and Reputation**: By providing expert information on your website, you establish confidence and trust that you are the subject matter expert through the information that you publish on your site.
2. **Generate Leads**: Your website is a great place to start the conversation with potential clients. From e-mail signup forms to lead collection forms, your website and landing pages present an opportunity to collect valuable information.
3. **Generate Sales / E-commerce**: With double-digit percentage increases each year and sales over $70 billion in online sales in 2012, e-commerce has carved out a specific niche of its own within the online world. Customers find online purchases to be less painful, cheaper, and faster than traditional retail purchases.
4. **Be Found / Equalizer:** Regardless of whether you have a memorable web address or people have never heard of your business, a majority of people will likely enter your website from a search engine results page.
5. **Provide Customer Service**: Your organization's website is likely one of the first places that customers turn for assistance with their problems.

When the purpose is defined, the focus and energy behind the digital efforts change. In 2010, PYA, a healthcare consulting client of mine, wanted to redesign their website. Their stated goal of the redesign was: "To drive more traffic to our website." Increased traffic isn't a goal; it's a result. Through a series of conversations we determined that the primary purpose of their website was to establish expertise, and as a result they wanted to generate more leads.

The structure of the website was built to accommodate the rich, expert content that they were already creating. Instead of setting a goal about the number of visitors, we set a goal to grow the number of content pages on the site with targeted content areas.

In both 2011 and 2012, the number of content pages on the site doubled. The first year saw only marginal traffic increases, but by 2012, traffic to the website doubled and the number of leads generated by the site quadrupled. Before the redesign, the focus was solely on traffic and search engine rankings. Now, the focus is on generating quality content and the website is generating real results. With proper website strategy, these kinds of results are possible for your brand too (see Table 8.1).

TABLE 8.1 The Importance of Purpose for Websites

WEBSITE WITH CLEAR PURPOSE	WEBSITE WITHOUT CLEAR PURPOSE
Content on the website is focused, supporting the central theme and purpose of the site.	Content is unfocused. Site architecture doesn't support a central theme.
Design and content consistently support the call to action.	There is either no call to action or it is buried in obscure locations on the website.
Analytics and reporting contrast the website performance against the stated goals.	Default reporting is not directive and provides no guidance to success of the site.
Visitors to the site clearly understand the products or services that you offer, they have enough information to inform their buying decision and they know how to engage with or contact you.	There are multiple business lines or product lines offered that leave the visitor confused, uninformed and with no reason to engage with or contact you.

The Website Needs Brief

Once you have determined the purpose of your website, you are ready to enter the first phase of the web project—the planning phase. At this point, you are in complete control and many of the strategic decisions that you make will impact the success of your website. Don't rush through this process to get to the design phase—the investment that you make in the planning phase will prevent many issues during the design. In this section, we will create a sample brief using a fictional company, Ishmael Consulting. Note that your needs brief should include all of the seven elements listed and can (and should) be much more detailed than our example:

1. **Purpose**: State the purpose of the website.
2. **Unique Selling Proposition (USP)**: State your USP. What are your points of differentiation from your

competitors in the marketplace? Does your USP answer these questions?

   a. Who is your customer?
   b. What is your customer's pain point?
   c. How are you going to solve it? (The answers to questions 2 and 3 establish the proposition.)
   d. Why is your organization in a better position than anyone else in your sandbox to solve their pain point?[1] (This establishes your uniqueness.)
   e. When does your customer need to act? (Effective USPs create urgency for them to act/buy now.)

3. **Goals**: In this section list specific, measurable, achievable, relevant, time-bound results that accomplish your goals.
4. **Identify Success Metrics**: Identify what actions a visitor takes on your website that supports your purpose (e.g., increase overall traffic by X percent, generate X leads per month).
5. **Audience**: Who are you talking to? Create a psychographic or demographic profile of your audience. This is especially important when developing the content on the site.
6. **Competition**: Who is the primary competition? Consider both online and offline.
7. **Inspirational Websites**: Spend some time browsing the web looking for websites that you like. Don't worry about staying within the same industry. Look for elements of websites that you are partial to and create a list of 10–12 websites with a description of what you specifically like about each one.

WEBSITE NEEDS BRIEF FOR ISHMAEL CONSULTING

Purpose of Ishmael's Website

Ishmael is in the business of professional consulting services and has a website at ishmaelconsulting.com. The primary purpose of this website is to generate leads for business development.

Additionally, the secondary purpose of Ishmael's website is a source of information for potential customers.

Unique Selling Proposition

Ishmael builds Fortune 500 Companies.

Goals for the Website

The website will generate 20 leads per month. Each lead that is generated on the site will be counted as our conversion.

Success Metrics

The pages per visit will increase from 2.3 to 4.6 by second quarter.

Audience

The primary audience for the website is executives within the business sector that are seeking consulting services. These customers are educated professionals that have limited time. Our audience character is Sandra Greer who is a 34-year-old attorney in Washington, DC. She's a foodie. She watches the Food Network and reads modern literature.

Competition

Ahab Consulting (ahabconsulting.com). The site is designed very well, perhaps too well. Some of the design made it hard to read and find the information that I was trying to find. They are much smaller and don't offer consulting services in the financial services where we do. There is a contact form on the contact page, but it doesn't seem that they are really trying to generate leads from the site.

Inspirational Websites

1. flask finishing.com—really cool video on the homepage
2. dagoodregs.com—landing page has a great USP
3. elijahenterprises.com—strong colors and graphics on the page

THE PROCESS AND CONSIDERATIONS FOR (RE)BUILDING YOUR WEBSITE

Once you know the purpose of your website, you must identify how you are going to execute it. This section identifies the overall process for developing a website. You will get a 30,000-foot view of the process from concept to site launch. In some of the more technically relevant areas, you will find a greater level of detail.

When beginning the process of (re)designing your website, there are a few general considerations. The website process consists of five phases. Depending on the complexity of the site, it may take as little as several days or as much as several months:

- **Phase I**: Planning (purpose, goals, and audience)
- **Phase II**: Design and content to fulfill Phase I
- **Phase III**: Development (overlap with Phase II)
- **Phase IV**: Test, tweak, and launch
- **Phase V**: Ongoing—measure and tweak

Like planning for a wedding, you can spend as much or as little as you want on a website, but the higher budgets allow you to do less work and have more features. This chapter presents options for both a "bootstrap" website and a professionally developed website. A do-it-yourself website can cost less than $1,000 using a themed WordPress[2] site, a few hours of a developer's time, and (optionally) a few hours of a designer's time. Alternatively, if you hire a professional web firm, a turnkey website may cost $10,000–$60,000 depending on design, photography, copywriting, website features, and custom development.

Determine the key decision criteria for building your website. If you are most concerned about price, you may want to do all of the groundwork yourself and hire a freelancer to assist with any of the more technical areas. If you don't want to develop the site yourself, you might consider developing a formal proposal request (RFP/RFQ) for the work in order to select a vendor that will provide the best price.

If you are going to work with freelancers, websites like guru.com, elance.com, and freelancer.com can help you find talented web designers and developers. You may also use your social networks to ask for recommendations. There are a number of developers that freelance in their spare time, so you may find someone in your community that you can meet face to face. Having the technical resource from the beginning is very important.

TEN STEPS: FROM DISCOVERY TO LAUNCH

Most people want to dive directly into the design of their website. Charles Eames said, "design depends largely on constraints," and spending the time in Phase I Planning builds the necessary constraints and ambitions required to produce a website that will return value on the investment.

Step 1: Discovery

During the discovery phase, share the website needs brief with your team. If you are working with a firm, the project manager will identify whether there will be application development needs, copywriting needs, and/or design needs, and will hold a kickoff meeting with the appropriate individuals. If you are working with freelancers, this will fall on your shoulders. While the developer may not be involved at the beginning of the project, it will be important to have their input as it may create additional constraints for the designer.

In addition, be prepared to provide the web team access to critical company information during the discovery meeting:

- Company branding guide and logos
- Personality of the brand
- Any *sacred cows* or non-negotiables
- Technical information like server and FTP information (if you already have web hosting)
- Shared contact information for the entire team

Project management software like *Basecamp* makes the sharing of this information quick and easy.[3]

Step 2: Information Architecture

Next, you will work with your web team to determine the information architecture. Your web team must consider the content and how it will be displayed in the pages of your site.

Jay Baer, one of the leading content marketers, says that content is an "information annuity" that doesn't have an expiration date.[4] It use to be common to scrap the site architecture and all pages within a site with every redesign as if it were disposable. Now, the content on your site is too important to risk driving a potential customer to the dreaded 404 page. As Mitch Joel says, "We live in a day and age when the content that is created is now all indexable, shareable, and findable forever."[5] This goes for the good as well as the bad.

If you already have a website, then you should review your existing site architecture against the backdrop of the website needs brief and ask the team whether the current architecture is achieving the fundamental purpose. If not, what changes need to be made to the architecture in order to achieve the purpose? If this is the first website for your organization, then you will have the luxury of a blank slate. Considering the fundamental purpose, what pages need to be at the top level of your site? What pages should be at deeper levels? In general, people prefer a broader, shallower infrastructure to avoid having to make too many clicks to arrive at their desired content.

Step 3: Content Layout

After the site architecture is in place, the next decision is where the content is going to be on the page. You may sketch this out on paper, or use a tool like Balsamiq to figure out where blocks of content are located on the page. Note, when you are laying out the content, you are not writing content or designing anything—you are simply identifying where the content will be placed on the page.

Usability Considerations

It is never too early to start thinking about usability considerations. Jakob Nielsen and Kara Pernice's *Eyetracking Web Usability* and Steve Krug's *Don't Make Me Think* are excellent resources when considering how visitors will interact with your design.

You should be aware of one important fact: You are much more interesting than your readers will find you to be. Yes, that's harsh, but true. The biggest pitfall when creating your website is thinking about the concerns of everyone but the user of your website. Based on years of research, user interface designers have a wealth of data to understand user behavior. Here are a few key items to understand about the general web audience.

1. People don't read text on the web.[6]
2. Visitors pay the most attention to the information at the top left of the screen.[7]
3. Customers will briefly glimpse your page like a billboard, if you don't catch their attention, they are gone.[8]

One consideration to make when building the structure of your site is how people behave with web content. Many websites use a similar navigation and content structure. Websites are one place where reinventing the wheel in the name of creativity may be detrimental to the goals of the site.

Jakob Nielsen, the web usability expert, has conducted numerous user interviews and observations over the last decade. This research reveals that visitors on websites interact with content differently than any other medium. Website visitors read in what Nielsen calls an *F pattern*.[9] That is, people place a primary emphasis on a top horizontal band. Secondly, they read a secondary horizontal band a bit further down the page. Thirdly, people scan the vertical band to the left down the page looking for keywords.

Step 4: Content Management Systems

At this point, it is best to decide what flavor content management system (CMS) you will use. There are few, if any, valid reasons to not use a CMS. The key advantage is that the site content is accessed through an administrative console and no coding or special software is necessary to update the content of the site. In addition, many SEO tools are built into these systems.

Depending on the size of and traffic to your site, you will want to investigate the best software to use, as each platform utilizes server resources in different ways. Discuss with your team what may be the best option for your site.

For simpler websites, or companies without large website budgets, Drupal and Joomla! are commonly options, and WordPress has become one of the most widely used systems available. Make sure that your developer has experience with the system that you pick.

If getting up a simple, prepackaged, and extremely cost-effective website is your goal, go with a predesigned theme from a website like ThemeForest.com. Each CMS has a number of elegantly designed themes or templates that are affordably priced or even available for free. These themes are predesigned with colors, fonts, sizing, etc., but they typically allow you to customize the style specifically to your needs. Pay particular attention to the following elements of the theme:

- **Responsive Design**: Does the theme have an adjustable layout for mobile, tablet, and desktop browsers?
- **Control Panel**: Can you change theme elements, including fonts, colors, and sizing?
- **SEO**: Does the theme mention search engine optimization?
- **Support**: Does the theme developer offer support? Is the theme compatible with the current version of the CMS?
- **Customization**: Are you going to be customizing your CMS with plugins? If so, will this theme work with your planned customizations?
- **Flexibility:** Does the theme offer enough flexibility with page templates that will work for all of the pages that you have sketched?
- **Personalization**: Does the CMS allow content to be segmented and personalized for each unique website visitor? (Many turnkey CMS systems don't, but for larger companies this is a must.)

Your developer should be able to make some modifications to the chosen theme to achieve your goals, but it is best to pick a theme that meets most of these criteria to avoid increased cost.

For medium- and large-company websites, where the design and development are generally done internally or by an agency partner, developers may be tempted to create a custom-tailored CMS application solution. However, before deciding to develop any applications, exhaust all other options. Custom development is costly and time consuming. Building and developing dozens of applications over the past decade, I know that customers typically end up paying two to three times the original budget, and it takes at least that much more time. The web is ripe with many off-the-shelf applications and plugins. There must be a clear need (that is not already being met), before setting out to develop any custom applications. If there is no apparent solution available, then go for it, but don't say that I didn't warn you.

Step 5: Design

Whether you are using a predesigned theme or you are creating the site from scratch, a designer's touch may make a huge difference in the effectiveness of your website. The web designer is charged with delivering a design that works within the identified constraints and will deliver to the established goals. They are going to look at things from color selection,[10] to the photos and graphics used on the site.

Some designers will create mood boards to determine which elements they will use in the design. Other designers prefer to create several mockups in Photoshop to get your feedback.

It is important to see the design with the eyes of the audience: "Would this motivate me to do something?" You may not like the color of the button on the right side of the page, but the question is not whether you like it. Will the potential customer act based on this design? Testing and analysis post-launch will tweak and improve upon your decisions, but it's certainly a good idea to start with a solid customer-centric design.

Once you give the designer approval on the mockup, your developer will code the mockup into files that can be used on the web: HTML, CSS, and JavaScript.

Step 6: Maintain a Voice Consistent With Your Purpose

As you saw in Chapter 3, your content is the most important element of your website. Period. In order for the presentation of your content to meet your website's purpose, it must clearly speak to your audience. Word choice, style, and tone of the copy that you use on your site represent the personality of your brand. Consider the difference in tone of the following HTML e-mail vendors:

Emma
Emma connects with the services you love
Do more with your online tools! Connect your favorite services with Emma to achieve figure-skating-pair-like synchronicity between your applications. (Sequins optional)
Constant Contact
Turn Fans Into Customers.
Run promotions and offers on your Facebook page with Social Campaigns that turn fans into customers so you can increase business. Create a great Facebook landing page for your offer with our features and free coaching. Then, promote it to your e-mail list and social networks to engage your existing audience and attract new fans.

Essentially, both of these paragraphs say the say same thing, right? Depending on the audience, they may find one of these paragraphs attractive and the other atrocious. Accordingly, the writers of the two pages were likely writing directly to their perceived audience. Write to the audience that you identified in the website needs brief.

Step 7: Search Engine Optimization and Content Marketing

Search engine optimization (SEO) has is a well-formed body of information—numerous books and blogs are devoted exclusively to SEO. For comprehensive coverage of SEO, see Chapter 4 on Search Marketing. Also, consider checking out the following blogs: Moz, SEO Book, and Search Engine Land, all of which discuss the latest on this topic. As Google says, remember to: "Provide high-quality content on your pages, especially your homepage. This is the single most important thing to do."[11]

Here are a few basic tips to keep in mind:

1. *Create linkworthy content.* Create expert content that only you can write.
2. *Invite social sharing.* Make it easy to share the content on your website.

3. *Have a focus keyword for each page.* Focus on one keyword per page. Your message will be more concise and your ranking for that page will be better.
4. *Use clear web addresses.* Make sure that the web address to the page includes the keywords.
5. *Incorporate keywords in the title of the page.* Include your keywords in the first four words of the page title.
6. *Create meta-tags and a meta-description.* Find an SEO plugin for your CMS and it will handle this for you.
7. *Let keyword density develop naturally.* Don't worry about the number of times a keyword appears in a page. Keep a content focus on the page and write naturally.
8. *Use the focus keyword in page headings.* Try to use the keyword in the first or second level headings on the page.
9. *Develop alternative text for images.* For every image on your site, make sure there is an alternative text description. This is how search engines "see" your pictures.
10. *Link social assets.* Your website is one location within your overall social web strategy. Make sure that there is a free flow of traffic between your website and your social assets.

Personalization for Effective Content Strategy

I've stopped using the term SEO, since we're generally really talking about content marketing, and the integration of content strategy and website strategy. Thinking of the hub-and-spoke approach presented back in Figure 8.1, the goal is to put your content out into the stream of content that people like, react to, and most importantly link to. This starts with effective two-way communication between your website and your other digital properties, but is ultimately tied together by integrating content between your website and these social channels.

This holistic, personalized, multichannel strategy starts with highly personal website content. When a person visits your brand's site, you have a great deal of data available to you, including:

- The geographic location of the person
- The device and browser they're accessing the site with

- The website the person was referred from
- How the person interacted with your site in the past (using cookies)

By combining this information, you can better understand the person's interests and can infer their need or desire to visit your site. This real-time information can be utilized to segment your audience and deliver a set of content that matches what is most likely to convert or create an impact with any given individual. Websites utilizing truly excellent personalization strategies serve a vastly different website, both in content and design, to every website visitor. By combining big data insights with this information provided by each user in real time, modern websites can be personalized beyond what you may have thought possible.

According to a study by Econsultancy, 52 percent of marketers agree that personalization of web content is fundamental to their online strategy, but only 32 percent say their CMS accelerates content personalization.[12] Anyone (re)building a website this year should be thinking very carefully about personalization strategy to improve website conversions—whatever your goal for the website may be. It may be a good idea to choose a CMS like OpenText[13] that has these abilities built in, if your website budget allows for it.

Step 8: To Blog, or Not To Blog?

Warning: Herein lies heresy. Not everyone should have a blog. In fact, 95 percent of the blog owners shouldn't have a blog.[14] Blogs may increase search engine rankings, build communities, establish expertise within a given field, provide a human side to your brand, engage customers, and become the vehicle to build loads of content. So, why do so many bloggers jump ship? Blogging is hard work.

You have permission to say "no" to the marketer or web designer that tells you, "and we'll throw your blog on there." Here are some of the stumbling blocks to creating and maintaining an effective blog:

- It takes time (more than many admit).
- Many thoughtful blog posts go unread.

- Establishing expertise requires, well, expertise.
- Your audience may not read blogs.
- Your number one keyword referral will not be what you expect.

When the *new* wears off, your blog will go months before it is updated. After carrying the unnecessary, blog-imposed guilt of not posting any new content (which is something that you never wanted to do in the first place), you'll sit down and write a post that says. "Betcha wondered where we've been?" or, "I know it's been a while since I've posted," which will only be read by exactly two people: You and the customer that you're trying to close who checked to see if you really update your blog. If blogging isn't a part of your content strategy from the beginning, save yourself the time, money, and stress of not keeping your blog updated.

On the other hand, there is probably no better way to tell your story than through your blog. In addition to the benefits highlighted in the first paragraph of this section, blogging is a powerful tool for growing international awareness through content alone. Blogging, coupled with effective use of social media tools, has led to the meteoric rise of net celebrities like famed marketing writer Seth Godin, wine connoisseur turned social media consultant Gary Vaynerchuk, and sales and marketing executive turned international rockstar social media consultant Mark Schaefer.

Many companies don't care to engage with their customers—they just want to sell their service or product. As Doc Searls says, "everything that happens in a marketplace falls into just three categories: transaction, conversation, and relationship. In our First World business culture, transaction matters most, conversation less, and relationship least."[15] For companies that understand their role as content publishers and their potential customers as consumers of that content, blogging becomes a natural starting point for conversation that in some cases leads to a lifelong, loyal relationship.

Step 9: Testing

So much anxiety. So much excitement! Ding. Your inbox awaits. It's here! Your test link! And it looks, well, a little weird. When you get the designer on the phone, he says, "Oh, are you on a PC?" Not to worry. The testing or sandbox site is just that—a place to play with the site and discover what needs to be changed before launch. While there may be a few issues with the site, you should test the site in the four main categories:

1. **Content and Style**:
   a. Has the site been proofread?
   b. Are spellings and word usage consistent?
   c. Is capitalization used consistently?
2. **Functionality:**
   a. Does search work?
   b. Does the navigation match the site architecture?
   c. Does the site render properly on all browsers, as well as on mobile devices?[16]
   d. Are all of the links working properly?
3. **Security:**
   a. Do you have a web file and database backup plan? (If you're using WordPress there are a number of backup plugin options available.)
   b. Have you changed the default usernames and/or passwords on your CMS?
4. **Performance:**
   a. Are measurement and tracking functions installed?
   b. Are you getting any errors?

Depending on your unique website, there are a number of website checklists available for download and modification. Box^{UK} provides the Ultimate Website Launch Checklist for free download, which covers 90 percent of the items that need to be tested before launch.[17]

Step 10: Launch

Once you are comfortable that the site has passed all of the initial tests, it is time to pull the trigger and launch it. You will want someone that is an expert in computer networking, hosting, and DNS involved during this stage. Perhaps you are just uploading the content to the old web server, but it is important to consider the following items:

1. **Redirects**: If you are changing domains or the URL paths to your pages, then work with your developer to create redirects to your new content.
2. **Favicon**: This is a little detail but can be a differentiator. Make sure that the small 16 × 16 pixel image that appears in the browser tab uniquely identifies your website.
3. **Security Certificate:** If you have a shopping cart or secure information on the site, work with your developer to make sure that you have a security certificate installed.
4. **Sitemap File**: Most CMSs offer the option to dynamically create and keep the sitemap updated. If not, there are multiple plugins that can generate the sitemap file.
5. **Google Webmaster Tools**: Add your website to Google Webmaster Tools. This allows you to see valuable information about how the search engines are indexing your site.
6. **Make It Live**: After everything is ready to go, work with the developer to make the necessary changes. It will take anywhere from one hour to two days for everyone to see the site. Check and make sure that everything is working correctly once it is "live."

TOOLS FOR SUCCESS

Now, we know why you have a website and how it is built. It probably seems like all of the painful work leading up to the launch of the site should begin generating results immediately. Sorry to say, the real work begins after the launch of the site. Now, it is critical to constantly measure the website goals against the established goals. Take a deep breath, they are not going to be right when you launch and that is completely normal.

Through the process of testing, analyzing, altering, and measuring your success, you will begin to understand more about your visitors. Now let's take a look at measurement and analytics.

Driving Success with Landing Pages and Pay Per Click

While not appropriate for all brands, landing pages are one tool to digital marketing success. Before investing tens of thousands of dollars in the complete website design and development, landing pages coupled with a small pay-per-click (PPC) campaign allow you to test your assumptions about your customers to see whether you will achieve your primary purpose. After the site launches, well-designed landing pages are a critical tool in the overall digital strategy.

Landing pages are different than other web pages on your site for three reasons: (1) The user visits this page as a destination from some other offer or call to action (CTA); (2) the landing page will have a measurable conversion in the CTA; and, (3) a landing page typically has limited off-page navigation. Landing pages are most commonly the destination from a PPC ad, but you may also link to your landing pages from blogs, social media campaigns, and traditional advertisements. In all likelihood, considering you have made some investment for the visitor to be on this page, it is wise to limit the number of outbound links on the page. Some of the best landing pages have only one exit door, which is through the CTA.

Landing pages must satisfy the offer made from the linking source. If, for example, someone clicks on a Google AdWords ad result for the search "24-inch silver Figaro chain," then the landing page must have the 24-inch Figaro chain immediately visible. If, however, the link directs the customer to the jeweler's home page, there's a 90 percent chance that the user will "bounce" and click the back button.

Remarketing

While bounce rates are covered in more depth in Chapter 9, a bounce rate is when someone hits the page and "bounces" before performing any action on the page. Remarketing programs offered by Google AdWords and AdRoll are a great way to increase exposure and overall conversions by displaying image ads to visitors to the landing page that bounce.

Tactics for Conversion

Let's consider some of the conversion tactics that you may use on your landing page and throughout your site. A number of these recommendations involve the visitor to your site providing you their e-mail address. This should not be taken lightly. These customers are giving you permission to disrupt their days. Respect them. Make your disruption of their time worthwhile. Unsubscribing is only a click away, and if you get in the habit of disrupting them too often with too little value, they will exercise that power.

While some of these recommendations are more appropriate for specific strategies than others, here are a few CTAs that you may consider using on your landing page:

- Include "premium content" on your website that is only available to registered members.
- Create an e-book or other premium content that provides information about your service or product that customers are sent via e-mail once they fill out a short form.
- Create compelling CTA: limited time offer for free service, free phone consultation, free on-site estimation or quote.
- Offer a coupon for the current purchase for subscribing to the sales e-mail newsletter.
- Register for a giveaway or contest by submitting a form on your website.

Measurement and Analytics

Measuring the traffic to your website against your goals is equally as important as creating your website. Many companies, however, rely on the conversions (sales, leads, or subscribers) as their primary metrics and only turn to analytics when there is a problem. Effectively measuring the way that people use your website will help you learn more about what motivates them and determine the driving factors behind their conversions.

Measuring and adjusting is an ongoing process. Applying the knowledge gained from the analysis of your web traffic and making adjustments to your website will change the overall results. Be careful not to make too many changes at once. Isolating variables is critical to understanding what is truly motivating your customers.

The following tools are used for different aspects of analysis. There is not a single tool that analyzes all behavior. Depending on the goals that you created in your website needs brief, identify the tools that will provide the most meaningful information to increase conversion. Test a few of the tools to see which work best, but be aware that each of these tools requires additional load time on your website. Using a staging or development version of your site will prevent any issues with your production website.

Google Analytics

Google Analytics, introduced in Chapter 6, and referenced in the Analytics Mini-Handbook in Chapter 9, is one of many website analytics tools available to measure traffic from your website. Mint [havemint.com], KISSmetrics [kissmetrics.com], and Mixpanel [mixpanel.com] are all alternatives that digital marketers use. Google Analytics, however, is free, widely used (thus has a large community), easy to setup, and is continuously updated by Google. For broad analysis and reporting of your website traffic, try several of the tools to see which works best for you. Make sure to take full advantage of goals, custom dashboards, and e-mail reports.

A/B Testing and Data-Driven Development

Once you are receiving data about the success of your conversions on the website, you can begin to fine tune the settings on the site to improve performance. A/B split testing is one of the easiest and most common methods to fine tune your website or landing page. Say, for example, that you wanted to increase the number of downloads on a landing page, you would create two versions of the same page: the control page (A) and the challenge or testing page (B). On the challenge page, you would change one variable, like the color of the download button. Then the software that you are using to perform the test would serve a "random assignment of new visitors to the version of the page that they see."[18]

MarketingProfs.com tested a "Signup for Social Media Campaigns" landing page with A/B testing on the header of the page. By including a benefit headline in the header and active voice in the headline, the A version of the page outperformed the control by 28 percent.

Factors to consider when A/B Testing:

- *Test one variable at a time.* Creating more than one variable may lead to misunderstanding about which variable attributed to success or failure.
- *Serve pages simultaneously.* The software used to conduct the test should serve an equal number of the control and test pages.
- *You may use multiple versions (A/B/C/D) to test the same variable.* For example, you may test four different headlines on a landing page.
- *Don't test indefinitely.* Test your pages for a set period of time, and then make the changes to your pages.
- *Test your pages on landing pages with PPC traffic.* A/B tests work especially well on landing pages with pay-per-click traffic because the conditions of the visitors are similar.

Optimizely.com offers a robust platform for A/B testing. Google Analytics also offers A/B testing within the Content > Experiments section.

Behavioral Analytics

Depending on the exact goals of your website, you will want to make sure that your reporting tools are delivering the information that you need to make informed decisions. Organized by type of reporting tool, here are a few other web applications to test.

- **Real-Time Visitor Reporting**
  - Woopra: This application allows you to see real-time visitors by location, referral source, and top page. In addition, you can tag visitors to measure recurring visitors. Woopra offers an on-site chat application, but is primarily a reporting software.

- Clicky Web Analytics: This is another real-time application that tracks visitors, location, referral source, and content. Custom alerts allow you to know in real-time when website visitors are performing desired actions.
- Google Analytics: In 2012, Google Analytics began testing real-time visitor reporting. This feature is not nearly as robust as that provided by the applications that are specifically dedicated to this function.

- **Visitor Visualization**
  - Crazyegg: This application is one of most affordable heat map and eye tracking applications. Look at heat maps of your pages and determine where specifically on the page they are clicking. Determine from this data whether your information and site are usable. Crazyegg also offers a scroll map, which displays how far visitors to the site are scrolling. This is especially valuable when determining whether information is posted below the fold.
  - ClickTale: In addition to the heat map, scroll map, and overlay offered in Crazyegg, ClickTale allows the owner of the site to view videos (including mouse movements) of users on the website. While it is premium software, ClickTale's features, including mouse maps, allow you to make informed decisions about how visitors are using your site.

CONCLUSION

In the current flow of the social web, some may begin to question the relevance of the company website. If anything, the growth of supporting networks have solidified and refined the purpose of having a website. It is the base camp of all digital marketing. Whatever purpose you have for your website, your social assets complement that purpose.

While some companies are creating the ninth major revision to their websites, doing it the way that it has always been done is a waste of time. Going through the process of planning and developing a website needs brief will communicate your expectations of and goals for the website, as well as unify the team that is working on your project. Your website requires constant cultivation of measurement and tweaking. Good luck!

ENDNOTES

1. See Jim Collins' website for a greater explanation of defining one's sandbox.
2. WordPress is a very popular blogging platform and website content management system (CMS) that makes it very easy to set up and manage a website.
3. www.Basecamp.com
4. http://convinceandconvert.com/convinceconvert/why-content-marketing-matters-to-me-and-should-to-you
5. http://www.twistimage.com/blog/archives/and-you-will-know-us-by-the-trail-of-content/
6. Krug, Steve, *Don't Make Me Think! A Common Sense Approach to Web Usability, 2nd ed.*, New Riders Publishing, Berkley CA, 2006. p. 22.
7. Nielsen Norman Group Research
8. Krug, Steve, *Don't Make Me Think! A Common Sense Approach to Web Usability, 2nd ed.*, New Riders Publishing, Berkley CA, 2006. p. 21.
9. http://www.nngroup.com/articles/f-shaped-pattern-reading-web-content/
10. Marketo released this helpful infographic on color theory: http://blog.marketo.com/blog/2012/06/true-colors-what-your-brand-colors-say-about-your-business.html
11. http://support.google.com/webmasters/bin/answer.py?hl=en&answer=40349
12. http://econsultancy.com/us/blog/10194-the-roi-of-personalisation-infographic
13. www.opentext.com
14. http://www.nytimes.com/2009/06/07/fashion/07blogs.html?_r=0

15. Rick Levine, Christopher Locke, Doc Searls, *The Cluetrain Manifesto: 10th Anniversary Edition*, Basic Books, 2009. p. 12
16. Adobe's browser lab allows you to check the appearance of the site in different browsers, for free. https://browserlab.adobe.com/en-us/index.html
17. http://www.boxuk.com/upload/pdf/relaunched_ultimate_website_checklist.pdf
18. Ash, Tim, *Landing Page Optimization: The Definitive Guide to Testing and Tuning For Conversions*, Wiley Publishing, 2008. p. 214

CHAPTER 9

MEASUREMENT AND ROI OF DIGITAL STRATEGIES

—by Rob Petersen

INTRODUCTION TO THE WORLD OF MEASUREMENT

"If you can't measure it, you can't manage it," said Peter Drucker,[1] who many consider the father of management and marketing. This succinct truth is the reason for this chapter.

According to former Google CEO Eric Schmidt, every two days the world produces as much data as was accumulated from the dawn of man until the year 2003.[2] New platforms are now needed to keep up with the daily explosion of data created from mobile devices, online transactions, sensors, and social networks. All these new measurements have created an industry known as *big data*, shorthand for the application of artificial intelligence, web-browsing data trails, social network communications, and sensor and surveillance data.

As a result, analytics, measurement, and ROI are more vital functions than ever to companies. In fact, it's estimated that

140,000 to 190,000 people with deep analytic skills, as well as 1.5 million managers and analysts, will be needed by 2018 to fill jobs in business that will be increasingly data-driven, according to McKinsey.[3]

For business leaders, the benefit of data and analytics is better decision making for every organization at every level—retailers, manufacturers, service providers, even governments. Business leaders believe in and agree on the value of measurements. What they can't seem to agree on, is how to translate these better decisions into ROI.

Consider these facts from a 2012 Columbia Business School Study:[4]

- Ninety-one percent of marketing leaders believe successful brands use customer data to drive business decisions.
- Eighty-seven percent agree capturing and sharing the right data is important to effectively measure ROI in their own company.
- Seventy-seven percent say getting traditional and digital marketing to work better together remains a major goal.
- Seventy percent say their marketing efforts are under greater scrutiny.
- Seventy percent report that a "cross-platform model" for ROI on their business is a major goal.
- Sixty-eight percent base their marketing budgets entirely or in part on "historical spending."
- Fifty-seven percent do not base their marketing budgets on any ROI analysis.
- Thirty-nine percent say it is important to spend only on marketing activities where financial effects can be measured.
- Thirty-seven percent did not mention financial outcomes when asked to define ROI.
- Thirty-seven percent claimed brand awareness is the universal metric they use to make marketing decisions.
- Twenty-two percent base marketing decisions on "gut instinct."

The statistics prove: More data and bigger data isn't better data unless you know what to do with it.

How do companies use digital data and analytics effectively? They use it to find actionable insights, discover new markets, and quickly implement innovations to win more contracts, get to market faster, and beat out rivals. Google, for example, used data-driven decisions to launch Gmail, Google+, the Android operating system, and Google Apps, all while Yahoo! was struggling to decide on its priorities in these areas.

How do you start to institute effective measurement practices at your company?

- *Carefully select key metrics to measure.* You are what you measure. There is usually no magic bullet, but taking the time to choose good metrics based on your objectives is critical to success
- *Be agile—look, learn, and take action.* Digital measurements occur in virtually real time. So it's less important to be right than to set up the practice of continually examining what's occurring. Success belongs to those who take action on the learning.
- *Integrate internal departments into decision making.* If data and measurements are being used to make and explain decisions, they touch everyone at the company and require interdependence within departments. Between IT, regulatory, marketing, sales and the C-suite, mutual cooperation, collaboration and accountability are required, both in general, and with regard to accuracy, regulatory compliance, timeliness, insights, privacy, execution, and optimization.
- *Recognize analytics is a people business.* When considering analytics as a resource and competency in your company, experts cite the 10/90 rule; that is, the software to generate, measure, and manage the data is 10 percent of the cost. The people to analyze it and identify the actionable insights are 90 percent. Allocate resources appropriately.

In this chapter, you'll learn what to do with the data, how to identify the key measurements for your business, and how to use analytics for better business decisions and to determine ROI. This chapter:

- Plays-off the digital paradigm described in Part I in evaluating digital marketing and investment through an ROI lens
- Connects the dots between digital market channels (e.g., search, social media, e-commerce, mobile technology) through cross-platform modeling and equivalent measurements
- Acquaints you with companies, tools, and resources who are leaders in data, analytics, and measurements
- Helps construct an actionable scorecard to keep business strategy on track with KPIs (key performance indicators) for better decision making

The two verbs Peter Drucker uses are *measure* and *manage*. Both are equally important when the goal is business growth in the near term, and profitable, scalable, and sustainable growth into the future.

THE IMPORTANCE OF MEASUREMENT

Digital media is the only media channel to grow in this decade. In 2013, digital technologies are the second largest media spending channel after television overtaking all forms of print advertising combined. By 2018, digital spending is expected to equal TV spending (source: eMarketer). While it's encouraging more business leaders are investing in digital, the more important question: Is it producing results?

"How do I measure return on investment (ROI)," is the number one question 3500+ marketers have asked for the past four years according to Social Media Examiner's Annual Survey.[5] ROI is the final word on the success of any marketing campaign.

How do you measure ROI? I reviewed the available definitions and formulas for ROI to get to the answer. You can read them at our company website, BarnRaisers, in my blog post, *11 definitions of ROI reveal a simple solution*.[6] Here's what I concluded: ROI is the final word for any marketing campaign because it proves how well a business is being managed. The formula for ROI is:

$$\text{ROI} = \frac{(\text{Investment Gain} - \text{Investment Cost}}{(\text{Investment Cost})} \times 100$$

The investment gain is return from sales or another income metric, depending upon what you're using for comparisons—it doesn't matter too much, as long as you stay consistent. Let's take an example: A business invests \$100,000 at the beginning of the year on either an ad or marketing campaign. At the end of the year, the gain is \$150,000. The ROI is: \$150,000 – \$100,000 = \$50,000/\$100,000 × 100 = 50 percent return on the investment or a 1.5-to-1 ROI.

But you have to set the criteria and goal for success:

- Identify business results in the "pre" period.
- Define ROI goals (e.g., 2-to–1, 3-to–1, etc.).
- Establish the "return" or gain (e.g., sales, profits, value to shareholders).
- Determine the time frame (e.g., 12 months, 18 months). This might be expressed as follows:
  - Double sales in a year and a half.
  - Increase profits by 25 percent within a year.
  - Gain 200 new customers within three months.
  - Generate a 25 percent increase in conversion within six months.
  - Decrease customer complaints by half within a year.

In addition to the ROI of your digital marketing program, you can also determine the ROI of each digital marketing channel (e.g., search engine optimization, paid search, video, social media, and e-mail marketing). This is called ROAI—return on advertising investment or return on advertising spend.

Return on investment measures the total margin that the total operation nets. This includes all operation costs in addition to just advertising expenditure. *Return on advertising investment* (ROAI) measures how much revenue you are making for every dollar you spend on each digital media channel.

Return on advertising investment is important because media is likely to be the largest investment in a digital marketing campaign. It is also the area that can be modified or reworked in the quickest amount of time to optimize results.

ROAI is calculated using the formula: sales from advertising/ad spending. For example, if your ad spending is $15,000 and your revenue from the ad spending is $20,000, your ROAI is:

ROAI = $20,000/$15,000 = 1.33 or 133 percent

ROAI can be calculated for every digital channel (e.g., paid search, sponsorships, video) because "cookies" or "tags" on digital media let you know what channels are driving how many visitors and how they behave (e.g., visit, register, download, buy).

With the numbers of visitors who perform the actions divided by the amount of spending per channel, you know the performance of each channel and can revise or optimize results based on learning.

Now, you put more emphasis on the channels that are working and pull back on those that aren't to increase results. ROAI is a business performance measure that is extremely useful in digital marketing but has no relevance to traditional marketing (e.g., TV, print, radio, outdoor).

In 1902, marketing pioneer John Wanamaker said, "Half the money I spend on advertising is wasted. The trouble is I don't know which half.[7]" If John were alive today, he'd know the answer for digital marketing.

Determining your return on investment (ROI) as well as your return on advertising investment (ROAI) is one of the more important topics for any business. It proves success, demonstrates marketing value, and shows how well the business is being managed.

DEMYSTIFYING THE BUZZWORD: THE DEFINITION OF ANALYTICS

Eighty-six percent of people are willing to pay more for a great customer experience with a brand.[8] A primary goal for any business is to create the best customer experience at the highest price consumers are willing to pay. Measurements and ROI help identify how to get there, when it is working, and what makes it work.

Once upon a time, companies differentiated themselves almost entirely based on the things they made. Companies obviously need to build innovative products and get them to market, but as their differences become more subtle, they are finding consumer experience to be that new differentiator.

Not long ago, digital marketing meant having a website. Now, it means having a strong presence in digital media (paid, owned, earned, and shared), search (organic and PPC), social media, and mobile. And, through analytics, digital marketers are able to understand consumer behavior and customer experience.

Analytics sounds complicated but it's not. Let's demystify digital analytics and ROI with four key strategic questions. Companies should answer these business questions before they establish their measurement plan:

1. *Why does your brand's website exist?* To establish a measurement plan and ROI, you need to begin with the business reasons why you created a digital presence. These reasons have to connect in some way to revenue (e.g., sell products, capture e-mail addresses, build a database, download relevant content). If you don't provide the revenue reasons why your brand is on the Internet, your digital marketing is an expense; one where you will be wondering how to recoup your investment.
2. *Who do you want to attract?* For every business, there is a wide disparity between best and worst customers. In digital marketing, as in life, there are people worth spending time with and people not worth wasting your time on. If you don't know who is who, you're likely to waste a lot

of unnecessary time, money, and resources. This is also known as the marketing discipline of *segmentation.*

3. *How do they find you?* People find your website in a variety of ways: search, referral from another website, through social networks, or they may simply come directly. Measurements of the channels through which people reach you are very much available. Find out how consumers come to your brand, and examine how it aligns with the way you are spending your time, money, and resources. See if you're attracting who you want.
4. *What action do you want them to take?* Once consumers find your brand, what do you want them to do? It is very important to be clear about this. The actions you want consumers to take should relate to the reason why your business is on the Internet, and who you are attracting, and how you can reach the most qualified targets.

These four questions (why, who, how, and what) give perspective and context. They give direction on how you expect to generate revenue and what are the criteria for selecting the measurements that matter most for your business.

Web Analytics

Web analytics is the measurement, collection, analysis, and reporting of Internet data for purposes of understanding and optimizing web usage. There are two categories of web analytics: off-site and on-site.

Off-site web analytics is the measurement of a potential audience (opportunity) on the Internet. It includes measurements like size and share of voice (visibility) and buzz (comments and reviews). It occurs regardless of whether you own or maintain a website.

On-site web analytics measure visitors' behavior once on your website. For example, the degree different landing pages are associated with online purchases. On-site web analytics measures the performance of your website in a commercial context. This data is typically compared against key performance indicators (KPIs) for performance, and used to improve website or marketing campaign response. We will cover KPIs shortly.

Although there are different services for looking and displaying analytics, what it most important is to have a clear sense of purpose and direction. While the methods and metrics for looking and displaying consumer behavior are evolving, the principles behind growing a profitable business are timeless.

MEASUREMENTS FOR A DIGITAL WORLD

So now let's talk about the measurements you need to win in today's digital space. This section covers what I consider key digital marketing measurements. You may not need all of them, but you should know about them. Let me help guide you to the ones that are most appropriate for the key strategic questions.

On-Site Analytics

On-site analytics (via a tool like Google Analytics) help answer the following questions:

- Why does your brand website exist?
- Who do you want to attract?
- What action do you want them to take?

Your website analytics tool is the GPS for your digital marketing program. It gives you a wealth of information as to how consumers interact with your brand online. Google Analytics is the most widely used of the analytics tools. The features and benefits of a number of analytic tools will be discussed in the "Tools of the Trade" section, but here are the measurements that are most important:

- **Unique Visitors:** This is the count of how many different people come to your website within a specified period of time, usually 30 days. Google Analytics software distinguishes cookies from the visitors who visit your site for the first time within a specified period. Every business has to create awareness to drive business growth. The Unique Visitors section of the software lets you know if you're building momentum and heading in the right direction.

- **Bounce Rate:** This is the percentage of people who view only one page of your website. Bounce rate is a measure of a site's relevance because, if the site is relevant, people are likely to view more than one page. A lower percentage is always better For example, if your bounce rate is 35 percent, then 65 percent of people view more than one page.
- **Segments (Segmentation):** For every business, there is a wide disparity between best and worst customers. Once you know how many visitors come to your site and its relevance, it's time to focus on the ones with the highest value to your business. Does your brand have a geographic skew? Do people who visit three or more times show a greater likelihood to buy? If you invest in media, what media generates the most visitors and sales? Segmentation can be easily viewed within Google Analytics on almost any dimension you set up using the tool's Advanced Segments feature.
- **Traffic Sources:** This metric gives you information on the sources of your digital traffic. These include: search, referral (e.g., social networks, e-mail, other sites), and direct. You can drill down to see the specific sources, where visitors come from (e.g., Google, Facebook, another website), how much time is spent from each specific source, and what the bounce rate is: visitors, time, and bounce rate for special properties in each. Once you know the percentage from each traffic source, you know how people find your brand online and you have a blueprint to create your outreach effort.
- **Keywords:** This measurement gives you insight into why viewers come to your site. Keywords are on your Google Analytics dashboard in the Traffic Sources section. A balance of keywords that includes your brand name words related to the category or industry you compete in is a good goal. This means people are finding your site both because they have an unmet need and because they know your brand.
- **Content:** What pages are viewed most often? Are your viewers taking the journey you want? This is answered by looking at the Content section in Google Analytics to see the pages viewed in rank order. If your bounce rate is not

where you think it should be, the result from your keywords and content measurements give the greatest insight into what needs to be corrected and helps to set you on the right path. Through Content Drilldown, Google Analytics gives rich information about every page.

- **Conversion:** What is the action you want visitors to take once they get to your website? This is the fundamental question for every business online. Do you want them to buy your product from the site? Or download a video, ebook, or white paper? Sign up for your e-mail or subscribe to your blog? These are examples of conversion, which is the action you want consumers to take when they visit your website. The answers can be found in the Conversion section of Google Analytics.
- **Average Shopper Value:** If you sell a product or service on your website, these last two metrics are for you. Average shopper value (or average value) is the best measurement to watch, giving you information that will allow you to take action to positively affect sales. Do customers buy one or two products when they buy? Or two or three? When you know average shopper value, you can put a plan in place to increase sales and measure the results, almost instantly.
- **Abandonment Rate:** This is the percent of people who signal their intention to buy by clicking on the add-to-cart button, but then fail to complete their order. Abandonment rate can vary, but usually is between 50 and 70 percent. If your conversion and average shopper value rates are not where you think they should be, abandonment rate is one of the first places to look for the culprit and the solution.

Off-Site Analytics

Digital media and search marketing measurements help determine ROAI. They let you know if the media is working because they answer the strategic questions:

- How do they find you?
- What actions do they take?

These measurements include:

- **CPC (Cost Per Click):** CPC represents the number of times a visitor clicks on a banner. Cost per click is often used when advertisers have a set daily budget. When the advertiser's budgeted cost is reached, the ad is removed from the rotation for the remainder of the period. For example, a website that has a CPC rate of $0.10 and provides 1,000 click-throughs would bill $100 ($0.10 × 1000).
- **CTR (Click-Through Rate):** CTR is defined as the number of clicks on an ad divided by the number of times the ad is shown (impressions), and is expressed as a percentage. For example, if a banner ad is delivered 100 times (100 impressions) and receives one click, then the click-through rate for the advertisement would be 1 percent. When banner ads first started to appear, it was not uncommon to have rates above 5 percent. They have fallen since then, and are currently averaging closer to 0.2 or 0.3 percent. In most cases, a 2 percent click-through rate would be considered very successful.
- **CPA (Cost Per Acquisition or Cost Per Action):** Cost per acquisition refers to the fact that most CPA offers by advertisers are about acquiring something (typically, they are trying to acquire new customers by making sales). Using the term *cost per acquisition* instead of *cost per action* is acceptable, as not all cost per action offers can be referred to as cost per acquisition. However, cost per action can go further to measure what the advertiser pays for each specified action (a purchase, a form submission, and so on) linked to the advertisement. This measurement is calculated by taking the: Digital media costs intended to drive the acquisitions or action (e.g., paid search, email marketing) divided by number of new leads acquired or new actions performed (e.g., new website visitors, new email addresses).
- **Keyword Rank:** Ninety percent of consumers go to a website on the first page of their search query and 46 percent click on the website in the number one position. It's important to

choose keywords where you achieve a high rank. Beyond the first page of results, your hopes for generating traffic drop significantly.

Although you do a lot in digital marketing to give customers the experience you think they want, you should listen to customers and include measurements that give feedback if you are providing what they want or they want something else.

Social media measurements play an important role in listening and being consumer-centric in the digital ecosystem. An *ecosystem* is defined as living organisms interacting with their environment, and that's exactly what's happening between consumers and your brand online.

Some key social media measurements are:

- **People Talking About** (Facebook Insights): Engagement is a key reason to use social media. People Talking About, available through Facebook Insights, is one of the best measurements of engagement. It is the number of unique people who have either *liked*, commented, shared, or mentioned your brand on Facebook. If *likes* and People Talking About are increasing, your brand is creating a positive buzz.
- **Followers and Competitors' Followers** (Twitter): These are people who take an interest in your brand. It is worth tracking for both your brand and your competitors. Followers also are a good metric if your brand is active on Pinterest.
- **Retweets** (TWITTER): In much the same way People Talking About measures engagement and involvement on Facebook, retweets (RT) work similarly on Twitter. They are the metric that measure the quality, rather than the quantity, of your tweets. If your brand is active on Pinterest, repins are an equivalent measure.
- **Comments and Pingbacks** (Blogs): If your brand has a blog, the number of comments and pingbacks should be tracked and measured. The latter are links from other blogs who have passed along your content to their readers. Imitation is the sincerest form of flattery.

- **Views** (YouTube): If your brand is on YouTube, views are valuable currency. Views are turbochargers to your search rank, especially since YouTube is the number two search engine. If you ever want your social media activity to go viral, case studies indicate it is more likely to happen on YouTube than any other social network.
- **Audience Retention** (YouTube Analytics): YouTube Analytics are some of the most sophisticated software on the internet. Mainly that's because YouTube is owned by Google. One metric that is particularly valuable is drop off, which measures or when people stop watching your video. If you put videos on YouTube and aren't paying attention to this metric, the only one that suffers is your brand.

Voice of the Customer

You should have feedback mechanisms that measure the voice of your customer. You build a digital presence around what you think consumers want, but only consumers can tell you what they really want. One method of determining this is a survey, administered from your website on a scheduled basis (e.g., quarterly, biannually) with some simple but actionable questions like:

- Why did you come to this website?
- What were you looking for?
- Did you find what you were looking for?
- Would you come back again?
- How can we make your next visit better?

Another method of getting customer feedback is by using A/B testing (also referred to as split testing). A/B testing is an experimental approach to web design (especially user experience design), which aims to identify changes to web pages that increase or maximize an outcome. For example, a company might test two offers to see which garners more customer interest:

- A call to action stating "Offer ends this Saturday!"
- A call to action stating "Limited time offer!"

When doing A/B testing or any online testing, companies should have a defined outcome that is measurable (e.g., number of sales made, click-rate conversion, number of people signing up/registering).

Key Performance Indicators

Now you know some of most important digital measurements, it's time to choose the ones most important for your business.

Key performance indicators (KPIs) are the key metrics that help you understand how you are doing against objectives. KPIs translate complex measures into simple indicators that allow decision makers to assess the current situation and act quickly. KPIs are the actionable scorecard to keep strategy on track.

If you and your team have looked at all the key measurements just described, you're now ready to determine what key metrics are most relevant to your business objective. You also need to know where to source the metrics and report on them regularly (usually either a monthly or quarterly schedule). When you meet to review the reports, you should be prepared to take action on the results. You want to choose measurements that are SMART:

- Specific
- Measurable
- Actionable
- Relevant
- Time-bound

The choice of KPIs is most effective when it's a collaborative process. For example, it might start off as a whiteboard discussion with your whole team present.

Next, identify the key metric and create your KPI scorecard. There don't need to be a lot of metrics because you've looked at everything and are ready to set up a measurement plan for the most important ones. What does matter is that you pick metrics you and your team are prepared to take action on when you meet to review them.

Don't worry if after you've begun, you change your mind. Measurements don't change and you can just substitute a measurement that isn't providing value for one that is. At this point, your KPI scorecard might be set up as shown in Table 9.1.

TABLE 9.1 KPI Scorecard: Choosing Metrics that Show How You're Doing Against Objectives Allow You to Take Appropriate Actions.

KPI	Qtr. 1	Qtr. 2	Qtr. 3
Sales metric #1			
Sales metric #2			
Website metric #1			
Website metric #2			
Website metric #3			
Social media metric #1			
Social media metric #2			

KPIs are next displayed as a dashboard like the one in Figure 9.1. The purpose of the dashboard is not only to display key metrics graphically, but to be able to drill down deeper in a key area if greater insight is required. A good KPI dashboard displays 4 to 10 different areas and shows them in a way where key segmentation can be seen for each key area as shown in the figure.

Let me demonstrate the value of KPIs with an example. Let's say the number of positive consumer reviews on the Internet for your brand is an important business metric. Positive consumer reviews are a relevant KPI for many businesses, as an increase or decrease of just one star on Yelp is now reported to be worth 9 percent in sales for a brand.

In the next measurement period, your brand's rating goes down one star on the basis of five stars. What do you do? You might want to drill down into the KPIs. If the overall ratings metric is determined from a compilation of the key sites where you collect the rating (e.g., Yelp, Reputation.com, Amazon.com), you could find

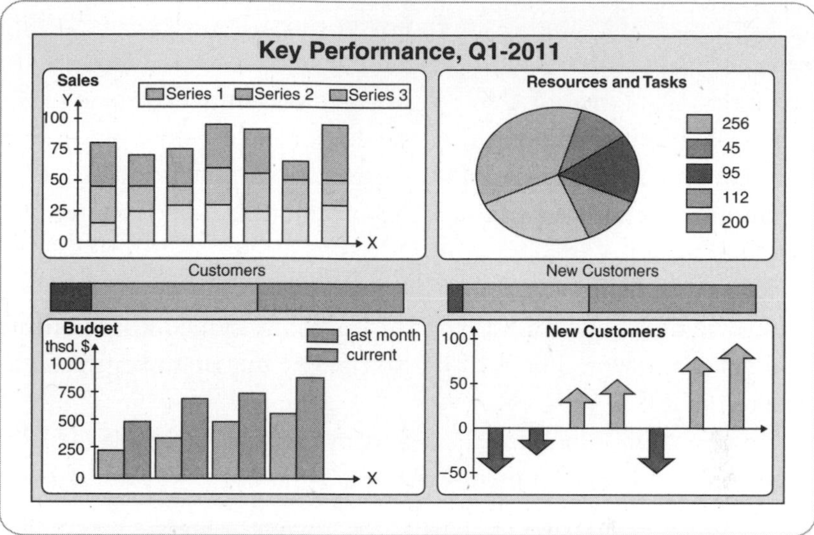

FIGURE 9.1 KPI Dashboard: A KPI dashboard displays metrics graphically and allows you to drill down into specific areas if additional insight is required.

the site where the biggest rating drops have occurred. Then, you might examine the content of the testimony in the last quarter to find out what has changed. Using this information, you can now take steps to address the problem from either a product, service, or customer relations standpoint. KPIs just helped you correct a business decline to keep your strategy on track.

If a performance indicator could potentially make a big difference in sales, it's worth measuring and taking action. Having carefully chosen your KPIs and taking action on the results, you've just make a difference in the bottom line. This is an example of how measurements help you win in the digital channel.

From KPIs to ROI

KPIs are the actionable scorecard to keep your business strategy on track. ROI measures the direct financial impact of the strategy on your business. ROI measures gains or losses from a sales and company operations standpoint. A company has to decide how they define their *gains*—sales, company growth, or profits.

Let's take an example. A company pursues digital marketing with the direct sales goal of driving consumers to their website to generate acceptance of a free trial offer or sample of their product. Trial offers are something the company has experience with and knows works. They know 5 percent of people offline take advantage of the offer, go buy the product, and become regular consumers.

The percentage of visitors who register for the trial offer online should be included as a KPI, so the company can compare online to offline behavior. The KPI is also the key metric to begin calculation for ROI.

To determine the annual sales from the trial offer, we identify the sales gain from the program:

(# who register for trial offer) × (% who become regular customers) × (Annual Customer Value)

Annual Customer Value is an important metric to obtain for an ROI calculation. Even if it's an estimate, every company should know what their average customer is worth on an annual basis. Some companies, like hotels, airlines, and cars even calculate the Lifetime Customer Value because their key customers have a value worth retaining.

With sales identified, the next step is to determine what are counted as investments. Some considerations in this example are: digital media, public relations, customer service, the cost of creating the website, staff, and overhead involved. This list is perhaps longer than what might be included, but the point is that a range of direct and operational investments is considered.

For some investments that may be around longer than the ROI reporting period, it may be worthwhile to amortize the investment. Say the website costs $75,000 to build but will be used for three years, the annual investment may be amortized to $25,000. With this information, we use the ROI calculation:

$$\text{ROI} = \frac{(\text{Investment Gain} - \text{Investment Cost}}{(\text{Investment Cost})} \times 100$$

The amount spent on digital media is then examined to determine ROAI. In the example, from information gained from cookies, tags, and measurements from the website analytics tool, we know which channels are driving visitors and how many from each channel take advantage of the trial offer. We then identify the under- and over-achievers by digital channel as:

$$\frac{\text{Sales from Advertising}}{\text{Ad Spend}}$$

Now you know how to create an actionable scorecard and understand its direct effect in terms of both ROI and ROAI.

MEASUREMENT TOOL MINI-HANDBOOK

As you might imagine, measurement tools and the selection of the right ones for your goal play an important role.

Fortunately, there are many tools available. There are digital marketing measurement tools to fit the ambitions and budget of any company. In terms of costs, they range from open source and free to highly customizable and with expensive monthly subscription fees.

What tools are right for your company and why? The answer depends on what your business objectives are, how you are using specific digital channels to achieve goals, and what your time frame is for desired results. As has been a consistent theme in this chapter, the tools to measure the data are not the issue; it's the key metrics you select to make better, data-driven decisions.

So now that you know what's available, here is a "toolkit" organized by digital channel. You should place a priority on tools in the areas where your business and company is most active.

Search Marketing Measurement Tools

If search engine optimization and a high search rank are high priorities for your business, then tools that can measure progress in search ranks and provide insight into opportunity for keywords, key content, and links are high on your list. Here is a list of tools to consider:

- **Google Trends:**[9] This tool tracks keyword volume and trends over time of the largest search engine library in the world. Google Trends is an essential and indispensable tool for all companies to measure and trend consumer demand over time for their products or services, as well as how consumers search for their unmet needs.
- **Google AdWords Keywords Tool:**[10] This tool allows you to measure search volume for keywords and competitiveness, as well as cost (CPC), if you are doing paid search. This is for all companies, but especially those who do paid-search marketing.
- **Trellian Keyword Discovery Tool:**[11] Keyword Discovery measures search volume and keyword rank. It is best for companies that do dedicated search tracking and measure search rank regularly and is available through a subscription service.
- **Wordtracker:**[12] This is a similar measurement tool to Keyword Discovery and is also available through a subscription service.

Competitive Intelligence

A primary use of digital measurements is to gain an advantage over the competition. You can know more about your competitors online than they might even know about themselves. Every business should have competitive tracking and business intelligence in place. Some companies and categories may place more reliance on this information than others. Ask yourself, how important is business intelligence at your company? Here are some resources to consider:

- **Alexa:**[13] This subsidiary of Amazon.com provides free information on traffic levels for websites, as well as keywords and demographics of visitors. It is a rich resource for competitive information but not as statistically accurate as the other available tools.

- **Quantcast:**[14] This service provides traffic and demographics for websites. The tool is primarily used by online advertisers looking to target specific demographics.
- **Compete:**[15] This company manages the largest panel of its kind in the industry, combining the online behaviors and attitudes from two million consumers across the United States. It is the most precise website tracking tool, measuring and even projecting consumer behavior. It is also primarily a subscription service with various plans geared to larger, enterprise organizations.

Website Analytics

A core area for any digital measurement program is the analytics of your website. A website analytics tool answers who, what, where, when, how, and why. It identifies your best and worst customers and tells how they find you. It is the epicenter of your digital measurement program. Google Analytics is a sophisticated and free website tool that has many capabilities and can fit the needs of most companies. However, if your business requires a more customizable solution to track specific areas not measured by Google Analytics, there are other services available to get to any level of detail:

- **Google Analytics:**[16] Google Analytics (GA) is a service offered by Google that generates detailed statistics about a website's traffic and traffic sources and measures conversions and sales. The product is aimed at marketers as opposed to webmasters and technologists from which the industry of web analytics originally grew. It is the most widely used website statistics service.
- **IBM Digital Analytics:** Coremetrics Web Analytics, a part of IBM Digital Analytics, is a powerful web analytics solution that is particularly suited to the Retail, Content/Media, Financial Services, Publishing and Travel verticals are also available.

Social Media

Does social media build your business? Is someone who *likes* your brand more likely to buy your brand or recommend it to a friend? What does "buzz" contribute to business building? How does that compare to *likes* and *comments* of your competitors? For companies that are active in social media, these are just some of the questions that can be answered through social media measuring and monitoring. This is a burgeoning area. Some of the major resources include:

- **Facebook Insights:**[17] This analytics tool is provided to Facebook page owners or platform administrators. Facebook Insights generates metrics that allow administrators to analyze trends about the activity on a given page such as "reach" and "People Talking About;" This measures people who have performed actions on your Facebook page such as: Clicked on the "Like" button, commented on a post, shared a post or responded to an event. It shows the level of interaction people are having with your Facebook Fan Page. It measure how people show *like*, comment, and share content about your brand.
- **Technorati:**[18] Technorati is an internet search engine for searching blogs and ranking their value through an "authority score."
- **Topsy:**[19] A social and sentiment analysis score of comments and content that receive the highest number of tweets on Twitter.
- **YouTube Analytics:**[20] This is a self-service tool that gives you detailed statistics on your videos and your viewers. It's an easy and powerful way to discover which videos and themes work best for your audience. How do viewers find you? How long do they watch your videos? When do they leave? YouTube Analytics gives you all the details, video by video or for all your videos at once, so you really understand your audience.
- **Salesforce Radian6:**[21] This social media monitoring platform from Salesforce is a full service social solution that helps you listen, measure, engage in, and discover online conversations so you can build your community and your business.

- **Lithium Technologies:**[22] Lithium makes social customer experience management software for the enterprise. Lithium Social Customer Experience Management Platform combines online customer community applications such as forums, blogs, innovation management, live chat, and tribal knowledge bases with the broader social Web and traditional CRM business processes, resulting in a wide range of online customer interaction methods.

Big Data and Dashboard Display Software

There is software to show and store major sources of data such as web-browsing data trails, social network communications, and sensor and surveillance data. Data visualization is one of the fastest growing areas in measurement software. The top players are:

- **Apache Hadoop:**[23] Hadoop is an Apache Software Foundation project and open source software platform for scalable, distributed computing. Hadoop can provide fast and reliable analysis of both structured data and unstructured data. Given its capabilities to handle large data sets, it's often associated with the phrase "big data."
- **Cloudera:**[24] The first big-data management solution that allows batch and real-time operations to be performed on unstructured or structured data all within the same scalable system. It is distributing Hadoop but moving it beyond batch, enabling data-driven enterprises to ask bigger questions.[25]
- **Tableau Public:**[26] Tableau Public is a free data visualization tool that helps people see and understand their data.

This should be enough to get you started. My advice is to pick the areas that are most important to your business and tests the tools available. Identify the measurements that matter and explore the capabilities of the tools you choose. See if they don't empower you to make better business decisions.

BEST-IN-CLASS EXAMPLES

The power of digital measurements is they help you build business by guiding you to making better decisions. Here are six best-in-class case study examples that prove how, today, "If you can measure it, you can manage it."

1. **Hertz:** With over 8300 locations worldwide in 146 countries, Hertz keeps its finger on the pulse of its customers with customer satisfaction surveys. The problem? How to collate the information and understand what customers were trying to tell them through these surveys? By applying advanced analytics solutions, the company was able to process the information much more quickly—in half the time it previously took—while at the same time providing a level of insight previously unavailable to the company. An example? While evaluating the solution, Hertz was able to identify a potential area for improvement in Philadelphia. Surveys and measurements indicated that delays were occurring for returns during specific times of the day. By investigating this anomaly, Hertz was able to quickly adjust their staffing levels at the Philadelphia office during those peak times, ensuring a manager was present to resolve any issues. This enhanced Hertz's performance, and increased customer satisfaction, all by parsing the volumes of data being generated from multiple sources.
2. **Hollywood Box Office Returns:** It's one of the great mysteries that movie studios face: How well will their next release do in the box office? To date, the answer to that question has involved a lot of guesswork and "gut checks." But with the advent of social media sites, as well as big data analytics, for the first time studios have a way to measure sentiment by accessing multiple big data sources. The solution: Examine how social media data feeds could be analyzed in order to better understand public sentiment. Initially the idea was to track social movements using social

media tools. The ability to understand how the public perceives a specific movie could go a long way towards informing the studio as to the efficacy of its marketing efforts, as well as the ability to better encourage interest. Of course, it could also give studios additional insights to help inform go/no-go decisions on everything from the breadth of distribution to whether it made sense to invest additional marketing muscle to push a movie over the public's awareness tipping point.

3. **T-Mobile:** Integrating big data across multiple IT systems, T-Mobile has used the combination of customer transaction and interactions data in order to better predict customer defections. By leveraging social media data along with transaction data from CRM and billing systems, T-Mobile USA was able to cut customer defections in half in a single quarter.
4. **Seton Healthcare:** Seton sought to address a need to reduce the occurrence of high cost congestive heart failure (CHF) readmissions. But, how could this be done? By proactively identifying patients likely to be readmitted on an emergent basis, Seton applied predictive models and providing analytics that providers can intuitively navigate, interpret, and take action. The benefit? For Seton, a reduction in costs and risks associated with complying with federal readmission targets. For Seton's patients, fewer visits to the hospital and overall improved patient care. Seton is able to identify patients likely to need readmission and introduce early interventions to reduce cost, mortality rates, and improved patient quality of life.
5. **U.S. Xpress:** A provider of a wide variety of transportation solutions, U.S. Xpress collects about a thousand data elements ranging from fuel usage to tire condition to truck engine operations to GPS information, and uses this data for optimal fleet management and to drive productivity. As a result, they save millions of dollars in operating costs each year. Measurement and analytics were both used for this purpose.
6. **H&R Block:** This tax services organization has learned in the weeks prior to April 15, that every question that is

not answered immediately is a lost sale. Tax preparation is a highly seasonal business. H&R Block had a heavy paid media scheduled but they also used Facebook and Twitter to provide immediate access to a tax professional for Q&A in the "Get It Right" social media campaign. The effort secured 1,500,000 unique visitors and answered 1,000,000 questions for a 15 percent lift in business compared to the prior year when there was no social media in the marketing mix.

BUDGETING FOR DIGITAL MEASUREMENT

How do you budget for the measurement plan at your company? Companies like Google, Cisco, Amazon, and Facebook benchmark measurement effectiveness in key areas to prove its value in achieving business goals. Areas in which they benchmark for budgeting and staffing are:

- **Quality:** How often does the data help choose the right course of action?
- **Speed:** How quickly are decisions made versus competitors?
- **Yield:** How often are the decisions executed as intended?
- **Effort:** What is the right amount of time, attention and resources put into making and executing decisions?

If measurement and ROI are going to be an asset for your business, learn from the successes of these companies and determine:

- **Benefits:** How much difference are better data and measurements going to make for improved decision making?
- **Results:** What are the expected results (e.g., greater actionability, time saved, increased competitive advantages, ability to enter more new markets with more new innovations) and estimated financial value?

- **Resources:** How many people are needed to analyze the data and provide actionable insights?
- **Specific Roles:** What are their specific roles, functions, and deliverables?
- **Software Costs:** What software is to be used?

As was said at the beginning of this chapter, digital analytics is a people business, so remember the 10/90 rule: That is, software and analytics tools required for the job should be only 10 percent of costs, and the people who analyze the data and find the insights should account for the remaining 90 percent.

Once you have quantified the impact a good measurement plan has on business results, establish a time frame for seeing the return on the investment of staff and their activities, insights, and actions.

THE FUTURE OF MEASUREMENT

"The best way to invent the future is to create it."[27]

—**Peter Drucker**

What's in store for digital measurements in the future? To show you, let me practice what I preach by using a tool of the trade discussed earlier. The tool is Google Trends, which allows the user to see how often specific keywords, subjects, and phrases have been queried over a specific period of time. What better way to identify what's in store for the future than seeing the areas of greatest need up to now, as measured through search queries on the largest resource in the world? I queried key topics covered in this book and measured them through Google Trends. The ones I included were:

- Digital marketing
- Social media marketing
- Search marketing
- Mobile marketing
- Big data

Here are six trends on the future of digital measurement from my examination and extrapolation of the data:

1. *Big data is a big deal.* Ninety percent of the world's total data has been created just within the past two years; 91 percent of marketing leaders believe successful brands use customer data to drive business decisions; and 87 percent agree that capturing and sharing the right data is important to effectively measuring ROI in their own company Although there are significant challenges such as data capture, curation, search, sharing, and visualization, the trend line indicates big data is already generating so much interest great strides will occur in overcoming these challenges.
2. *Digital is headed toward the cloud.* One reason to explain not only the rise of big data but the heightened interest in digital marketing in general is that information is getting easier to store in computer clouds. Cloud computing is a technology that measures trends to watch. Consumers and businesses are moving more of their data off their computers and into rich Internet applications that are available everywhere. You can experience this for yourself on sites like Yahoo! Mail, Google Docs, Salesforce.com, and Mint.com. While there are process and security issues to be worked out in the cloud for big data, the cost savings compared to storage on servers will push businesses to find solutions.
3. *Search marketing is helped by social metrics.* Queries for search marketing have declined. Does this mean interest in search is declining? No. It means the value of search is now working in greater integration with social media and mobile technologies. Here's what the experts at Google have to say about search marketing: "…We do use [tweeted links and RTs] as a signal. iTweeted Links and RTs, for example, are used as a signal in our organic and news rankings. We also use them to enhance our news universal by marking how many people shared an article." A representative of Bing stated, "We do look at the social authority of a user. We

look at how many people you follow, how many follow you, and this can add a little weight to a listing in regular search results."[28]

4. *Mobile search drives mobile marketing.* By 2014, more people are expected to access the Internet from mobile devices than from desktops or laptops.[29] So why is the trend line for mobile marketing flat? When we look more closely at the trends with mobile marketing, we see search is the area generating the most interest and growing at the fastest rate. Table 9.2 tracks the following terms: mobile marketing, mobile commerce, mobile search, and SMS marketing. Ninety-five percent use a search engine. Search is the number one Internet activity on mobile devices. Search will drive mobile just like Internet search drives our online behavior. Mobile search metrics will be one of the most important areas to watch.
5. *Strategy is a key priority for social media.* When we drill down into keywords driving social media growth, they include phrases like: social media strategy, social marketing plan, and marketing strategy. It certainly seems that social media adoption has moved beyond having a Facebook page to having the strategy to evaluate what a social presence is achieving And a measurement plan to keep the social strategy on track. and a measurement plan to prove.

Measurements and ROI are the way you win in today's digital world. But, don't worry, you don't have to master them on Day 1. Table 9.2 summarizes the path you take toward analytics mastery.

It's a process, and you have to work the process. Like everything you do, you get better with practice. This chapter has attempted to equip you with the resources, ideas, and budget requirements so your business wins.

To get where you want to go, get started and just put one foot in front of the other. Enjoy the learning process and delight in the insights when you find them. I believe you'll find your way.

TABLE 9.2 Measurement and ROI

"If you can measure it, you can manage it."

Crawl	Walk	Run	Thrive
• Define business goals • Determine success metrics for behaviors and benefits • Establish KPIs • Align with campaign & IMC objectives	• Use Google Analytics and available open-source measures: - Traffic/visitors - Source of traffic - Time/page views - Site interaction - Actions	• Determine broader digital campaign effectiveness: - Creative evaluation - Media dynamics - Marketing mix - Brand impact - Sales impact	• Understand and optimize ROI: - Choose ROI scenario Brand/DR - Establish success benchmarks - Identify what works to optimize and sustain results

ENDNOTES

1. Harvard Business Review/http://hbr.org/2012/10/big-data-the-management-revolution
2. http://techcrunch.com/2010/08/04/schmidt-data/
3. http://spotfire.tibco.com/blog/?p=6886
4. BRITE Study (Columbia Business School and NYAMA), 2012 http://www.iab.net/media/file/2012-BRITE-NYAMA-Marketing-ROI-Study.pdf
5. http://www.socialmediaexaminer.com/SocialMediaMarketingIndustryReport2012.pdf
6. http://barnraisersllc.com/2012/11/11-definitions-roi-simple-solution
7. Penn State University Library/ http://pabook.libraries.psu.edu/palitmap/bios/Wanamaker__John.html
8. BRITE/NYAMA
9. http://google.com/trends
10. http://adwords.google.com/o/KeywordTool.com
11. http://www.keyworddiscovery.com

12. http:// wordtracker.com
13. http://www.alexa.com
14. https://www.quantcast.com
15. https://www.compete.com
16. http://www.google.com/analytics
17. http://www.facebook.com/insights
18. http://technorati.com
19. http://topsy.com
20. http://www.youtube.com/yt/playbook/yt-analytics.html
21. http://www.salesforcemarketingcloud.com/listen
22. http://lithium.com
23. http://hadoop.apache.org
24. http://cloudera.com
25. http://www.marketwatch.com/story/cloudera-announces-game-changing-real-time-query-on-hadoop-and-leads-a-new-era-of-data-management–2012–10–24
26. http://www.tableausoftware.com/public
27. The Drucker School – Claremount Graduate University http://www.cgu.edu/PDFFiles/Drucker/MBA_FE%20brochure.pdf
28. Search marketing is helped by social metrics (Google and Bing Quotes) http://searchengineland.com/what-social-signals-do-google-bing-really-count–55389
29. Mobile marketing: Mary Meeker, Morgan Stanley http://gigaom.com/2010/04/12/mary-meeker-mobile-internet-will-soon-overtake-fixed-internet/

CHAPTER 10

UNDERSTANDING THE LAW IN DIGITAL MARKETING

—*by Glen Gilmore*

KEEPING PACE WITH THE LAW IN DIGITAL MARKETING

One of the most daunting tasks for businesses in an age of *social business* (i.e., a time when digital marketing is inextricably intertwined with "social"), is coming to grips with the legal risks associated with social media marketing. Businesses are expected to engage with customers "in real time", while often having little clarity on what the actual do's and don'ts of digital marketing might be. For some businesses, this is because their industry has been given little guidance from their regulators, as in the case of those within the pharmaceutical space. For other companies, bluntly, it is because they have not invested the resources in tracking down the rules of the road and providing the guidelines and training necessary to give employees the confidence to ply their trade effectively and in compliance with the current state of digital marketing law. Complicating the task of digital marketing compliance is the simple fact that the law is evolving in starts and stops, while the digital technologies and social platforms move forward at break-neck speeds.

In this chapter, we will explore the current state of social media marketing law, compliance strategies for your business, and trends that will create new challenges for compliant digital marketing.

As You Market in the Social Space, Be Ever Mindful of the Rules and Regulations that Govern Your Business or Profession in the "Real World": They Also Govern Your Conduct in Social Media Marketing

As a licensed attorney, I am governed by rules that are unique to my profession. I am always mindful of the special risks and responsibilities that come with being an attorney.

For example, I understand that I can create a special relationship with special responsibilities anytime I offer legal advice or create a situation where someone might think that because of my words or actions an attorney–client connection has been created. I realize that this can happen even when I simply write or speak about the subject of law. To lessen the chances of this happening, I must affirmatively confront the issue.

You, depending on your profession, for example, if you are in the medical or financial field, may face similar hazards and may need to take similar precautions when you are in the digital space to ensure that you do not create a situation where, unintentionally, you have exposed yourself and your enterprise to unnecessary liability. Without being cautious, your blog post, your tweet, your pin, your post, could expose you or your company to liability.

As I like to tell my students and clients, "Whatever you tweet, pin, post, Google+, or blog, may be held against you in a court of law, should a violation of the law occur." It is happening with greater frequency that content from the social web is finding its way into our courts when disputes occur. It has been commonplace in family court for Facebook intrigues and photos to be used to demonstrate infidelity and deceit, but, other posts and social communications are finding their way into other courts in all types of legal disputes. So think before you tweet, pin, or post—or let others do so on behalf of your business!

Do In the Digital Space What You Must Do in the Real World, e.g., "Because I Am a Lawyer, I Must Give You, Dear "Followers," "Friends" (Readers), Some Disclaimers…."

- *This is not legal advice.* Although we are examining the law as it applies to the digital and social space, nothing in this chapter should be considered legal advice. WARNING: The application of the law often varies depending on the applicable jurisdictions and the specific circumstances of a particular matter. If you have a legal question, you should speak with an attorney from your own jurisdiction (state, nation).
- *I am not a "social media" lawyer.* "What?!"… While it is true that I teach Social Media Law at Rutgers and that I have written and lectured somewhat extensively on the topic, there is no certification, as may be found in other areas of the law, such as in Family Law, covering this new area of the law within my governing jurisdiction. I do not want anyone to assume that I am asserting a specialty qualification in the field of social media law where one does not exist … at this particular point in time!

The Digital Lesson of this Disclaimer: "The Medium Doesn't Matter"

So back to the digital lesson of this disclaimer: Apply to the social and digital spaces the rules that you know ordinarily govern your conduct and communications in the real world and apply them, as best you can, to the digital and social spaces. This means, for example, that in the profile of my niche Twitter account, @SocialMediaLaw1, I include a statement that "Tweets do not equal legal advice." I'll also include disclosures with a tweet or blog post itself, depending on the nature of the content being shared. In short, consider your own professional or business rules of conduct and apply them accordingly.

"The Medium Doesn't Matter"… However, DIGITAL AND SOCIAL TEND TO AMPLIFY WORDS AND DEEDS

Do not think for a moment that simply because you are tweeting on Twitter or pinning on Pinterest, that the rules of your trade do not apply. They do. And, be warned, that any missteps or transgressions will be amplified by the medium of social media so that they are likely to be heard by your industry regulators (often with the help of your competitors, who will be intently listening).

Social Media Monitoring Equals Business Intelligence

Social media monitoring makes competitive business intelligence accessible to anyone willing to invest a little time in tracking their competition. There are no whispers in the social space.

A Blog Post May Constitute Consumer Fraud, Just a Tweet May Be Defamatory

A blog post slightly exaggerating the benefits of your products or services? Consumer fraud. A tweet that spreads a lie about a competitor or coworker? Defamation (i.e., a false statement of fact about a person or business to someone other than the person or business being communicated about that causes damage to the person or business being falsely communicated about; it forms a basis for suing the person spreading the falsehood). There is no license to bend or ignore the law in social media. (And yes, if it is an employee or partner of yours who is using social media in a way that harms another, your business might also be dragged into court or sanctioned, perhaps, in part, because of your failure to establish a social media policy or training.)

CREATING A FRAMEWORK FOR SOCIAL MEDIA GOVERNANCE AND COMPLIANCE

Whether you are a small business or a larger enterprise, you must put into place a framework for social media marketing governance and compliance. Naturally, how each looks will depend much on the size of your enterprise and your industry.

I understand that if you are a small business, you may be the HR department, the legal department, and the marketing department, all wrapped up into one. That's okay. The framework should still help small business owners get a good sense of the prominent compliance issues that should be considered when using social media for marketing.

"Embedding" Social Media within Your Enterprise: Creating a "Social" Corporate Culture

At its best, leveraging social business includes "embedding social" within your organization. This means achieving a comfort level with compliant social media engagement that will enable everyone within the organization to participate in the social space with confidence, agility, and creativity. This won't happen overnight, but it will happen over time, with a commitment to training, teamwork, and supervision.

Guideposts for Creating a Social Media Governance and Compliance Framework

- *Get "buy-in" from the C-suite.* Upper management must approve of your journey into the social space or it will be doomed to failure from the start without adequate resources. Be sure that you can make a business case for becoming social.
- *Align your social media marketing goals to your business goals.* Sounds simple enough, but it is something that is often overlooked. When you are using social media for business, it must become part of your business plan and review. Simply "being there" in social, is not enough; it requires a plan, a commitment of resources, and oversight.
- *Create a social media governance team.* Ideally, you will embed social into your business's culture, as discussed earlier, meaning that you will help all of your organization's members understand the value of being "social" and how to be so in a way that furthers the enterprise's objectives. Still, having a team dedicated to social media excellence is an important foundation for getting social right. This means a team that meets regularly to review best practices,

gauge what is working and what is not, and continually considers how social media training can improve the organization. This group should represent a cross section of your organization, from IT to legal to marketing to HR, so that it can advance all of the functions of your organization through social media. This team should also designate assignments concerning social media monitoring, engagement, and overall planning. It should be this team that works with legal to hammer out a social media policy and auditing procedures.

- *Provide a social media policy, a playbook, a decision tree, and training.* Having a social media policy without social media training simply doesn't work. It's not enough. To improve your enterprise's prospects of compliant, real-time engagement, you must couple your policy, which sets the limits of engagement, with a playbook that provides examples of best practices. A decision tree that helps employees know what paths to take depending on the situations they confront should also be created, one that is unique to the organizational and regulatory concerns of your enterprise. Finally, ongoing training is a must to keep everyone on top of the ever-evolving technologies, platforms, and best practices. (Know that the benchmarks outlined in this bullet point, in particular, mirror what regulatory agencies are beginning to sketch as foundational requirements for responsible and compliant social media participation.)
- *In creating or applying a social media policy, get to know the National Labor Relations Act (NLRA), as interpreted by the National Labor Relations Board (NLRB).* Many social media policies include warnings that employees must not say anything bad about the company or the supervisors they work for. Such warnings, generally speaking, are themselves a violation of the National Labor Relations Act, *29 U.S.C. §§ 151–169*, which prohibits companies from creating or enforcing policies that are likely to have a "chilling effect" on the right of employees to communicate in a "concerted fashion" about the "terms or conditions of their employment."

In releasing a report on the subject of social media policies in January of 2012, the National Labor Relations Board

(NLRB), an independent federal agency that protects the rights of private sector employees through the implementation of the NLRA, warned both employers and employees of the competing interests balanced by the board when it comes to social media communications and social media policies:

- *Employer policies should not be so sweeping that they prohibit the kinds of activity protected by federal labor law, such as the discussion of wages or working conditions among employees.*
- *An employee's comments on social media are generally not protected if they are mere gripes not made in relation to group activity among employees.*[1]

Under the NLRB's guidance and review, how difficult has it become to write a social media policy that does not itself violate the law? Very. Even simply telling employees to be "respectful" or to keep confidential information confidential can be deemed to violate the NLRA law, if the language of the policy does not elaborate on such points to make it very clear that the employer does not intend to have a chilling effect on the right of employees to talk about the terms and conditions of their employment. Simply including a boilerplate statement within a social media policy that the policy is not intended to contradict the NLRA or that the NLRA trumps the social media policy, is not enough to remedy a policy that contains language that could reasonably be construed as having a chilling effect on the right of employees to speak (tweet, post, blog, or pin, etc.) about the terms and conditions of their employment in a concerted fashion. Even if an attorney is drafting your social media policy, it would be wise to be sure that the attorney has carefully studied the NLRB's guidance on this subject.

- *Expect a crisis and train for a crisis.* Know that your organization will have a social media crisis. Real-time, human engagement on evolving platforms makes it a near certainty that you will have a crisis with your social media participation. It may be a matter of having your account hacked, as has happened to Lady Gaga, the President of the United States, and countless others. Or it may be a "mistweet" (a tweet that wasn't meant to be sent from the account it has been sent from), as has happened to the

American Red Cross and Chrysler, or an employee of your organization will be shown on YouTube doing something they shouldn't (too many examples to cite!). You must consider what types of real crises are most likely to occur within your own industry, as well as those that are common to social media, and plan how to integrate a social media response into your overall response.

- *Audit and adjust your social media engagement.* When a business is found to have run afoul of the rules of compliant social media marketing, it is usually the FTC that will have done the policing and cleaning up. The clean-up of a digital marketing mess that involves the FTC usually includes a settlement that provides for outside auditing. As with the case of Facebook's alleged privacy violations, the FTC settlement called for certified, outside auditing of compliance procedures for a period of 20 years.[2] Whether done by an outside firm or an in-house team, regular auditing of your social media and digital marketing for compliance-related issues should become a company standard.

UNDERSTANDING THE FTC's SOCIAL MEDIA MARKETING GUIDELINES

Now, as you have been reading this chapter, you may have already said to yourself, "I'm not a lawyer or doctor or financial advisor, so it really doesn't seem that I have to concern myself too much about regulatory issues in the social space." You may even have given a sigh of relief, saying, "Thankfully, I don't have a regulator breathing down my neck." Think again.

Ever heard of the FTC?

"Sure."

Know what they do?

"Ah, not really."

I'll help you out. The FTC is the Federal Trade Commission, a national regulatory authority that has called itself "the nation's consumer protection agency." They have also become the nation's primary privacy watchdog and enforcement authority for the social space as well. If you market, they are your regulator.

Ever hear of the FTC's Social Media Guidelines? If not, you are in good company. If you are like most marketers (purely anecdotal evidence, from asking hundreds of marketers around the country), you somehow missed the FTC's 2009 revision of its endorsement guidelines to specifically include social media marketing. And, yes, I did say "2009."

Let's drill right down to the nitty-gritty of the FTC social media endorsement guidelines.

16 CFR Part 255, Guides Concerning the Use of Endorsements and Testimonials in Advertising

Section 255.5 of the FTC revised guidelines[3] requires the "disclosure of material connections" in marketing communications, whether the communication occurs in traditional media or on Facebook, Twitter, or any other social network. If you are a business or marketer using social media to promote your products or services, it is this section of the FTC's guidelines, which the revisions explicitly extend to social media, that is most likely to get you in trouble, as it is the requirement most often ignored by marketers in their social media marketing.

From the FTC's perspective, the disclosure of material connections is all about truth in advertising—and the obligation applies regardless of the type of business or enterprise involved, or the medium (traditional or new) used for the marketing communication.

What Is a "Material Connection"?

Under *Section 255.5*, a *material connection* exists between a business and an endorser when the connection between the two is such that if the nature of the connection were known by the audience, it "might materially affect the weight or credibility of the endorsement." In other words, absent a disclosure by the endorser, the nature of the connection to the business behind the product or service being endorsed would not be reasonably be expected by the audience hearing/viewing the endorsement.

In its simplest form, a material connection exists when someone is paid to make an endorsement of a product, service, or a brand, generally speaking. In the social space, the "payment" may not necessarily be a monetary one, but one that comes in the form of a blogger receiving free products or services, such as spa products or a spa treatment. If a blogger posts about how wonderful a spa experience was and the products that the spa used without saying that the treatment and products were free, it is unlikely that a reader, absent a disclosure by the blogger, would expect that the treatment or products would have been free, or that anything other than a spa-and-client relationship existed. The ringing endorsement in a blog post that states "This is the greatest spa with the greatest products I have ever experienced," would be sure to inspire interest and possibly added business for the spa.

Would a disclosure by the blogger that the spa treatment and products blogged about were free "materially affect the weight or credibility of the endorsement" given by readers of the blog post? Probably so. As such, there exists a "material connection" between the spa and the blogger that must be disclosed by the blogger within the blog post.

To underscore this point, the FTC's updated endorsement guidelines include the example of a college student who blogs about computer games and receives a free sample of a game from a game manufacturer who simply asks the student to blog about the game. Evaluating the scenario, the FTC outlines the duties that exist in a sponsored-blogger relationship:

> Because his review is disseminated via a form of consumer-generated media in which his relationship to the advertiser is not inherently obvious [social media], readers are unlikely to know that he has received the video game system free of charge in exchange for his review of the product, and given the value of the video game system, this fact likely would materially affect the credibility they attach to his endorsement. Accordingly, the blogger should clearly and conspicuously disclose that he received the gaming system free of charge. The manufacturer should advise him at the time it provides the gaming system that this connection should be disclosed, and it

should have procedures in place to try to monitor his postings for compliance.[4]

The blogging example provided by the FTC articulates some specific obligations in a sponsored – blogger relationship:

- *Advertiser–blogger relationships are not inherently obvious.* Unlike in television, when there is a break in a show for a commercial, or in print media where the advertisements are typically clearly delineated from the print content, in the medium of new media (Facebook, Twitter, blogs, etc.), sponsored-blogger relationships are often not obvious unless they are disclosed by the blogger. Importantly, the FTC notes that advertiser–blogger relationships are not "inherently obvious," because of the very nature of "consumer-generated media," triggering a heightened duty to disclose.
- *In a sponsored – blogger scenario, the blogger should "clearly and conspicuously" disclose the material connection.* Though the example does not define "clear and conspicuous," the standard has been fleshed out to mean something other than a disclosure within a profile page or a so-called "disclosure tab," badge, or link. Clear and conspicuous disclosure under FTC guidance has come to mean disclosure that is positioned close to the content where an endorsement takes place.
- *A disclosure tab or link does not satisfy the FTC's duty of clear and conspicuous disclosure.* The FTC has noted that in online social conversations, consumers might never leave the social "conversation" to inspect someone's profile page. Even if a consumer observed a blogger's profile biography which clearly stated the name of the blogger's employer, the consumer still might be unaware of the fact that the product being chatted or tweeted about was one produced by the blogger's employer. For example, one might not realize that a company known for making birth control pills is also the company that manufactures a common line of contact lenses. If a connection is not obvious, it must be disclosed.

FIRST CASE STUDY FOR THE FTC's NEW SOCIAL MEDIA ENDORSEMENT GUIDELINES

Three months after the FTC published its updated Endorsement Guides which, for the first time, specifically addressed social media marketing, Ann Taylor LOFT decided to hold a blogger event to trumpet its summer clothing collection. Bloggers were invited to preview the collection and given the chance to win prizes if they blogged about the collection within 24 hours of the event. The FTC launched an investigation when it learned about the event and became concerned that the bloggers who attended the event might fail "to disclose that they received gifts for posting blog content about the event," according to a no action letter from the FTC. (A *no-action letter* is a notice of a decision not to pursue enforcement; it is not a determination of guilt or innocence.) The closing letter noted that "an advertiser's provision of a gift to a blogger for posting blog content about an event could constitute a material connection that is not reasonably expected by readers of the blog."[5]

A Sign Does Not Constitute Disclosure

Seemingly mindful of the FTC's new social media disclosure guidelines, the LOFT had posted a sign at the preview that "told bloggers that they should disclose the gifts if they posted about the preview." Though this seems to have been a good-faith effort by the LOFT to comply with the FTC's guidelines, it was not sufficient compliance from the FTC's perspective. In a footnote to its closing letter to the LOFT, the FTC simply observed that it was not clear "how many bloggers actually saw that sign."

Written Disclosure Policy and Monitoring for Compliance Weigh Against FTC Enforcement Action

In the case of the FTC's investigation of the LOFT's blogging event, the FTC announced that it had "determined not to recommend enforcement action at this time." The FTC outlined the considerations that weighed against it pursuing an enforcement action.

The FTC noted that the event was the retailer's first such blogging event and that "a very small number of bloggers posted content about the preview and several of those bloggers disclosed that LOFT had provided them gifts at the preview." After the event, the retailer also adopted a written policy stating that it would "not issue any gift to any blogger without first telling the blogger that the blogger must disclose the gift in his or her blog." The FTC further noted that the retailer would "take reasonable steps to monitor bloggers' compliance with the obligation to disclose gifts they receive from LOFT."

Monitoring Sponsored Bloggers for Compliance with Their Duty to Disclose

The FTC does not say how sponsored bloggers should be monitored for compliance with their duty to disclose, only that it must be done. It is up to the sponsor to determine how best to comply with the obligation. Given that in this instance the FTC actually followed up to see how invited bloggers complied with the duty to disclose that they had received gifts, it seems pretty clear that, at a minimum, some actual auditing and monitoring of the invited bloggers must take place. Simply monitoring the social space for brand mentions would not be enough.

TWO TWEETS AND NIKE RUNS INTO REGULATORY PROBLEMS: THE ETHOS OF TRANSPARENCY

In the world of social media marketing, an ethos of transparency is transcending national boundaries as the standard when it comes to social media marketing. For example, in the United Kingdom, the Advertising Standards Authority (ASA) performs a similar function to that of the FTC in the United States. It describes itself as the "U.K.'s independent regulator of advertising across all media." Looking at its rules shows a definite parallel to those found in the United States, particularly with regard to the duty of disclosure.

Under the U.K.'s Code, Marketing Must Be "Obviously Identifiable as Such"

Similar to the U.S.'s requirement of "clear and conspicuous" disclosure of sponsored blog posts, the U.K.'s Advertising Code, Section 2.1, which is applicable to social media, mandates that marketing communications "must be obviously identifiable as such."[6]

In June of 2012, the ASA announced its adjudication of a complaint against Nike based on two tweets by two of the country's most famous soccer players—tweets that appeared not on Nike's Twitter account, but on the accounts of the two players.[7]

The Offending Tweets

The first tweet that was the subject of the ASA's Nike investigation, was tweeted by a footballer who proclaimed, "My resolution—to start the year as a champion, and finish it as a champion ... #makeitcount gonike.me/makeitcount." The second tweet announced, "In 2012, I will come back for my club—and be ready for my country. #makeitcount.gonike.me/ Makeitcount"

An unidentified complainant challenged "whether both tweets were obviously identifiable as marketing communications," as mandated under British advertising law. (Yes, sponsored tweets—or posts or pluses—can be considered "ads" for regulatory purposes when they are used to convey a commercial message.)

Nike Asserts Team and Player Sponsorships Were Well Known

According to the ASA, Nike asserted, in response to the complaint, that both players were "were well known for being sponsored by Nike, as were the teams for which they played," preventing the players' Twitter followers from being misled about the nature of the tweets or the relationship between the players and the company.

Nike further asserted that the presence of Nike web addresses within the tweets that directed viewers to the company's site would also have alerted viewers to the marketing nature of the tweet.

British Advertising Authority Bans Nike's Twitter Campaign

The ASA considered the nature of the social network Twitter and how people customarily use the network. The ASA observed that "the average Twitter user would follow a number of people on the site and they would receive a number of tweets throughout the day, which they may scroll through quickly." Dismissing Nike's defense, the ASA noted that the country's advertising code does not simply require that ads be "identifiable as marketing communications but that they must be ***obviously identifiable*** as such." (Emphasis supplied.)

The ASA dismissed the notion that the Nike link or hashtag #makeitcount would be sufficient to alert viewers of the commercial nature of the tweets. The ASA also observed that "not all Twitter users would be aware of the footballers' and their teams' sponsorship deal with Nike."

In sum, the ASA concluded:

> There was nothing obvious in the tweets to indicate they were Nike marketing communications. In the absence of such an indication, for example #ad, we considered the tweets were not obviously identifiable as Nike marketing communications and therefore concluded they breached the Code.[8]

UNDERSTANDING THE FTC'S NEW PRIVACY FRAMEWORK: PRIVACY BY DESIGN, SIMPLIFIED CHOICE, AND GREATER TRANSPARENCY

In March of 2012, the FTC issued its privacy policy framework, *Protecting Consumer Privacy in an Era of Rapid Change*. The report contained three primary recommendations for businesses:[9]

1. **Privacy by Design:** Companies should build in consumers' privacy protections at every stage in developing their products. These include reasonable security for consumer data, limited collection and retention of such data, and reasonable procedures to promote data accuracy.
2. **Simplified Choice for Businesses and Consumers:** Companies should give consumers the option to decide what information is shared about them, and with whom.

This should include a Do-Not-Track mechanism that would provide a simple, easy way for consumers to control the tracking of their online activities.

3. **Greater Transparency:** Companies should disclose details about their collection and use of consumers' information, and provide consumers access to the data collected about them.

In its privacy settlement with Facebook, mentioned earlier, the FTC included a very practical provision within its consent agreement, a provision that mandated that Facebook designate "an employee or employees to coordinate and be responsible for the privacy program."[10] Consider the size of a business such as Facebook, then consider the FTC's mandate that they formally designate *someone* or a group of individuals as being responsible for the organization's privacy program. The FTC has reasoned on this topic that if everyone is in charge of a business's privacy program, no one is. It's good advice. Have someone within your enterprise, even if it's you, tasked with asking, "How are we protecting consumer data in this new marketing initiative?" It will help you stay on the right side of the FTC, at the very least.

UNDERSTANDING THE CHILDREN'S ONLINE PRIVACY PROTECTION ACT

The Children's Online Privacy Protection Act (COPPA), *16 CFR Part 312*, requires verifiable, parental consent before an online site directed to children (or any site that has actual knowledge that it is collecting information from children under thirteen), regardless of whether that "site" is a social networking forum or an app, may begin the collection, storage, use, or transfer of the personal information of a child under the age of 13. The site must provide a prominent link to its privacy policy and information on how parental consent may be received, and outline the site operator's responsibilities to protect a child's privacy and online safety.[11] The COPPA rule gives parents the right to know what information has been collected about their children and the right to have that data deleted. Operators, for their part, are not permitted to collect from children any more data than is necessary for use of the site.

The FTC has outlined methods of obtaining "verifiable parental consent":

- Getting a signed form from the parent via postal mail or facsimile
- Accepting and verifying a credit card number in connection with a transaction
- Taking calls from parents, through a toll-free telephone number staffed by trained personnel
- E-mail accompanied by digital signature[12]

Social Networking App "Path" Settles FTC COPPA Violation Claim for $800,000

Underscoring the seriousness with which the FTC views COPPA violations, the FTC, in February of 2013, announced an $800,000 settlement it had reached with the social networking mobile application, Path. Though the application promised users privacy by default and only a limited collection of user data, according to the FTC, Path broke both of these promises. The FTC's complaint charged that Path had actual knowledge that it was collecting data from about 3,000 kids under the age of 13, without ever obtaining parental consent as required by COPPA.[13]

As the FTC continually warns, be especially careful when it comes to kids!

"PIN THIS": COPYRIGHT AND FAIR USE, THE BASICS

The right to share a work belongs strictly to the owner of a work, whether the work is a song, a blog post, or a photograph. The right of exclusive control of a work is protected, once the work is created, by a legal protection known as a *copyright*. Contrary to popular belief, a work does not need to have a copyright symbol to be copyrighted.

The subject of copyright, the legal privilege of the exclusive right to control a work, boiled over with the arrival on the social scene of Pinterest, a site that primarily invites users to post photographs and other visuals.

Why would everyone be so worried about violating the copyright on a photograph, but not worry as much about the copyright on a blog post? There is a practical reason. A cottage industry exists in which most photos found on the web are owned by an extremely large corporate entity, which this writer guesses makes more money threatening users of its photos with legal action than it does from selling standard licenses for any of its photographs. Photographs tend to be tracked by their owners with a vociferousness rarely shared by authors of posts, who are generally glad to see their works shared with attribution.

The bottom line? If you are going to share the work of another, get their permission, or risk legal action, especially if what you are sharing is a photograph!

U.S. Copyright Office

For a wealth of easy-to-understand information about copyright issues, a visit to the U.S. Copyright Office online is the perfect resource at: www.Copyright.gov. There are links to information on the subject of trademarks as well.

Fair Use

Among one of the most frequently asked questions concerning the issue of copyrighted works, is the question of when can a copyrighted work be used without the copyright owner's permission. Citing *Sections 107–118 of Title 17 of the U.S. Code*, the Copyright Office explains that four factors are to be considered in determining whether or not a particular use is "fair" (i.e., permissible without the copyright owner's permission):

1. The purpose and character of the use, including whether such use is of commercial nature or is for nonprofit educational purposes
2. The nature of the copyrighted work
3. The amount and substantiality of the portion used in relation to the copyrighted work as a whole
4. The effect of the use upon the potential market for, or value of, the copyrighted work.[14]

Copyright Infringement Versus "Fair Use"

Importantly, after outlining the four factors to be considered in determining whether a use is a "fair use," versus an "infringement," the Copyright Office warns:

> The distinction between what is fair use and what is infringement in a particular case will not always be clear or easily defined. There is no specific number of words, lines, or notes that may safely be taken without permission. Acknowledging the source of the copyrighted material does not substitute for obtaining permission.

The Copyright Office offers a better solution than trying to fit a work within the "fair use" privilege, it recommends that you get the copyright holder's permission!

MARKETING ON THE WORLDWIDE WEB REQUIRES COMPLIANCE WITH INTERNATIONAL LAW

In 1995, the European Parliament issued a directive regarding the protection of personal, online data.[15] That directive continues to guide European policy regarding online data protection, and it established a standard of privacy protection that is higher than that mandated in the United States.

The European Parliament's directive on data protection recognized data protection as a "fundamental right" and called upon member nations to protect personal data. This strongly worded directive continues to set a high bar for privacy compliance and creates significant hurdles for those seeking to market to a European audience.

THERE'S AN APP FOR NEARLY EVERYTHING—AND THERE ARE GUIDELINES FOR APPS

According to the FTC, about a thousand new mobile applications (apps) enter the market each day. They raise significant privacy issues and carry equally significant liability issues for those who develop or sponsor them (i.e., the company that causes them to be created), and even for those who simply market them. In February of 2013, the FTC released a report, *Mobile Privacy Disclosures: Building Trust Through Transparency*, that outlined numerous best practices concerning the making, marketing, and use of mobile applications.

Establishing a privacy policy, providing transparency about data collection through disclosures, and care concerning the collection, maintenance, or use of data from children by observance of the *Children's Online Privacy Protection Act, 15 U.S.C. Sec. 6501–6508*, are minimum thresholds for basic protection of consumer data as called for by the FTC in the realm of mobile applications.

STAYING ON THE RIGHT SIDE OF THE LAW IN SOCIAL MEDIA CONTESTS

Social media "contests" are governed both by the "law of the land" and the "law of the social networks." If you get either "law" wrong, it could have substantial consequences to both you and your business, either from the imposition of fines, criminal sanctions by a regulatory authority, or the shutting down of your account by a social network. What follows is simply an overview of some of the issues you need to be aware of when holding a game promotion. Unfortunately, the do's and don'ts are too extensive to be listed here. Beware.

You Must Abide by the "Law of the Networks"

Despite the prevalence of social media contests, the rules that go along with such sponsored promotions can be rather complicated. Know that each social network gets to set its own rules concerning social media contests, and that a violation of those rules can result in a suspension of your account without a process of appeal. Consider which social platforms you plan to use, then carefully study their rules. (Contrary to what you might commonly see, "liking" an account is not permitted by Facebook to be part of a contest, just as "retweeting to win" is not permitted by Twitter.)

You Must Abide by the "Law of the Land"

Once you've nailed down the latest rules posted by the social network of your choice concerning how a social media contest must be run in connection with their platform, considering the "law of the land" becomes the next hurdle.

For all states, clarity and accessibility of promotion rules are a must

For all states, your rules must be clear and accessible from where you advertise the promotion. State the eligibility and geographic scope of your contest, who and where the sponsor is, when the start/end dates are, and how to find out the winners. Get confirmation from the participants that they have complied with the rules, have submitted only original works, given permission to use their name, likeness and works, and provided necessary information for payment of taxes on prizes over $500.[16] Keep a record of winners for at least four years (durations vary for states).

Three states require registration: Rhode Island, Florida, and New York

Rhode Island, Florida, New York, and each require registration of contests that are targeted to their residents. Rhode Island's registration is triggered where the total retail value of prizes exceeds $500, while Florida and New York's registrations are triggered when the total value of prizes exceeds $5,000. New York's registration must be submitted 30 days before the start of the promotion, and Florida's, 7. Both New York and Florida require bonding for the value of the promised prizes.

Not All Contests Are Created Equal: Lottery, "Contest", Sweepstake

There are three types of sponsored game promotions, one that is unlawful for you to hold, a *lottery*, and two others, a *contest* and a *sweepstake*, that you may be permitted to hold, depending on your strict compliance with various requirements. This section will explore the elements of each broadly. Know that it is always advisable to seek the counsel of a lawyer anytime you have questions about a legal matter, especially when the issues are complicated, as with online, sponsored games.

Lotteries

Unless you are the government or have been specifically licensed by the government, you cannot hold a lottery, as it is generally deemed to be unlawful gambling. A lottery has three elements:

1. **Consideration:** *Consideration* is a legal term meaning something of value; it does not have to be money, and can even be something as seemingly innocuous as filling out a marketing survey. Beware!
2. **Chance:** A winner selected by pure luck, without any consideration to skill.
3. **Prize:** Something of value.

As you prepare to hold a contest or sweepstake, carefully consider the three elements that make up a lottery and be sure that you have eliminated one of them.

Contests = A Competition Based on Skill + A Prize (Consideration, i.e., something of value, may or may not be required)

Contests are defined as a competition based on skill where usually the winner receives a prize (consideration; i.e., something of value). The important point in a competition is to be sure that the winners are judged on skill, with objective criteria, by judges who have credentials to assess the skill that decides the winners. Have a back-up plan for addressing any irregularities because the competition must go on; you can't decide your winner on a coin toss or any factor of chance because you have detected problems with your entries. Your rules must address such contingencies or you could find yourself hosting an illegal lottery or being sued by contestants for a mid-contest rule change. It is also important to state the number of rounds to get to a winner.

A quick warning on community voting: A community vote could well be deemed by a court to lack objective criteria and also cause you to run afoul of the law. Stick with credentialed judges deciding the winners!

Sweepstakes: A game of chance with a prize *AND NO FEE OR PURCHASE NECESSARY!*

Just as I titled this section with the words capitalized and in bold, "NO FEE OR PURCHASE NECESSARY," you should include similar language at the beginning of your rules—and be sure that you mean it! Asking entrants to do something small, whether it's filling out a survey or paying "handling" fees could get your sweepstake judged an unlawful lottery.

To lessen the chance of having an unlawful lottery, include an alternative mode of entry (AMOE) that should be prominently discussed in your rules, not buried, and make it clear that using the AMOE provides entrants with the same chances of winning as if they had entered using the other defined method of entry. The AMOE should look to further exclude any actions or things that could possibly been deemed to be "consideration" (i.e., something of value).

DIGITAL MARKETING COMPLIANCE IN HIGHLY-REGULATED INDUSTRIES

If you happen to work within a highly regulated industry, such as pharmaceuticals or finance, you likely already follow the regulations of your primary regulatory agency, whether it is the FDA, FINRA, or any other acronym-known authority. You must also carefully mind the guidance, to the extent it exists, of that authority within the social space. Do not overlook, however, the guidance of the FTC, as the FTC has made it clear on multiple occasions that it has overlapping authority when it comes to marketing and privacy.

TRENDS AND THE FUTURE OF DIGITAL MARKETING LAW

The good news? Regulatory authorities are beginning to "get" social media and provide clearer guidance on the subject. The bad news? If your business ignores the regulatory guidance and laws that are evolving in the social space, your business will face the prospects of even greater sanctions for any missteps. Keeping transparency as your guide and being mindful of the issues reviewed in this chapter should help you minimize the legal risks of being social. When in doubt, however, check with a lawyer!

ENDNOTES

1. *NLRB Report: Acting General Counsel issues second social media report*, January 25, 2012
2. See, *In the Matter of Facebook, Inc., FTC File No. 092–3184, Agreement Containing Consent Order.*
3. http://www.ftc.gov/os/2009/10/091005revisedendorsementguides.pdf
4. http://ftc.gov/os/2009/10/091005revisedendorsementguides.pdf
5. See *AnnTaylor Stores Corp., File no. 102–3147, FTC Closing Letter*
6. CAP Code http://www.cap.org.uk/Advertising-Codes/Non-Broadcast/CAP-Code/CAP-Code-Item.aspx?q=CAP%20Code%20new_General%20Sections_02%20Recognition%20of%20marketing%20communications_Rules#c49
7. *Complaint Ref:* A12–183247. ASA Adjudication on Nike (UK) Ltd. http://www.asa.org.uk/Rulings/Adjudications/2012/6/Nike-(UK)-Ltd/SHP_ADJ_183247.aspx
8. ASA Adjudication on Nike (UK) Ltd. http://www.asa.org.uk/Rulings/Adjudications/2012/6/Nike-(UK)-Ltd/SHP_ADJ_183247.aspx
9. FTC Release, 03/26/2012, FTC Issues Final Commission Report on Protecting Consumer Privacy: Agency Calls on Companies to Adopt Best Privacy Practices

10. In the Matter of Facebook, Inc., a corporation, FTC File No. 092 3184. http://www.ftc.gov/os/caselist/0923184/111129facebookagree.pdf
11. 16 CFR Part 312, Children's Online Privacy Protection Rule; Final Rule 16 CFR Part 312. http://www.ftc.gov/os/1999/10/64fr59888.htm
12. *How to Comply with the Children's Online Privacy Protection Rule, FTC guide. A Guide For Business and Parents and Small Entity Compliance Guide* (revised July 2013) http://business.ftc.gov/documents/Complying-with-COPPA-Frequently-Asked-Questions
13. *FTC Path case helps app developers stay on the right, path, FTC Business Center advisory. United States of America v. Path, Inc., Consent Decree and Order for Civil Penalties, Permanent Injunction and Other Relief.*
14. U.S. Copyright Office: Fair Use http://www.copyright.gov/fls/fl102.html
15. *Directive 95/46/EC of the European Parliament and of the Council of 24 October 1995 on the protection of individuals with regard to the processing of personal data and on the free movement of such data Official Journal L 281, 23/11/1995 P. 0031 – 0050*
16. *See IRS Form 1099-Misc.*

PART 3

COMPLETING THE DIGITAL TRANSFORMATION

CHAPTER 11

DIGITAL LEADERSHIP PRINCIPLES

—by Bob Pearson

HOW WE DIGITALLY TRANSFORM OURSELVES AND OUR ORGANIZATIONS

"The entrepreneur always searches for change, responds to it, and exploits it as an opportunity."

— Peter F. Drucker

I have to admit I was stunned when I realized who my biggest competitor had been for many years. It was a competitor that I knew quite well. It was me.

It made me feel a bit ashamed for a few minutes, since I realized how much time I must have wasted over the years. But then I started to realize that it was, in many respects, the greatest gift I could receive on a business level.

Once we realize that innovation occurs more strategically and more rapidly when we unlock ourselves, rather than counting on others, our impact on an organization can be transformational, or game-changing, or whatever phrase you want to pick. You get the point.

Think about how we act now inside our organizations. We are all excellent at explaining why we don't have enough resources, or senior level commitment, or something else that prevents us from innovating. It's not us. It's someone else who is preventing us from achieving our goals.

When we do decide to innovate, we often anticipate what our organization can handle in terms of change, so we introduce new ideas at the pace that our colleagues will accept. We are taught to not surprise people—to ensure that all levels of management are informed before we move on to something new. Basically, we have a system in place that makes it very hard to innovate.

We've become experts over the years at how to not innovate at a pace that will keep up with the marketplace. It's a fact.

And it is a fact that is easily changed.

I've been fortunate to have worked with and spoken with leaders at hundreds of the Fortune 1000 companies in the world on the subject of digital innovation over the last seven years. I've also had the opportunity to build the Fortune 500's first global social media function with a great team at Dell back in 2006.

It's funny how we approach innovation sometimes.

We have a tendency, when we want to learn, to absorb ourselves in data, slides, and meetings. In the case of digital, we memorize the pace of device growth by market, or we contemplate a net promoter=score change of 2 percent month-over-month, or we form committees to explore what is next.

I used to do this until I realized that this was unrelated to innovating in a manner that can create unique competitive advantage for a company.

So the digital principles I will share, that will help you transform yourself and your company, involve about five million frequent flyer miles and hundreds of meetings with innovative leaders—leaders who desire to innovate throughout the world. All I can tell you is that these principles are rooted in success and are related to effectively changing. This chapter presents what I have found to be important across more than 25 years of practice.

ADDRESS THE LARGEST BARRIER TO INNOVATION FIRST

If you look in the mirror, you'll see what I saw. You are your own largest barrier to innovation.

I'll never forget when I asked Michael Dell if he was ok if I developed a customer response policy for the company, in terms of how we respond to customers with an issue online. He agreed this was important and I rounded up the key leaders to develop the new policy. In my mind, if we could agree on a policy where we responded within 24 hours of the complaint, we would be in great shape, since I was worried about waiting days to respond.

We finished the policy and I e-mailed it to Michael for a last review before we announced it internally. Without giving me a chance to get a cup of coffee, my phone rang. It was Michael, and he said that the 24-hour response policy looked good. He thanked me for the effort and I felt pretty proud of myself. But then in typical Michael style, he said "But you did make one typo." I was surprised, and said, "Where did I make a typo?" His answer said it all. "You missed a period between the 2 and the 4."

I laughed and then I cringed. He was right. His point to me was that I should have started at zero and worked my way from the optimal scenario. Instead, I had thought of what the organization could handle and then tried to make that happen.

I was my own barrier to innovation.

When I reflected on past innovations I was involved in, I started to realize that I was not fully unlocking what I was capable of doing. Right then and there, I resolved "never again."

Think about your own organization. We are very creative in how we create barriers to change. Do any of these examples sound familiar to you?

"That's a great idea. Let's benchmark the industry first and then see where it takes us."

"Excellent work. Let's form a committee of xyz and see what it tells us."

"Love it. Just don't have any budget. Let's readdress what we can do next quarter."

"Great initiative. Thank you (no follow-up described)."

"We came to a similar conclusion a few years ago."

(No follow-up intended.)

Leaders who have yet to develop transformational innovation skills are expert at *almost* getting things done. They *almost* take chances. They *almost* reallocate resources. But they *never* do it in time with the market.

We have developed a term for people like this. We call them "antibodies." Keep in mind that everyone of us is an antibody at some point in time. If you think you have never been one, your mind is not open enough to innovate.

Here's a test for you to implement next week: Invite a multi-function team to a one-hour meeting that you call the "Digital Innovation Meeting." Outline the rules for the meeting, which you will now hold every month. Members cannot discuss the past. They cannot discuss the present. They can only discuss the future and describe how an innovation will work at your company. They cannot describe how it *will not* work. They can only describe how it *will* work.

I've done this with much success. It is amazing to see for yourself how often we rely on the past to get our way; or how often people are lost in the moment and only want to describe what they are doing right now. It is actually hard to hold the conversation for the first few meetings.

We have to force ourselves to think outside the box. We have to make it easier to do so as a team; and the only way to really do this well is to practice.

The world's best soccer players practice continually, no matter how good they have become.

The world's best leaders practice innovating every day.

Malcolm Gladwell has eloquently told us that we need to do things 10,000 times, or put in 10,000 hours, to become an expert in a given area.[1] How will you get to 10,000?

Let me summarize this section with six ways you can improve your own personal innovation:

1. *Change what you read.* Take 10 minutes, think about how you consume content each day, and change it. Start reading techmeme.com or go to CIO.com—even if you are not a CIO—to learn about technology trends. Read *Internet Retailer* to learn about social commerce. Figure out which mobile publications fit your needs. Change it up. Don't just read about your industry. You already know your industry. Make sure 50 percent of your reading is new.
2. *Embrace the antibody concept.* Make it acceptable to call people out for being an antibody. Have fun with it. Improve the habits of your team, as a result.
3. *Create a forum to innovate out loud as a team.* Make it ok to ask questions, learn together, and not always be right. You'll be surprised at how many ideas are inside your employees' heads that you never knew existed. Start with yourself. If you show you are open to learning and you don't know everything, it becomes ok if your employees don't know everything either.
4. *Sponsor small, inexpensive pilots to test new concepts.* Take an idea now, and test it. Don't set up a perfect pilot. If you do, it will be dead on arrival. Let your team try new things on their own with minimal guidance. Let innovation continue outside the room. Don't innovate in the room and then put the perfect pilot clamps on the project. That squelches what you might create.
5. *Embrace the work and succeed fast or fail fast.* We often learn more from failures. Both outcomes are fine. The key is we learn from each and share those lessons. Remember that a great baseball player gets out seven of ten times. Steve Jobs didn't succeed wildly with every project. Neither will you. If you haven't failed recently, you are holding back value from your team and your organization.
6. Determine *what you're chasing.* Innovation works best when it creates something or solves something. Decide up front what it is. On February 11, 2000, David Neeleman launched JetBlue. What was he chasing? Simple. Neeleman was intent on answering the question, "How can we make people smile again when traveling?"

THE IMPORTANCE OF FORWARD-LEANING LEARNING

Our online world is going through amazing change. Since 2006, when I started tracking specific statistics related to change, an average of 325,000 people go online every day for the first time in their lives. That is about 900 million new people who have arrived online with new search habits, new preferences for the device of choice (phone vs. tablet vs. PC), new e-commerce needs, and new influencers they count on for advice.

We've never had marketplace change this fast in the history of the world. And this is what has led me to the realization that forward-leaning learning is most important for leaders to innovate in digital.

Entrepreneurs create new ideas that lead to companies by deeply learning how a marketplace is working. They either spot a flaw or an unmet need, and they are onto the next new brand, service, or company.

Steve Jobs is a great example. He didn't technically write the code or invent new technology. Rather, he was so forward-leaning that he saw trends before we did and had the vision to put together new products that we wanted—even though we didn't ask for them.

Leaders who innovate in digital for their organizations are forward-leaning. They intensely learn their marketplace, constantly consume new information, speak to everyone who has an idea, and before you know it, the new way to go becomes obvious.

In my book, *Pre-Commerce*, I interviewed more than 30 leaders, ranging from Sona Chawla, president of Walgreens.com, to Marc Benioff, founder and CEO of Salesforce.com. What they all had in common was an intense desire to learn, a tremendous gut feel for their marketplace, a willingness to change plans based on customer insights, and an ability to go right around antibodies that put up barriers. No one gets in the way of their innovation.

For today's leader in an organization, what do you do to become more forward-leaning?

Well, one of the best ways is to toss out your case studies and start studying the next practices that matter for your industry.

Case studies focus on the past. They are always out of date. They are always wonderfully successful. And they are often used to further one's career. Not much innovation comes out of self-promotion.

Next practices involve analyzing who is succeeding in the areas that you care about inside your company, or (more commonly) outside of it. You study how they are doing well, and you spend an equal amount of time on how they are failing. You focus on the learning's that you can apply today in your business.

There are two related points for next practices: (1) When you review your internal work, remember to catalogue what worked and what did not work. Ensure that your internal reviews lead to positive criticism on how to improve. And, (2) when you are looking to study next practices, realize that no one company does it all well. In fact, you have to figure out what you want, and then study a wide range of companies. For example:

Intuit is excellent at customer-driven community forums.
Starbucks does a great job gathering and acting on customer ideas.
Google Labs is constantly innovating with relation to search and paid media.
Hershey knows how to build communities on Facebook.

The key with next practices is that you outline what you want to learn about, develop the list of specific brands you want to follow, and then proactively track their progress. This way, you can learn about a next practice before it is memorialized for the rest of the company to learn about.

At our firm today, based on this approach, we have anywhere from 10 to 20 emerging ideas at any one time that we are looking at bringing to the market. Every one of them has the potential to build competitive advantage for our clients.

HOW TO UNDERGO TRANSFORMATIONAL CHANGE IN YOUR COMPANY

It is fine if you are improving processes, systems, or skills related to digital innovation. That's great. Just keep in mind that where you need to move from is *process* change to *transformational* change.

With transformational change, you are challenging the current business model in a rapidly changing marketplace. Your evolving mindset requires a strategic view, clarity on organizing principles and how you behave, and a culture that embraces forward-leaning innovators.

When I say this, it sounds like a lot. It can sound like it is impossible. It's not, of course, if we break down transformational change into key steps you can make in your organization over time.

Here are five key ways to transform. Be sure to also see the digital transformation framework presented in Chapter 13, which builds on these concepts.

1. *Intellectually scale your models.* An organization needs to know what the code words are. They must understand the official way to do something. We all want this type of information, yet we often complain about it when we receive it. It is because we often dump information on our employees, rather than intellectually scaling our models and approach to a market. For example, in the digital arena, what is the company approach to how you identify influencers who drive share of conversation (see Figure 11.1)? What is your definition of share of conversation? How do you measure results so you know if you are actually shaping behavior that will lead to sales?

   When employees understand the logic of why you have chosen a certain model or have embraced specific metrics, they will adopt this behavior themselves. We intellectually accept change when we comprehend the context. We reject change when we don't or it is forced upon us. See Figure 11.2. We grew up with the four P's of marketing—price, product, place, promotion. These are still important, but now that we live in a digital world, it is critical that we measure how passion is catalyzed in the market and how the most important customers share content with their ecosystem. The 4A model measures both conversational and behavioral analytics to understand if a campaign or topic is successfully reaching its audience. And behind the model, you know exactly who is driving the positive or negative share of the conversation. No more guessing in today's world.

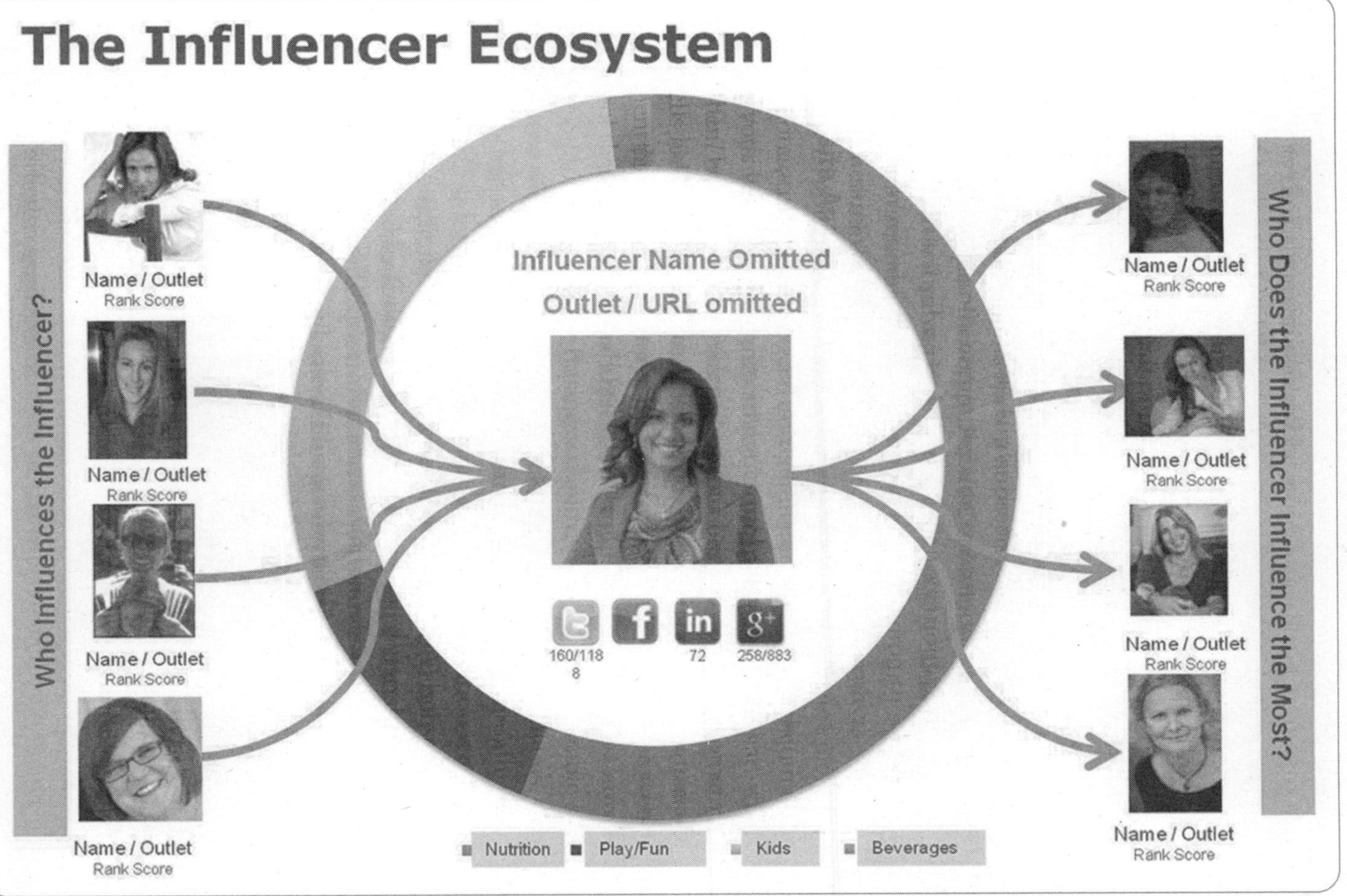

FIGURE 11.1 The Influencer Ecosystem: Understanding influencers, and their impact on your community, is crucial to effective digital strategy.

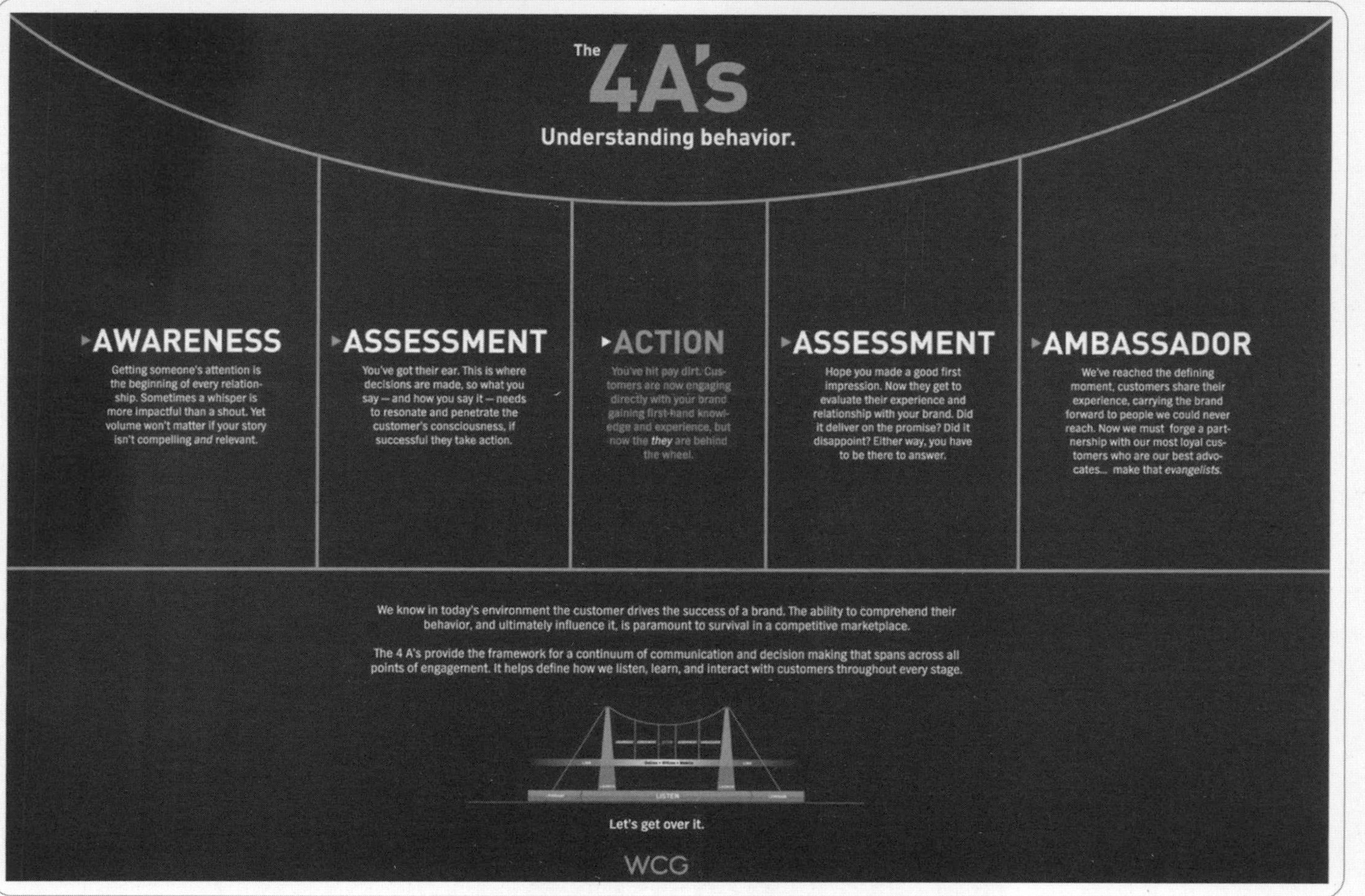

FIGURE 11.2 The 4A Model: The 4A's provide a framework for a continuum of communication and decision-making that spans across all points of engagement.

2. *Use training to embed intellectual scaling.* Too often, a training program is either nonexistent or it is done by a dedicated part of your organization, so the opportunity to embed your models and thinking into the larger company is missed. If training enables your leaders to hear about models and metrics, question them, learn from examples, and then determine how they will pragmatically use them when they return home, you are on the right track. Said another way, a disconnect between your models and your training is unacceptable.
3. *Open up your "organizational brain."* Think about how you can use technology to improve your organization and teach your colleagues new ways to do business. Two great examples relate to idea communities and predictive questioning. If you put in place an idea community for your team, division, or company, they can tell you what matters most via peer voting and commenting. The most important ideas will rise to the top. Some excellent ideas that don't gain traction, yet have high potential, will be towards the bottom. You have just opened up the *organizational brain* of your company. To go a step further, you can use predictive questioning via software from companies, like Consensus Point. Imagine asking 300 sales reps what the price of a new product should be when it launches in six months. Most likely, their responses will be more accurate than the results of your traditional research.
4. *Walk the talk.* Are you sponsoring digital innovation initiatives in your company? If you are, you are walking the talk. Are you personally participating in social media? If you are, you are walking the talk. If you are not, you're an antibody, since your actions are telling your team that you might talk about digital opportunities as important, but its not really important.
5. *Talk the talk.* Scientists and researchers publish and present at meetings all of the time. They find it to be the best way to share innovation, learn from their peers, pick up new ideas and continue to iteratively innovate. It's no different for digital innovation. You need to talk inside your

company about what is new and why it might matter—and you need to do the same outside of your company. Thought leadership, innovation, and transformational change are cousins. There aren't many successful innovators who have decided not to hop on the public stage to share and learn. Remember, you'll get back more than you give in terms of new ideas. This is not an ego thing.

Ok, so you are now thinking about how you will transform yourself and your organization. If you're like me, you're wondering, "How will I know I am on the right track?" It's a legitimate question when you are pioneering new territory.

Whether I was meeting with P&G for their digital advisory board or partnering with Intel on new ideas, I would always keep thinking about what traits are most important for success? Years later, I've seen up close how dozens of leading companies make a positive change in how they approach online challenges. You learn a lot when you can take the time to listen and observe.

TEN TRAITS OF DIGITAL LEADERSHIP

When we develop new analytics models for our clients, we like to mention that human beings follow very predictable patterns. We often don't know what they are, but once we do, it is easy to figure out how to succeed. Interestingly enough, this same idea applies to how we lead digitally. When we are successful in making a difference at our company, what we do is not all that different than our peers at the company across the street.

We are all doing the same thing, in a sense. We want to help a group of human beings, our colleagues, move in a certain direction to improve the company. We often make it more complex than this, but it really isn't.

And this leads to the key question. What is it that leaders do well to transform their organizations digitally? After years of thinking about this and, more importantly, watching dozens of the leading companies in the world in action, I can say that this top ten list has only been reinforced in importance:

1. *Transform your company, not a department.* If a department becomes savvy in the digital arena, but the rest of the company is not, we have a problem. This is why I always say that the leaders of a company must embrace digital innovation. It's not an option. If a company is willing to transform, it will. Part of this success is to form a Center of Excellence that truly serves the entire company and is fully integrated with divisions and regions.
2. *Think of all current models as old school.* Media relations, paid search, community management, keyword analysis, editorial content, advertising—think of every area of your company and just say to yourself, "The model we use today is old school. I am going to determine how to evolve this model." Then, you move. Whether it is how you recruit new employees or how you protect your reputation, what worked a few years ago is old school. With our ability to understand what is happening online, we can develop new insights, new ways to share content, understand exactly which words drive behavior, and know the priority order of influencers who matter to our brand. Many of us like the show Mad Men. We're in the midst of creating a new show. Not sure what the name should be yet, but it sure ain't Mad Men.
3. *Centralize strategy, decentralize execution.* Your Center of Excellence team can build out the official models and the way to operate. This is all part of intellectual scaling. They can build out your digital roadmap, ensure it is integrated with the IT roadmap, and much more. But there is a limit. Headquarters can centralize strategy. The local countries, divisions, and brands execute. They are the ones who implement, learn, and shoot back their learning's to the Center so we can all improve together. Decentralizing innovation, by the way, leads to chaos. Your organization won't scale in how it is learning and you will fall way behind your competitors who work as a streamlined team.
4. *Realize your consultants are learning too.* Let's say that you successfully build a Center of Excellence. You have your

own digital models, and intellectual scaling is going great. Congrats! Just one more thing. Your partner agencies are also learning, and if you don't include them, you will end up rapidly innovating and they will be selling you yesterday's solutions. The divide will only grow. The key here is that agencies also need to be willing to admit they are learning. Consultants really don't know everything. They just sometimes say they do. Learn from the leaders and teach your agencies, in real-time, as a team.

5. *Learn how to fail fast.* Always tell corporate leaders that they are great at succeeding fast, but not at failing fast. The room always breaks out into smiles. We all know we need to change here. What we need to do, in our minds, is realize a very simple principle. Pilots are meant to provide learning so our next project benefits. Pilots are not meant to succeed 100 percent of the time. If they do, they aren't pilots.

   My experience is that you need to provide minimal guidance, and let your team innovate. If you overly prescribe exactly how to do it, and put pressure on the team that upper management has their eyes on it, it probably won't achieve the desired results. One of my favorite innovations was the creation of www.ideastorm.com at Dell. We didn't tell the world we were going to do it. A handful of us quietly built the plan, then the site, and then we launched it. Was it exhausting? You bet. Did it work? It did—and we learned a lot.

6. *Focus on ROI from the beginning.* The digital world is also a quantitatively based world. We can track all we do. I like to remind leaders that we should never guess. We need to set up the ROI we expect, and then identify the metrics that get us as close as possible to understanding the value of what we are doing and see what it tells us. If a project leader can't tell you what they are measuring and why, they haven't gone far enough yet. And remember, don't accept yesterday's metrics. For example, website visits and page views don't measure success. We want to know how many people recommended our brand, shared our content (and

with whom), and signed up for more information—and much more.

7. *Never guess.* The answers are right in front of us. If your analytics are strong, your insights will be targeted. Ask yourself these questions:

   Do I know the top five questions being asked by our customers right now?

   What are the top 15 keywords that drive the majority of search behavior, and are we using them in all of our content?

   Who are the top 50 influencers who drive the majority share of conversation for our brand?

   What time of day is the peak time for content consumption by our target audience each day of the week?

   When we build our audience for a channel, e.g., Twitter, are we following the exact people who are aligned with our interests?

   You get the point. Precision is available. If you are guessing what is being said in the market about your brand (or a specific issue) right now as you read this, you're behind. It's time to catch up.

8. *Innovators will drive change. Find them.* Your most successful team members may not report to you. But who cares? My own personal experience is that this is irrelevant. Identify who wants to innovate and, more importantly, who has the passion and mindset you need, and empower them tomorrow. Never look back. The rest of your team will eventually catch up to them.

9. *Antibodies protect yesterday's models at all costs.* Watch out for antibodies. Unfortunately, these antibodies often have power within the organization. And they will do all they can to protect the models of yesteryear. Old regimes falter and fail. We see it happen time and time again around the world. Regimes inside your company will suffer the same fate with time. My advice is to help these folks learn how to change. Generally, they are willing to change once they realize the business value.

This requires a brief moment on why some senior leaders are resistant. I am finding that it is related to three simple issues: (1) They are super busy and believe they don't have time to learn new models. (2) They feel responsible for reaching the company's financial goals and don't want to decrease their chances by innovating. And, (3) they are looking after their personal interests, because if they make today's goals, they get their bonus. In some respects, they don't care about the future. That is someone else's problem.

This is why it is critical for the leaders of an organization to lead by example and make it clear, and acceptable, that digital innovation will occur to improve the short-, mid-, and long-term value of the organization. I remember presenting to Lee Scott, then CEO of Walmart, and his top 75 managers in Bentonville towards the end of 2008. During my talk, Lee stood up and asked if he could speak. He then said to his team that it was time for Walmart to become excellent in social media and how to utilize it to build value for its customers. I have to admit I've never seen more note-taking when I have given a talk then after Lee stood up.

Suffice it to say, Walmart is now considered a leader in online retail and has built an industry-leading team since then. They decided to lead.

10. *Become a student of the digital world.* We grew up learning. We went to school for 13 years, then college for 4 years, and some of us continued in graduate schools for even longer. We know how to learn, yet once we get our jobs, we seem to lock in to learning that is very rote. We keep up with the industry we are in and we attend the mandatory classes given by our company. If we are lucky, we go to special seminars or industry meetings now and then.

For some reason, we have stopped learning at the same pace that made us into who we are.

It is time for us to turn that switch back on and become students of the digital world. When you do, you learn new things. You realize that 10 languages reach 82 percent of people in the world online. You can see that understanding which smartphone apps are of highest value is more relevant than knowing how many smartphones are sold. You start realizing that forensic analytics can develop advantage for you if you learn how to do it well—perhaps substituting for the primary research you are heavily invested in today. You will reprogram yourself on how to think differently and your organization and your career will benefit.

In the spirit of the journey, you will embrace the changing digital landscape as a student, and as a leader who will transform your organization. Thus, I'll leave with you these thoughts on future trends that are in the process of changing how we do business. Each ends with a question for you.

- *C2C will replace B2B or B2C as the most important model to reach consumers.* On its face, it is rather obvious. Peers look to fellow peers for purchase decisions. We count heavily on our friends to inform us on what to do next. The next generation of successful brands will become a relevant peer of their customer communities and empower customers to work with other customers directly. *How will our approach to customers change?*
- *Storytizing, the subject of my next book, will replace advertising as top dog for media.* Advertising interrupts us, gains our attention, and then quickly tells us something, hopefully intriguing us enough to click or call or visit for more information. Storytizing will deliver the entire brand's story (ad, slides, FAQs, reviews, and more) directly to the customer where they hang out, with the information they prefer to get. Paid media will become the supporting actor to earned, owned, and shared media. *How will we optimize our media spend and plan?*
- *Forensic analytics will require us to think more like detectives.* If we become excellent at understanding what our customers are doing online, we are swimming in a world of clues. Which clues matter, what do they tell us, and how do we gain advantage via these insights? We will become detectives. *How do we develop clues today?*

- *Psychology, physics, statistics, and economic models will enable us to think outside the box in the world of marketing.* We too often rely on past models for answers to future questions. This will change as we realize that we can determine conversation elasticity for a brand, if we model it against pricing elasticity. Or, if we know the 4,500 adjectives that matter the most in the English language, we can see how we are shaping behavior more effectively, since we will understand how behavior is changing based on word choice (and before an open declaration). Or we'll look at the mass, force, and velocity of our content to better understand what we should provide to our customers. *What models do we use today and what do I really know about them?*
- *Customer service will become a profit center.* This will occur as we realize how we can connect the answering of a question online with the connection to related products. After all, more than 90 percent of a company's customers never call or inquire in a given year. We need to improve how we reach our customers who have an issue. *How will the customer experience change?*
- *Social CRM will revolve more about how we build the right audience in the social cloud.* Nothing against databases, but we don't need them as much if we can identify who is likely to enjoy our brand, outreach to them with highly specific information in a relevant way, and form a two-way bond that goes across the social channels they care about. Notice how I didn't mention websites here. They are just one more channel. *Where are our customers online and how do we know we are meeting their needs today?*

The list could go on, but you get the point.

We are just beginning to understand the value of digital innovation to our organizations, brands, and services. This is why it is so critical for us to ensure that we transform all three, plus our agencies and ourselves, to succeed in this journey.

It all starts with us—being honest about how we view things, and whether we are up for challenging the existing order. Rather than pursue incremental growth or a feel-good existence, we need to learn from Alan Mulally, who, when joining Ford as CEO, canvassed the entire organization and posed the one question needed to catalyze the company's future–"Are we building the right products?"

The question cut right through the very heart of the business and bypassed the myriad symptoms being faced by the problems the company created. It opened up new thinking and innovation that led to an array of fresh, technology-rich, and environmentally sound products.

Take a look in the mirror . . . what do you see?

ENDNOTES

1. http://en.wikipedia.org/wiki/Outliers_(book)

CHAPTER 12

DESIGNING ORGANIZATIONS FOR DIGITAL SUCCESS

—by Amy Kates

INTRODUCTION

The introduction of digital products, services, channels, and interfaces over the past 15 years has posed a challenge for leaders of traditional companies considering how best to design their organizations. Digital technology introduces a dimension of the organization that rarely stands on its own; it must be linked and integrated into the other parts of the company.

Consider these scenarios:

At *Scottrade*, a pioneer of online consumer securities trading, the product is a digital platform. Should it be owned internally by the IT organization or by the marketing function? What is the best design for the product development process, given that it spans both these arenas?

The Keurig unit at Green Mountain Coffee Roasters sells brewers from its Keurig.com site as well as the single serve "K-Cups®" used in the brewers. The site is also an important brand-building component of the firm's marketing strategy. Should the e-commerce channel be managed by marketing, as a brand, or by sales, as a distribution channel?

Levi Strauss & Co. sells clothing around the world through large retailers, its own branded retail stores, and direct to consumers through its Levi.com site. How does it successfully create an omni-channel strategy that avoids internal competition and cannibalization of sales?

LexisNexis Risk Solutions aggregates public data and sells it back to the government and to other businesses. The company adds value to this information by making connections between discrete data points to improve everything from the tracking of tax fraud to the targeting of marketing campaigns against microdemographic segments. When your product is information, how do you design your "factory"?

We will examine these dilemmas through the lens of organization design—the process of configuring a company's resources to execute on a given strategy. Through this lens, we'll highlight ways that traditional organizations can harness the inherent tensions that the new organizational dimension of digital content and delivery introduces into productive new capabilities.

WHAT DO WE MEAN BY "DIGITAL"?

Digital technology, which transformed the media industry, is now transforming many other industries. As the examples above illustrate, the definition of *digital* differs by company.

Our definition here is broad. Scott Brinker, a marketing technologist, makes a helpful distinction between types of digital technologies. *Internal technologies* include analytics, search engine optimization, competitive intelligence, and social media monitoring. *External technologies* consist of the platforms used to reach customers and deliver content—website, ads, landing pages, e-mail campaigns, and apps of all kinds. *Product technology* includes social sharing features, GPS, RFID, and all forms of connectivity.[1] All of these are digital and none fit neatly in the traditional domains of marketing, product development, or information technology (IT) functions.

Our focus here is not on the digital natives—companies founded on the premise of an interactive experience such as Amazon, Google, or LinkedIn. Rather, our focus is on well-established companies that are adding digital offerings such as analytics, mobility, social media, and smart-embedded devices into their core businesses. Many of these companies are already pursuing complex strategies with multidimensional organizations comprised of a matrix of product lines, customer segments, regions, and functions. Jay Galbraith suggests that digital technology, and particularly its manifestation as big data analytics, will become a fifth strategic dimension needing to be accounted for in many companies.[2] More and more firms will need to find a way to integrate this capability into their existing business models.

In addition to the digital natives, many established firms are well on their way to fully integrating technology into all aspects of their business. UPS describes itself as a technology company that delivers packages. The Warner Music Group is still in the business of promoting artists, but digital technology is no longer just another distribution channel; it is fast becoming the only channel. For companies like these, the technology and the product are on their way to becoming almost inseparable.

Plenty of companies, however, use digital content and delivery as an adjunct to a core business. Digital technologies are used to create user and consumer communities, provide brand building and e-commerce channels, or embed differentiating product features into their core offerings. For example, John Deere adds technology to its vehicles that can use real-time weather and GPS data to determine when best to sow seeds. Welch Allyn, a 90-year old medical-device maker, hired a software executive out of Silicon Valley to be its most recent CEO. The company is developing a software platform that doctors can use to connect all of their frontline diagnostic equipment. Temperature, heart rate, blood pressure, and other readings are now fed directly into a medical record.

We observe the biggest organizational tensions occuring in companies where digital considerations are an adjunct to the core business. Managers struggle with the questions of whether digital work should be centralized or decentralized. Who should manage digital strategy and where should it sit in the business? How should it be linked to other functions and operating units? Who governs investment decisions and priorities? How is success measured—is it overhead cost or a profit and loss center? How is the talent profile different than for traditional marketing and technology staff?

These questions are best considered in the context of a framework for organization design.

THE STAR™ MODEL FOR ORGANIZATION DESIGN

Organization design is the art and science of aligning structure (power), lateral connections (linkage), metrics, and people practices to achieve a given strategy. Each company, even those in the same industry with similar products or customers, will have a unique organizational configuration. The design of your company needs to reflect your particular formula for success. The right alignment of components provides a source of competitive advantage, as it ensures that your organization is purpose-fit for your particular context.

A useful model for thinking about organization design is Jay Galbraith's Star Model, shown in Figure 12.1, which has served as the core framework for organization alignment for complex and global companies for nearly 30 years.

As with all good models, the power of the Star Model is in its apparent simplicity. Successful organizations start with answers to basic strategy questions—what are we trying to achieve, what is our unique position in the marketplace, what capabilities differentiate us from competitors and are hard to copy?

The organization can then be seen as a mechanism of strategy execution. A leader should not have a goal of getting the organization "right"; rather, the goal should be an organization that aligns the energy and talents of the firm toward achieving the strategic goals. When the strategy or environment changes,

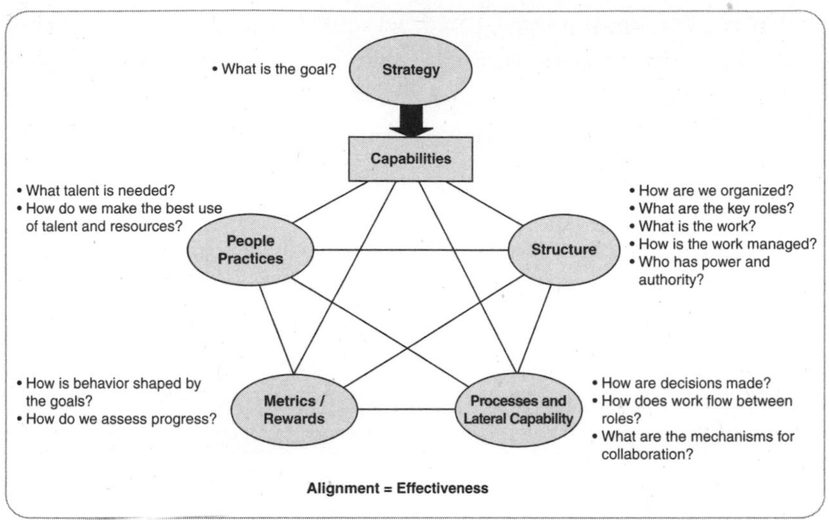

FIGURE 12.1 The STAR™ Model: Jay Galbraith's model ensures a holistic perspective on organization design.

or the company outgrows its organization, then the organization configuration must change and evolve to get the new work done.

Capabilities are the elements of the strategy that differentiate and are hard for competitors to copy. They represent the "organizational muscle" that is built through deliberate management attention and practice. For digital technologies, a capability might be "turning customer and operational data into insights that feed the product development process." Another might be "creating an engaged and loyal consumer community." A third could be to "turn data and insights into a monetized service offering."

Structure, lateral connections, metrics, and people practices—these encompass the tangible decisions that a leader can make to create the right conditions for building needed capabilities. Culture, behaviors, and performance are all outcomes of organization design. They are identified as part of the strategy work. The other four elements then are configured to make it easy for employees to come to work and create the culture and business performance that you want.

Our research reveals a set of questions that leaders in more traditional companies seeking to build digital capability should consider. The answers presented here are based on our consulting work, in-depth interviews with marketing and technology leaders across a range of industries, and a review of major studies recently conducted by MIT, econsultancy.com, and others examining this topic. For further resources, please see the suggested reading list at the end of this chapter.

In the next section, we will review the design questions associated with each of the points in Jay Galbraith's Star Model.

ASKING THE RIGHT QUESTIONS IN DIGITAL ORGANIZATION DESIGN

Structure Design

As much as the popular business press would like us to believe that we are past the time of structures and hierarchies in organizations, the question of how to group resources and allocate decision authority has not gone away. In fact, as business strategies become more complex and many companies add product lines, customer segments, and geographic markets, the need to organize and coordinate becomes even more important. Structure is just one lever for creating an aligned organization, but it is still an essential one.

Should digital work be managed as a function?

When considering a digital strategy, the first question many leaders face is where should this capability live in the organization and who should "own" it. While digital responsibility can be housed in a number of places successfully, it benefits from strong functional leadership.

As with most new work, digital endeavors tend to start in a fragmented way, with managers in various departments—typically marketing, sales, and technology—recruiting people that have some skills in this area. As activity increases, leaders find they need to consolidate oversight of the digital work in order to afford specialists, ensure everyone is using common tools, and make sure that digital projects are coordinated where they need to be. Consolidating the work into a function with a dedicated leader allows for focus, accountability, and the ability to create common technology platforms and build deep technical skills.

A 2011 survey of almost 200 digital and e-commerce managers across a range of industries confirmed the expected advantages of configuring digital work into a dedicated function:[3]

- **Shared Learning**: Experts and specialists benefit from close connection to colleagues for learning, idea sharing, and mentoring.
- **Consistency and Control**: Oversight of processes, practices, terminology, standards, methodologies, tools, and measures can be provided by a single department.
- **Governance**: This ensures that scare resources are applied to the most important projects.
- **Economies of Scale**: Whether using internal staff or contracting with vendors or partners, a benefit of a function is the ability to afford specialized resources that are available across the enterprise.

These benefits are difficult, if not impossible, to realize if left to employees to self-organize, no matter how well intentioned. Gaining these advantages requires a strong leadership that can connect a digital vision to the business strategy.

What belongs in the center and what should be embedded in the business units?

When a company has multiple business units, customer segments, or geographies, the next question that arises is what activities and decisions should reside in the center (corporate, headquarters), and which should be embedded in the operating units. Many leaders make the mistake of swinging between the extremes of centralization and decentralization, never getting the best of both. We find the concept of *center-led* to be helpful here. Center-led is a granular approach that looks closely at what work and decisions are best made at what level in order to balance the often competing objectives of speed and scale. Figure 12.2 illustrates the concept that the center provides an important role in setting standards and making decisions for a small subset of high-value or high-risk decisions for the enterprise. This might include technology platforms, brand guidelines, and vendor contracts. It might also include shared services for utility functions such as analytics that can be leveraged across the company. The operating units, which tend to be closer to the customer and competing in local and niche markets, are then provided some freedom to make decisions and investments in the people, skills, and work arrangements that make the most sense for them.

Even where digital staff in the operating units have a high degree of autonomy, it is useful for them to have a strong connection back to the central group and to peers in other units to ensure the maintenance of deep functional expertise. This can be accomplished through communities of practice, rotational assignments, shared learning and development activities, and forums for best practice sharing. In this way you gain the benefits of both strong centralized guidance where consistency pays off for the enterprise, and local speed where variability is needed to meet the specific needs of customers.

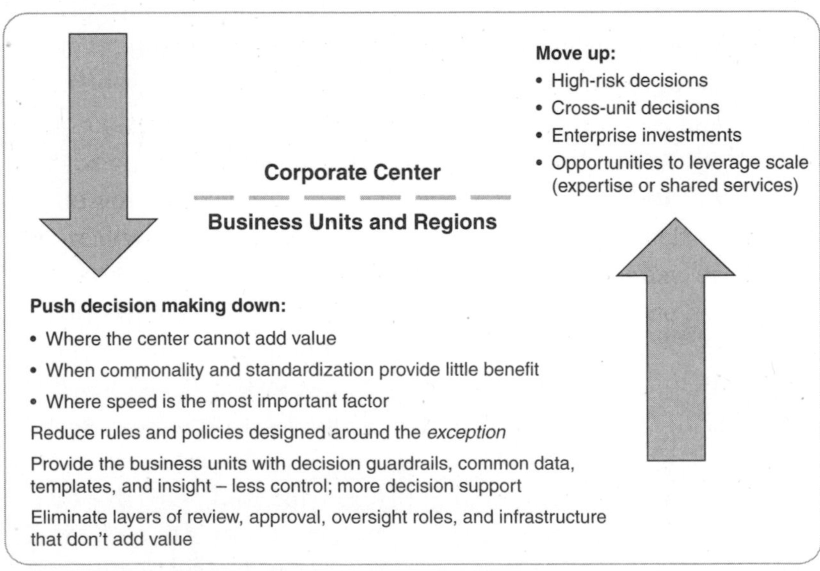

FIGURE 12.2 Using the Center-Led Approach: The center-led approach helps organizations to avoid getting caught in the centralization/decentralization trap.

When should digital work stand alone and when should it be embedded in other parts of the organization?

With the lines between marketing, product development, and technology blurring when it comes to digital work, a case can be made for many places for the function to sit. A study of 30 firms found that in large companies there is often a "Director of Digital" role reporting into marketing.[4] In another study, the majority of respondents (66 percent) had less than 10 people allocated specifically to digital work and these small teams were mainly housed within the marketing or communications function.[5]

E-commerce is often the most difficult digital function to find a natural home. When e-commerce is still a relatively small sales channel, it is often a part of marketing and a peer to the digital marketing team or embedded in another function. For example, Keurig.com is both a brand-building website and an e-commerce channel. For now, its primary function is to serve as a portal into the brand and to tell the brand story so that it differentiates Keurig. However, the e-commerce channel is growing rapidly. In 2012, it represented $0.5 billion sales channel out of the total brewer and K-Cup portion pack revenue of about $3.5 billion. Perhaps most importantly, it is the most profitable place that Keurig sells its brewers and portion packs. At Levi Strauss & Co., e-commerce lives in the retail unit.

When e-commerce represents a significant source of revenue, it is often pulled out to stand on its own. At Warner Music, digital sales grew from a rounded error on total revenue in 2005 to over 50 percent of revenue in 2010. The digital function was pulled out to report directly to the CEO, reflecting the importance that digital sales and the monetization, through advertising, of Warner Music's over 1,000 artist websites now represented to the company.

What is the typical work of a digital function?

A core set of sub-functions typically comprise digital work. However, there are multiple ways to group this work within the digital team, and not every company will need all sub-functions. Many of these sub-functions overlap with marketing and technology

Traditional Marketing	Digital Sub-Functions	Traditional Technology
Brand Customer segmentation Content Customer insights	Digital strategy Web analytics data CRM Social media Affiliates and partnerships Mobile marketing and mobile apps Community management Content marketing Paid search Search engine optimization User interface Web design	Platforms and systems Tech support Web build

FIGURE 12.3 Typical Digital Components: Digital endeavors typically overlap with traditional marketing and technology functions.

work and, if not housed in a dedicated digital group, may often be placed in one of those functions (see Figure 12.3).

Who owns social media?

A recent survey found that many businesses outsource management of their social media sites and online communities to a marketing agency. Social media management is not perceived as a core competency by these companies, but rather a specialized channel that is best monitored by an experienced partner.

However, it appears that firms that see their social presence as a differentiating element of their strategy keep social media close to home. Clearly this is important for consumer-focused companies, but community building is also moving into the business-to-business world. Two examples illustrate this.

Scottrade is one of the few financial services firms actively communicating with investors and providing customer service support through social media networking communities and through social media outlets. *Scottrade* is in a highly-regulated industry and many financial services firms have yet to even dabble in social media.

> What began as "listening" has evolved into a social strategy focused on providing value through customer interactions. We maintain two Facebook pages, four Twitter handles, one YouTube channel, a company blog, and a Flickr page. These channels work together to engage customers and further connect them to the *Scottrade* brand. We manage all the conversations in real time, so we need to own this. The social media team (in the marketing group) will answer some questions that come up directly. If the question or comment is about a specific account, then it goes to the service team or to a branch. We have immediate response. Within 15 minutes of an issue being posted it is escalated to a service team, which will then respond to the client directly.
>
> We also have a closed community of *Scottrade* clients that we launched in 2008. We have found that the more engaged they are—panels, contests, interacting with one another—the more activity they do with us. Social engagement is one of our top priorities. In 2010, we launched a Chinese-language online community. We've done the same for registered investment advisors so that they can collaborate and meet other like-minded financial professionals. We manage these communities and they have become as much a part of our brand as our other products and services.[6]
>
> **—Kim Wells, Chief Marketing and Digital Officer, Scottrade**

At Keurig, they call it the "on-going hand hold" with customers. In 2012, there were hundreds of social media interactions on Facebook and other sites each day that mentioned Keurig, with either compliments or complaints. The social media team responds to issues within five minutes of a post. It becomes a way to surprise and delight customers. This emphasis made Keurig.com number four in customer satisfaction among the top 100 websites in 2012.

> We don't farm out our social media. The way we interact with our customers is a proprietary advantage. The social media group sits right down the hall from me. If something blows up on Facebook, we can make decisions real time and react in real time. People expect that we are listening to them. And we are. Marketing is real time today. You can't hire this out—you can't outsource it. If you are just getting reports, then you are not really involved with your consumer.[7]
>
> **—Dave Manly**

In addition, Keurig has a database of five million people that they can communicate with proactively. This is an advantage for companies that have both e-commerce and brand-building sites. Direct access to consumers allows for analytics, insights, and touch points that other companies don't have.

Compare this to Coca-Cola, one of the most valuable brands in the world. In November 2012, Coke announced a complete revamping of its website for the first time since 2005. Since it doesn't have e-commerce, the intention of the change was to engage with customers through content. Ashley Brown, director for digital communications and social media, explained the strategy to the *New York Times*:[8]

> The hot thing is to talk about being publishers. We have this belief in great, real content and creating content that can be spread through any medium as part of our "liquid and linked" strategy. My team has been re-formed in the last year to look more like an editorial team at a magazine with a production schedule and an editorial calendar.

Who owns the user experience?

The user experience sub-function is one of the most important for digital work. It is here that the interface is created and the brand is brought to life as customers interact with the site or app. User experience has a high degree of impact on whether customers stick with a site and a product or service.

User experience typically is located within a marketing group, but where it sits—with a digital team or with a customer segmentation team—can vary. What is important is that this person or group is set up to be neutral—the Switzerland on the marketing team. The user experience folks are there to represent the best interests of the customer. They have to be independent of the brand teams and the demands of the product launch schedules. They need to challenge the product developers, marketers, and technologists to design from the customer backward.

How should we manage continuous change in the digital space?

Your digital groups are unlikely to look like other functions that you traditionally find in organizations such as legal, finance,

HR, compliance, or sales. Digital capabilities and customer expectations are evolving quite quickly. As of this writing, while the consensus seems to be that pulling it out and providing focus is a smart way to get started, that may not hold for long. At some point, when digital thinking and skills become part of the company DNA, "digital" may even cease to be called out as a separate element and this whole discussion may seem quite old-fashioned.

For now, because digital capabilities are distinct and touch so many aspects of any organization, including customer interface, marketing insights, product development, sales, technology, and IT, digital staff and their work and decisions must be closely linked to the groups they collaborate with and support. Small teams, with strong digital players and their cross-functional counterparts configured around projects and opportunities, provide the speed and agility needed. You may start with some people at the center and a few in your operating units and then shift the balance of skills and focus as your customer needs change and your capabilities mature. The next section focuses on how to do this.

Process and Lateral Connections

Leaders frequently lament the organizational silos that prevent people from working together. The fact is, all structures create silos. Whenever people are grouped according to one logic, boundaries are created that make it difficult for them to interact with groups formed according to a different logic. This is not a problem if the strategy does not require a high level of interaction or collaboration across these boundaries. But if the strategy does require collaboration, then the organization's structure—no matter how well thought out—will likely create some barriers. Collaboration, however, requires an investment in new roles and processes, as well as of management attention and time spent on internal coordination. Leaders have to believe that this investment will pay off.

We have made the case that many companies will benefit from bringing their digital staff together under strong functional leadership. The predictable downside of this approach is that a dedicated function creates new organizational boundaries. Leaders responding to the MIT study called out three organizational challenges created by forming a functional digital group:

- **Learning**: Separating out digital expertise from general marketing and other functions makes it more difficult to increase the level of knowledge of digital marketing among nondigital specialist staff.
- **Hand-offs Rather than Cocreation**: It may be more difficult to integrate digital work right from the start and join up data more effectively across departments and within the organization if the digital work stands alone. This can be a potential hindrance to multichannel marketing and integrated product development and technology projects.
- **Priority Setting**: A third potential risk is that a dedicated function will focus on fulfilling the needs of larger business units, leading to frustration among the smaller business units if they are unable get projects prioritized.

Further, respondents in the study concluded that when their companies lacked effective coordination they did not get the most value possible from their digital transformation initiatives.

What are my options for linking digital into other functions and work?

The organizational challenge is how to bridge internal boundaries and integrate activities. As a leader, you have a number of options. They can be arrayed from low to high along a scale that indicates how much management time and attention is required and how much internal complexity is introduced (see Figure 12.4):

- **Communities of Practice**: In your firm, digital work may be a piece of many people's roles. Or, the digital needs of your various product lines or markets may be so varied that the benefits of consolidating into one function may be outweighed by the need for differentiation and speed. Digital staff embedded in the operating units, although focused on their own customer needs, will still require a

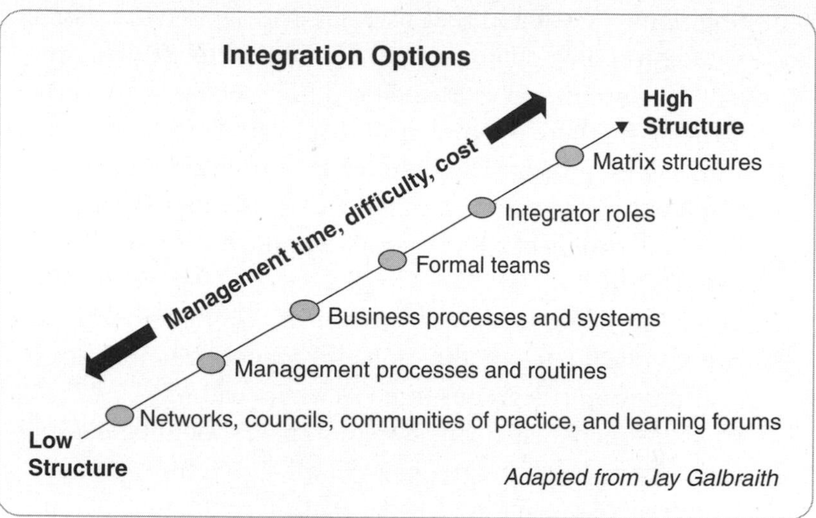

FIGURE 12.4 Integrating the Digital Function: Always start with the lightest touch possible to minimize complexity.

way to connect with one another. In this case, a community of practice can help to create some alignment, sharing of best practices, and network building. A community of practice is different from a formal team in that it has no set objectives, outputs, or accountabilities. A successful community of practice does need to be designed and supported, however. This can be done through helping staff meet each other, management encouragement, and a travel budget for in-person meetings.

- **Colocation**: Just having technologists and marketers sit together, regardless of reporting relationships, can be a powerful way to create the common digital language that draws from both these domains. Despite all the advances in virtual communication tools over the past 15 years, there is still no substitute for face-to-face communication when complex problems need to be tackled from diverse perspectives.
- **Management Processes**: Of course, anytime you have a scarce resource, such as developers of analytic algorithms, there will be conflicts over priorities. At LexisNexis Risk

Solutions, they found that a strong priority-setting process based on return on investment is essential to ensuring that data is viewed as an asset and used for the greatest return. Otherwise, there is a danger of in-demand digital resources working on projects based on other, wrong criteria: what is interesting to the staff, influence of a strong project leader, demands of a low priority customer, or executive pet projects.

- **Decision Rights**: Clear accountability for decision making can also facilitate coordination and reduce organizational tensions. Some decisions, such as what customer relationship management system to use, should be made centrally or by clear agreement of all the operating units. Common platforms are the foundation for analytics. On the other hand, decisions regarding search advertising and customization of landing pages can be made by the business units that know the local market best. This level of specificity and clarity helps to speed decision making and reduce tensions.
- **Teams**: Teams are formal groups that cut across the structure to get project or ongoing work accomplished. For example, new product development teams that include representatives from the digital function at the earliest possible stage help avoid design and customer issues later. Teams, when given a clear charter and support, can be a powerful way to quickly reconfigure resources around problems and opportunities. Amazon Web Services has been described as looking like a collection of 40 start-ups with the build-out accomplished by 800 small teams. Jeff Bezos, CEO of Amazon, believes in limiting team size to what he calls a "two-pizza team." Eight to ten is the number of people that can be fed by two large pizzas and seems to him like the ideal number to balance the need for speed with gaining the benefit of diverse viewpoints and expertise.[9]
- **Joint Accountability or Matrix Management:** At the top of our integration spectrum is the creation of formal linkages through shared reporting and accountability.

> For example, at *Scottrade*, marketing product managers and technology architects are jointly accountable for the product roadmap. Rather than a hand-off, they have joint metrics. The same approach is used when development is outsourced to a vendor. Vice-president-level staff from the two functions are jointly accountable for the product being right and meeting the project timeline. *Scottrade* has found that this helps the company move faster in a cohesive manner.

With a matrix, one person is accountable for the outcome, but that person has dual-reporting responsibility to two managers; for example, one in marketing and one in technology. This can work well to knit the organization together, but should be used sparingly. Matrix management—sharing of resources—introduces complexity that requires a sophisticated and highly functioning management team. Only a few key roles at a fairly high level should be in dual reporting. At levels below, keep it simple. For example, at a heavy construction equipment manufacturer, a Digital Solutions Group has responsibility for developing the smart GPS and other technology that is being built into the vehicles. Executive leaders rightly concluded that this group (with 1,000 employees) needs to be tightly connected to marketing, product engineering, and technology. However, they have done this through four levels of matrix reporting. While all of this matrix reporting certainly forces the right conversations and brings together the right perspectives, the company's leaders found that the internal complexity slowed decision making and diffused accountability for results. They are now redesigning to better balance accountability and focus with integration and linkage.

In organization design, there are always trade-offs to be made. In general, first design for focus and accountability. Then add in the integrating mechanisms as needed, always using the lightest touch possible.

How can we assure an integrated technology platform?

Collecting data from customers and internal operations continues to become easier and cheaper. Making sense of this data and turning it into insights that guide decision making is much harder. At many firms, data is just a by-product of the more tangible service or product that is the core business. Systems are not designed to connect and analytics is a weak muscle at best. In fact, many of the conflicts that we see in multidimensional companies occur because there is more than one source of truth. If different data sets are used, even if the same logic is applied, managers come to different conclusions regarding investments and performance. Econsultancy.com's survey found that "legacy systems and processes" and "difficulty joining up data" were identified by respondents as the top two barriers to digital progress for their companies.

For companies that are looking to gain more from their data, studying a company for which data is the product can be instructive. At LexisNexis Risk Solutions, the business unit front ends are organized around three market segments: insurance, financial services, and government. These front ends are primarily focused on product management, marketing, and sales.

Content operations is a shared utility that purchases and manages the data that all of the business units use. For example, a data set might be names and phone numbers within a region. Within the content operations function is the core of the company—the "factory," so to speak. This is a proprietary platform called the high performance computing cloud (HPCC). Getting this platform right, including continual investments in upgrades, is the foundation of the company's success. From this foundation, hundreds of developers create the algorithms that link the various sets of data and mine the "smart decisioning" analytics that provide insights for Risk Solutions' customers.

Compare this approach to the hodgepodge of systems at a typical company that don't interact with one another, and the frustration for managers to get analytics on operational data, insights into customer behavior, or even a current org chart.

Metrics

Metrics and rewards align individual behaviors and performance with the organization's goals. For employees, a company's scorecard and reward system communicate what the company values more clearly than any written statement. In complex organizations, the overriding challenge in designing metrics and rewards is how to create incentives for collaborative behavior and keep everyone aligned toward the same goal.

Once an organization has defined its digital vision, leaders must translate that vision into a set of targets that drive success. Even if the digital function is not measured as a business, it should have clear performance indicators that create accountability and serve as guideposts of progress.

How should we measure success of digital initiatives?

In the first Internet boom of the early 2000s, many start-ups defined success by volume of clicks or "eyeballs" on a website. But when the clicks and scans didn't translate into revenue, those pioneer firms were soon gone. Just as with the second wave of Internet sites, which have found how to monetize page views, traditional companies building successful digital capability today are quite clear about which metrics represent success.

At *Scottrade*, success is a person clicking the "open account" button and following through, or depositing more assets into an existing account as the result of a marketing campaign. The team works back from that metric to create a set of customized landing pages that will draw in a customer based upon where they started from on the web or what search term was used. A Google search, a Yahoo! ad, or a link in a Motley Fool newsletter will all go to customized pages reflecting the likely profile of the person searching.

At Keurig, a similar approach is taken. The annual operating plan will have a clear target for selling portion packs through the website channel. The digital team creates algorithms for traffic volume and conversion rates. Skills on the team are organized to optimize each step required to meet these goals. Marketers create the promotions targeted to microsegments of consumers. Internal experts in search and in building partnerships with other sites create ways to drive people to the site. Other staff, who know how to convert browsers into buyers, create the engaging user interface and work to continually simplify the checkout process.

> This is as much engineering as marketing. We have to get the formula right. But then we organize by the formula and continually measure against the formula. If our goal is to sell 30 million portion packs and we miss, then we can see where we missed and fix or change the formula. Analytics are real time, with people who can analyze and make decisions quickly. We'll try three campaigns and see after 10,000 e-mails how we are doing and then make a change.
>
> **—Dave Manly**

How should channel conflicts be managed?

One of the knottiest problems in designing for digital marketing is to get the metrics right across sales channels when an e-commerce site can be seen as a threat to wholesale customers, a retail business, or even other internal sites. The MIT study found that channel conflict is a major source of tension between managers in traditional units and those in the digital function, especially when the former see themselves losing when new businesses gain.

At Keurig, with e-commerce representing about 10 percent of total sales, the site managers are careful to never conflict with retailers or sell brewers below the price of the retailers. They will promote discounts to customers through their loyalty club, but not on the open website.

The primary channel for Levi Strauss & Co.'s (LS&Co.) brands—Levi's® and Dockers®—is through third-party retailers. LS&Co. also operates nearly 500 of its own stores and approximately 1,800 franchise stores, and sells through retailers' e-commerce sites (for example, Amazon.com, Macys.com) as well. When the Levis.com site was set up to sell directly to consumers through the web, it was soon clear that the LS&Co. organization was not aligned to support this. Attracting consumers and delivering merchandise was the easy part. But the retail stores and e-commerce site were measured independently. Therefore, store managers had little incentive to direct consumers to the Levi.com site.

The solution was to redefine success from the customer's point of view. It is fine if the shopper tries on the product in the store and then buys it online, or explores the product online and then buys in the store.

> The goal is to become channel agnostic. If someone buys the product at Macy's or Macys.com or our site or our store or Amazon, it's all OK. We found that 60 percent of people who visit our site plan on making an off-line purchase. People still want to see and try on clothing. When we start looking at this as a system, rather than channels, then it puts a different justification on the investment in digital.[10]
>
> —**Jen Sey**

While an e-commerce function should have clear accountabilities and metrics of success, it is not so clear that it makes sense to give it a profit and loss and consider it a business unit. Since your customers usually don't distinguish the retail and dot-com channels as separate, measuring them as separate businesses creates unnecessary internal conflict. To avoid unhealthy internal competition, senior executives need to set a clear vision from the top that spells out the role of e-commerce in the strategy, and then work through the right set of metrics that will make cooperative, customer-centric behaviors rational and easy to demonstrate.

People Practices

Leadership and technical staffing are clearly critical elements of the transition that companies must manage in the transition to a digitally focused strategy and capability. Know-how and mindsets must change in order for digital strategies to thrive as an integrated portion of the business.

What is the profile for the digital workforce?

A success profile emerges from the literature and discussions with leaders hiring and managing digital staff. In the not-so-distant future, this skill set and mindset may become more widespread, but for now they represent a distinct profile.

While technical and marketing domain knowledge is needed, that seems easier to find than the deep systems thinking needed to understand how all the channels and digital properties work together and can then create strategies to optimize and integrate them. At the design firm IDEO, they have coined the term *T-shaped* people. The vertical in the T represents a deep skill, an area of expertise that can be contributed to a team. The horizontal represents the breadth of business understanding that allows this expert to collaborate with people from other disciplines.[11]

While this type of mindset seems valuable in any role, it is particularly critical to the digital function, because of its position at the intersection of other disciplines. As digital work evolves from simply messaging and transactions to the creation of true digital experiences with and for customers, channel integration becomes more important. People who are able to apply deep vertical skills yet collaborate with others will be highly sought after. Ben Malbon, managing director of Google Creative Lab in New York is quoted as saying "We need people fluent in one language but literate in many."

For many firms this deep understanding of customer and consumer, and how the business model plays out and interacts across multiple channels needs to be nurtured in-house, not outsourced or bought only when needed.

> I call it digital DNA. You have it or you don't and I can't teach it. But I can tell in the first six months whether or not you are going to get it. My best staff are digital systems thinkers. They may be deep in a channel, but they understand across how clients consume digital. My head of e-mail thinks about how to get a person to open the e-mail, get them to click, where the click takes them and then how to measure it.
>
> The profile is someone who values and knows how to use the research from our clients. The background could be technology, user experience, or content, but they have to be passionate about all three. I find that they tend to think visually. I don't see that anyone is teaching this in colleges today.[12]
>
> **—Kim Wells**

The profile is one of a deep digital technologist, not a generalist marketer with some exposure to technology. Companies are looking for people who live and breathe this and have grown up in digital, not just added it to their toolkit along the way.

The LexisNexis Risk Solutions business model underscores the need for digital staff that are able to work at a faster pace than traditional marketing or IT personnel. Lee Rivas, CEO of Public

Sector and Healthcare at LexisNexis Risk Solutions provided us with this profile.

> When data is your business, markets can change very quickly, even on a daily basis, requiring a change in functionality or user interface for a customer. Our business requires people that are comfortable dealing with ambiguity; people who can look at trends and statistics, and make a call how we should proceed or alter our course.

This is felt at traditional companies adding in digital capabilities, as explained by Jen Sey at LS&Co.:

> I need people in e-commerce that are comfortable making decisions without complete information. It's a completely different mindset than wholesale marketing. Whatever we're doing now, in six months it's going to change. We have to operate in real time at the pace of the consumer.

Do marketers now have to become technologists?

Scott Brinker makes the case that a whole new competence has emerged: the "technology savvy marketer." Web apps, widgets, phone and tablet apps, interactive ads, landing pages, micro-sites, social media outposts, and even the connected features of products are now part of marketing's realm.

Brinker goes further to propose a new role—the chief marketing technologist—reporting into the chief marketing officer. The profile is of a technologist, with a strong background in software and technology management, but with a focus, passion, and allegiance to the company's marketing mission. He sees the marketing CTO perched at the intersection of marketing, product development, and technology.

> Instead of marketers having to take what those other technologists say at face value—which leads to challenges when incentives and end-to-end business objectives are not perfectly aligned—the marketing CTO can provide checks and balances. Timeframes, technical specifications, architecture

> choices, and final deliverables can all be reviewed by an expert who is perfectly aligned with marketing's agenda...that is how marketing must embrace technology—as a new fundamental building block of its DNA. Technology must become infused into marketing's culture.

This type of integrative role may help to mitigate the tension that often exists between marketing and technology functions when trying to determine who owns marketing technology. Brinker goes on to say:

> IT and marketing simply have different incentives and priorities. IT is primarily concerned with stability, security, economy, standardization, and functional specs. Marketing is more concerned with speed, agility, innovation, market impact, differentiation, and customer experience. It's not that IT doesn't appreciate marketing's priorities—or vice versa. It's just that their incentives cause them to value their own respective priorities more.

What is the right approach to sourcing and developing digital talent?

The challenge of finding staff with suitable digital skills was listed as the fourth most significant barrier to progress in e-consultancy.com's study. Analytics and insights comprised the skill set perceived as the most difficult to recruit for. It requires someone with both marketing and computer science skills, sometimes called computational marketing. Digital leaders identified social media, content marketing, search engine optimization, website design and build, and mobile marketing and mobile commerce as the other scarcest skills sets in the labor market.

Interestingly, this survey of over 100 digital leaders also found that having an office located outside a major urban area was a major barrier to attracting people with desired digital skills profiles. Despite the inherent nature of digital technology lending itself to virtual ways of work, those who work in the digital realm prefer to live in dense, urban areas with other like-minded people.

The MIT survey of digital leaders found that most hired the skills they needed after trying to unsuccessfully retrain existing employees. However, internal high potentials that may be short on experience but high on energy and enthusiasm can be harnessed to work with vendors to incubate and grow needed capabilities. In addition, there is actually a role where being an insider provides an advantage. Highly regarded senior executives who embrace the digital vision will have more credibility when advocating for change than hotshot stars brought in from the outside. These insiders should be used to lead the business element of the digital change and sponsor the coordination necessary across various functions. While outsiders are often necessary to bring the vision and skills, successful culture change is much more likely when long-tenured internals embrace it and champion it.

CONCLUSION

The Star Model of organization design provides a path for leaders that want to build digital capability in a traditional organization:

- **Strategy and Capabilities**: Start with a clear vision of the contribution that digital investments will make and the capabilities that will make a difference for your context. Although digital thinking is all about twenty-first century ways of work, it requires strong leadership and management attention from the top. If you allow it to self-organize from the bottom up and fragment across the company, you will miss opportunities to invest in the platforms and technologies required for analytics and other tools. While this may seem self-evident, one of the top three barriers to digital success uncovered by the MIT survey was a lack of "senior management buy-in for investment in resourcing and training." Many digital efforts fail because actions on the ground don't match stated ambitions.

- **Structure**: Many structural configurations and placements can work. While digital teams typically live in marketing functions today, whether these staff are centralized at a corporate level or include embedded staff in the operating units depends on the diversity of your business portfolio and which decisions are best made at the center, and which are best left to local discretion. Regardless of the structure, digital success requires strong functional leadership to guide investments, build skills, and configure the right resources around problems and opportunities.
- **Lateral Connections**: Digital strategy is all about linking, primarily the links between the marketing, technology, and product development staff. Whether you use a light touch, such as a community of practice, or a more formal connection through matrix reporting, these linkages have to be deliberately designed to ensure the right people are having the right conversations.
- **Metrics**: These are perhaps some of the most important, and often overlooked, elements of organization design. Set targets in a way that make it easy and logical for people to collaborate and align their work agendas across the various departments that are essential to digital success.
- **People Practices**: The talent management aspect of digital work requires attracting, developing, and rewarding people that have the currently scarce digital DNA—systems thinkers, deep in marketing and technology, that can move at the pace of your customers and competitors.

SUGGESTED READING

Booz-Allen & Hamilton. *The Shape of the Digital Organization: From Shared Services to Allianced Services*. New York, NY: Booz-Allen & Hamilton Inc., 2000.

Espinel, Jorge. "What Is the Ideal Organizational Structure for a Digital Media Company?" SpectatorBytes.com 26 Feb. 2009. <http://spectatorbytes.com/2009/02/26/what-is-the-ideal-organizational-structure-for-a-digital-media-company/>.

Kesler, Greg and Amy Kates. *Leading Organization Design.* (Jossey-Bass, 2010).

Slawsky, Richard. "Understanding the Relationship Between DigitalTechnologyandLocation-BasedMarketing."DigitalSignage Today.com. 2012. Sponsored by: Nanonation.www.nanonation.net/about-us/downloads/WP_Location-BasedMarketing.pdf?id=18645&na=1.

ENDNOTES

1. Brinker, Scott, "Rise of the Marketing Technologist." Chiefmartec.com 18 Apr. 2010. <http://chiefmartec.com/2010/04/rise-of-the-marketing-technologist/>
2. Galbraith, Jay R., "The Evolution of Enterprise Organization Designs" (August 2012). *Journal of Organization Design*, Vol. 1, No. 2, pp. 1–13, 2012. Available at SSRN: http://ssrn.com/abstract=2181930
3. Digital Marketing: Organisational Structures and Resourcing Best Practice Guide, December 2011, http://econsultancy.com
4. Daniels, Matt, "How 30 Undercurrent Clients Design Their Digital and Social Organizational Structure." Undercurrent.com 13 Mar. 2012. <http://undercurrent.com/post/how–30-undercurrent-clients-design-their-digital-and-social-organizational-structure/>
5. MIT Center for Digital Business and Capgemini Consulting, *Digital Transformation: A Roadmap for Billion-Dollar Organizations.* Cambridge, MA: MIT Center for Digital Business and Capgemini Consulting, 2011
6. Kim Wells, Chief Marketing and Digital Officer, *Scottrade*
7. Dave Manly, Vice President, New Business Creation and General Manager, Digital Marketing, Keurig
8. Coke Revamps Web Site to Tell Its Story, *New York Times*, Nov 11, 2012
9. Brandt, Richard L., "Birth of a Salesman," WSJ.com 15 October 2011. <http://online.wsj.com/article/SB10001424052970203914304576627102996831200.html?mod=WSJ_article_comments#articleTabs%3Darticle>

10. Jen Sey, SVP, Global ecommerce, LS&Co.
11. Hanson, Morton T., "IDEOCEO Tim Brown: T-Shaped Stars: The Backbone of IDEO's Collaborative Culture" ChiefExecutive.net 21 Jan 2010. <http://chiefexecutive.net/ideo-ceo-tim-brown-t-shaped-stars-the-backbone-of-ideoae™s-collaborative-culture>
12. Kim Wells, *Scottrade*.

CHAPTER 13

THE PATH TO AN INNOVATIVE, DIGITAL-CENTRIC ORGANIZATION

—by Alexander Kates and Eric Greenberg

SIX HABITS OF HIGHLY SUCCESSFUL FIRMS

When devising effective digital marketing strategy, we firmly believe that *standing on the shoulders of giants* is a great starting point for determining which direction to head. When it comes to designing and reforming an organization to be equipped for the digital world, we should start in the same place. Rather than marketing pioneers and thought leaders, the *giants* we speak of in this case are high-growth, high-impact companies that embrace our digital world. They are the companies that are driving the innovation behind the cultural shifts we observe, and arguably have the largest impact on the way marketing has evolved over the last decade. These companies include Google, Amazon.com, Facebook, and Apple, among several others that might also be called *true innovators* on a global scale. These four companies have collectively tripled in size and market value over the last five years, and are among the most talked-about companies in the media.

In analyzing company structures, policies, and philosophies, we've noticed certain consistencies among these top innovative companies—aside from the obvious focus on social, mobile, and web technologies. While your own company may operate in a vastly different space, the fundamental ideologies that help these companies deliver customer value apply universally. These companies all see technology as enablers of opportunity, and eagerly embrace new processes and systems that utilize them to deliver value. They also understand the modern consumer, and invest heavily in new technologies to drive innovation. Here are six habits of these top-innovating companies that drive their success—and that your company can learn from.

1. Platform Convergence, not Product Conformity

In studying the operating activities of these companies, it is often difficult to determine exactly what space each of them operates in. How would you describe Google's operating space? The company's mission statement has always been " ... to organize the world's information and make it universally accessible and useful."[1] It makes no reference to its products or services at all, let alone which areas it operates in. If one studies the evolution of Google, it is apparent that they've held to this mission. Google has reached its innovative tendrils into virtually every technology and information space one can think of—including many spaces that have yet to be formally acknowledged as operating spaces.

Each of these other aforementioned companies lives by the same philosophy. They began in their own respective niches, but now all compete directly with one another on multiple levels, and across multiple channels. Apple was first to create branded mobile hardware, but Google and Amazon quickly followed suit. Apple was also the first to create an app store, but Google, Amazon, and Facebook all have stores of their own now. Google was known for its dominance in search, but now Facebook and Amazon have each become the go-to search platforms for people/brands and shopping, respectively. These companies are entering each other's operating spaces head-on, but with different solutions and ways to attack the same problems. Are these companies just running out of horizontal and vertical growth in their niche areas? We might argue this isn't the case at all. These companies understand that technology is converging the competitive landscape, and that their brands can use technology to reach into existing spaces in new ways. They also understand that when every brand thinks this way, everyone is potentially a competitor. Can you imagine how companies in analogous spaces—or even these companies we've mentioned—might soon be your company's direct competitors?

These innovative companies know that the companies who will win in the next decade are the ones that consumers first think of for a particular task, and use their brands as gateways to everything else they do. This is the reason why Google has aggressively expanded its open-source Android operating system worldwide, and why it puts significant effort into developing beautiful apps for Apple's iOS, despite Apple being its largest competitor in mobile. It's why Amazon sells its Kindle tablets at cost, why it pushes its *Prime* membership services, and why it created a colossal marketplace for third-party merchants to sell products through its platform. It's the reason Apple so aggressively invests in and promotes its app store and cloud services. It's also why Facebook is resolved to get companies, places, and people all onto its network to create an organized mini-web of its own. It's worth noting that while these companies are all aggressively investing in technology, they are investing particularly heavily in mobile platforms and solutions. The most innovative companies understand that technology provides a plethora of opportunities, but that consumer attention spans are shrinking as the technology landscape becomes more crowded. Becoming the gateway to a particular set of activities, and even more so making that gateway accessible on the go, is key to success. Can your brand find a way to use technology to become the unifying platform or hub in your space?

2. Big Data, not Blind Deductions

These innovative firms rely heavily on collected and mined data to drive their decisions. Today's fractured world of media generates data at an alarming rate, and effective analytics is the solution to collecting, organizing, and utilizing this data to generate positive outcomes. Just as we now rely on machines to perform various tasks more consistently than error-prone humans, innovative companies rely on data ahead of employee deductions when choosing between viable alternatives and when optimizing existing products and services. It is unsurprising then, that top-performing companies do analytics better than other firms. In turn, they not only have ample data at their fingertips to make good decisions, but they also draw profound insights from seemingly uninteresting large data sets.

Furthermore, the *test and learn* methodology is rooted deeply into these companies' operating activities. For example, rather than Google focusing on building a product to its exact vision, it utilizes engineers to whip up several concept iterations, and then thoroughly tests them using its real customers (and in real time) to determine which have the best outcomes. Innovative companies encourage employees to generate new ideas, and to test them quickly and cost-effectively. This way, ideas that perform well don't slip through the cracks, and certainly don't die on the vine of bureaucracy when a manager dislikes the concept. Nonperforming ideas are discarded rapidly, and performing ones are explored with more testing. This *idea-meritocracy* helps top firms innovate swiftly, and reduces the number of costly mistakes dramatically. Is your organization using data effectively to make decisions?

3. Customer Experiences, not Conventional Expectations

The most innovative and successful companies are fiercely focused on customers. They relentlessly pursue more engaging and refined user experiences for their products and services. For IT companies, this includes (but is not limited to) user interfaces (UI) on web and mobile platforms. Google's search, Amazon's e-commerce solutions, Facebook's social network, and Apple's iPods, iPads, and iPhones are all known, above all, for having incredibly beautiful and intuitive interfaces. They are also all interoperable across multiple channels and across all device types. Extra effort is exerted by these companies to ensure that a seamless and intuitive experience can be had from anywhere, and from any device—and that switching from one type of device to another is painless. Test drive the iPad apps from Google, Amazon, Facebook, and eBay, and you'll quickly ascertain how watertight the experiences are, and how they provide a full immersion from any device.

Lastly, the most innovative firms ensure that all customer experiences are intensely personalized. When consumers visit the owned properties of these brands, they are greeted with an experience that is tailored to their specific habits and needs. For example, Google's search (and its new Google Now mobile platform) provides results specific to users' past searches, current location, link-click history, and even their listed interests and activities on other Google services. In addition to Facebook's core services being intensely personal around your friends' activities, its new graph search provides intelligent and personal results. Amazon provides targeted product recommendations based on purchase and browsing history. These companies all utilize both individual and aggregated customer data to create personalized experiences in real time.

Real-time personalization, coupled with great multichannel support and intuitive interfaces, are a recipe for keeping customers coming back time and time again. Even if your operating space is completely outside of IT, custom experiences are always more appreciated than canned offerings. Does your organization relentlessly pursue a flawless customer experience?

4. Networks, not Bulwarks

The most innovative firms understand the importance of their networks. These include the networks of consumers that use their products, as well their network of corporate partners that make their businesses possible.

Understanding the network of consumers that use and interact with your products is crucial, and these firms know this. They put time and effort into identifying and guiding brand influencers who are most likely to interact in digital channels, and thus have the ability to convert fence-sitters into loyal customers. The most innovative brands understand the entire continuum of users better than others through the use of analytics, and by mapping the entire usage ecosystem to make strategic initiatives and investments. The sum total of their activities results in managing and directing the consumer network to maximize usage and sales. Is your business actively identifying, managing, and rewarding brand advocates?

A company's network of corporate partners is equally important, and innovative firms put immense effort into building this network. In today's demanding consumer environment, no company, no matter how innovative, can create and own the entire experience themselves without aid. Top firms view themselves as a crucial piece of an overall ecosystem, and seek partnerships that drive competitive advantage. In many cases, these firms understand that their partners are also competitors on many levels—but nevertheless must leverage their unique positions and expertise for growth. Amazon's tightly-knit relationships with third-party merchants and mail carriers, and Google's extensive partnerships with mobile handset manufacturers, are prime examples of these beneficial partnerships. Even Apple, which traditionally maintains control of its entire product from design to sales, has been utilizing more partnerships with chipmakers and panel manufacturers to focus on its core competencies. Is your brand leveraging its partnerships effectively to maximize value?

5. Top Talent, not Hired Hands

The most innovative firms understand that their human capital is their best asset and actively seek the absolute best talent available. These firms are willing to pay the highest salaries for the most intelligent and talented people, and firmly understand that one salaried employee at $200,000 can often be many times more valuable than two at $100,000—even with the same number of years of industry experience. Unsurprisingly, firms like Google and Facebook have among the highest starting salaries for young employees, and their jobs are the most sought after by this demographic. Firms that believe they have the infrastructure or culture that can turn very good and sufficiently talented employees into brilliant and outstanding ones are mistaken. The best firms know that innovation starts with top talent, and no number of employees or policies is going to change that.

To make the most effective use of top talent, innovative firms create an organizationwide culture that thrusts innovation and creativity into the spotlight. Google does this very effectively using its 70/20/10 rule. Former CEO Eric Schmidt pioneered this model of resource management back in 2005, and it is still utilized by Google today. Under this model, 70 percent of an employee's time is dedicated to core business tasks, 20 percent is dedicated to tasks related to the employee's core business, and 10 percent is devoted to projects completely unrelated to the core business. Employees collectively spend nearly one-third of their office time working on creative projects that may not have immediate benefits to the company. This schema benefits employees by allowing them to exercise their creativity to explore projects on Google's dime. The company, in return, gains ownership of a plethora of potentially lucrative ideas that can be exploited for innovation.[2]

Pulling 30 percent of employees' time away from their core tasks seems frightening, but in today's complex technological world, this mode of thinking is a necessity. Our best and most innovative ideas no longer generally come from management, but rather from our top engineers, and from talented employees organizationwide across all seniority levels. Large organizations especially must empower employees to innovate, and must incentivize them to do so as well. Many managers believe their organizations simply can't afford to do this. Budgets are always tight, deadlines are always near, business units are always understaffed, and change is never easy. However, we must innovate today to be sure our brands can compete two to four years down the road in our quickly evolving world. The real question organizations should be asking is: "Can our company afford *not* to do this, and still survive into the 2020s?" The best firms understand this well, and ensure top talent has the freedom and flexibility to create value for the future.

6. Innovation, not Immediate Gratification

The absolute best firms understand that to compete in the world of tomorrow, they must begin investing in the future today. Firms like Google and Apple are investing in research and development for products that may not even be useful at the present time. Each company secured more than 1,000 patents in 2012,[3] many of which revolve around technologies that will not see the light of day for many years—if ever. Some of these concepts are even turned into products inside the company, despite not having any real practical application at this time.

Google is perhaps the greatest culprit of this. In early 2013, the company unveiled a prototype pair of sneakers that can connect to users' smartphones to message their contacts, and can even speak 250 different phrases based on the wearer's environment or movements. However, the company has no intention of releasing *connected shoes*. So why bother investing time and money into developing a product without commercial use? And why bother to create professional YouTube videos to promote it? Well, we believe this concept gives us a glimpse into the inner-workings of Google. The company is constantly innovating and testing concepts of every conceivable type. Employees are, after all, forced to spend a significant chunk of their work-time working on projects of their own creation. We imagine that this one was chosen among many others to be promoted and shared with the world because it's humorous and shows that Google is always thinking outside the box to innovate. We'd guess that many teams inside Google are dreaming up ways to use the information Google collects and organizes to improve our daily lives, and this video reminds us of that. It's worth noting that the video showcasing the concept did receive nearly one million views in its first month on YouTube[4]—not too shabby for a pet project—and good PR to boot.

We don't recommend that your company start intentionally researching and manufacturing useless products. However, we can all learn lessons from Google. The company is working on dreaming up products for the future—ones that will be useful in the world of tomorrow, rather than the one we live in today. They know that much of what they create is not suited for commercial purposes now, and may not ever be. However, the insights they gain by investing heavily in creative R&D helps the company understand what tomorrow will bring. The company can then keep these concepts, innovations, and knowledge in its back pocket when creating new products. This is how the most innovative companies help us create the future. We can be sure that many of the bizarre concepts dreamed up in Mountain View, California, will somehow make their way into the everyday products and services of tomorrow. In this way, Google ensures that it will not only survive into the 2020s, but that it will continue to be an innovator and thought leader for many more years to come.

No matter what space you operate in, it is important to invest in technology and R&D, and to spend time designing products for what the world will look like in the near future. Many companies are intensely focused on the present, which will likely cause them to slip behind as the world evolves at an ever-increasing pace.

In addition to these six habits, the most innovative and digital-centric firms exhibit several other similarities, such as effective content strategy, and similar organizational structures and principles. The digital transformation framework we propose is an eleven-step process that helps guide firms toward preparing themselves for the digital world.

DIGITAL TRANSFORMATION FRAMEWORK

"Everybody wants better, no one wants change."

Firms face a plethora of obstacles when it comes to effecting change. These include longstanding organizational structures and procedures, corporate culture, and stodgy individuals (who we call *dinosaurs*) who are unwilling to risk change to make progress. For large organizations especially, change isn't easy. Very frequently, without the understanding and support of our superiors and our peers, our hopes for change die on the vine.

This three-part, eleven-step framework provides a set of guidelines that most traditional organizations can follow in order to transform themselves into digitally inclined organizations (see Figure 13.1). Since most businesses originated prior to (or were not originally impacted by) the information age, we feel this framework applies nearly universally across all sectors and company sizes.

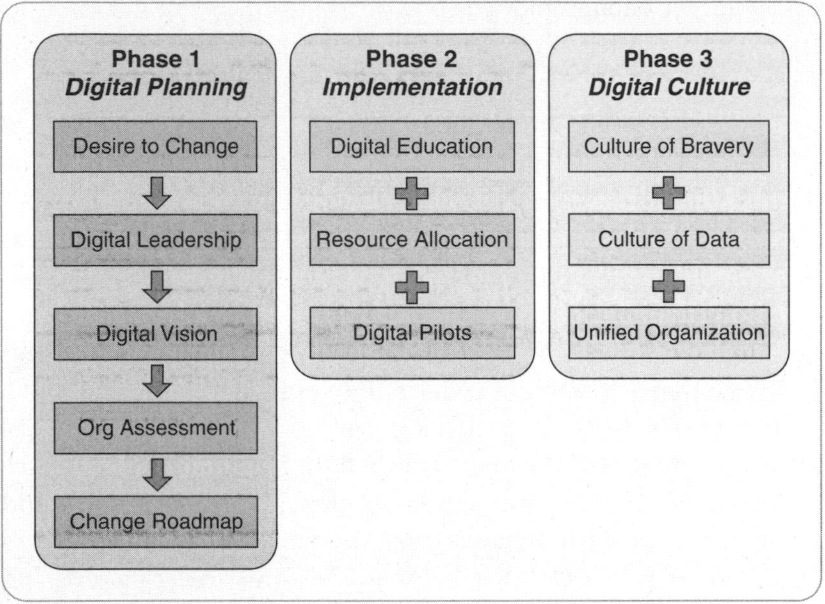

FIGURE 13.1 Digital Transformation Framework: Digital Planning is a five-step, chronological process for planning change. Implementation and Digital Culture each contain three non-linear steps toward achieving a digital-centric organization.

Phase One: Planning the Digital Transformation

1. Desire to Change

Any good transformation framework starts with the correct mindset and a sense of urgency. The organization, from top to bottom, must accept and embrace the fact that the world is changing—and changing rapidly. Employees need to acknowledge the profound effect technology has had, and will continue to have, on culture and the future of the firm's business. Most importantly, senior management must make openness to change a priority and perpetuate that message down through every level of the organization. This desire to change represents the cornerstone of organizational digital transformation, and is a necessary foundation for all organizations that hope to compete in the digital world of tomorrow. Not everyone in an organization will immediately be willing to break the molds they have clung to for decades, and not every senior leader will be on board at first. However, organizations must garner enough momentum from within so that the need for rapid change is felt throughout the organization.

2. Digital Leadership

When a critical mass within an organization (including upper management) is willing to embrace change, it becomes necessary for an organization to identify and cultivate the key agents of that change. Companies need employees across all levels and functional areas to champion the digital paradigm, and to actively spread the word about the digital opportunity. Ideally these digital leaders are senior managers with a great deal of influence. However, frequently they are mid-level managers with a sound understanding of digital media and a strong desire to change their organization for the better. The desire to embrace digital is often spread upward through the organization to senior leaders, and downward to young employees in key departments. In many cases these digital leaders across the company naturally organize and band together, creating digital thought-centers.

Digital leaders throughout the organization, as well as informal digital thought-centers, should be formally organized and brought together to create a cohesive and unified Digital Board. We highly recommend that this board represent all of the company's significant business units and functional areas, including HR, Legal and Compliance, IT, etc. To organize a Digital Board that feels empowered and has a true sense of purpose, usually several very senior leaders (including the C-suite) must be behind the initiative for change and take the Board's recommendations seriously.

3. Vision for a Digital Organization

When the Digital Board meets, it has a single goal in mind. It should seek to answer the question: "What should our organization-of-the-future look like to embrace our rapidly evolving digital world?" Although tempting, at first this should not be based on specific reformations of current structures and policies. Instead, it's about crafting a vision for an ideal or aspirational version of the organization that maximizes efficiency and agility, while simultaneously staying true to the company's mission and core values. Rebuild the entire organization from the ground up, being careful to account for all important functional areas, as if no structures currently exist. We should note that the larger and more decentralized the organization, the more difficult this process is. Large organizations will also require more input from more digital thought-leaders, and hence more time and effort to create a single, cohesive vision.

This vision should be thoroughly documented and codified, visually and otherwise, so that it is clear and digestible for senior management. This vision is almost always a complete departure from the present reality of the company, and that's okay. In fact, various parts of the vision may be impossible to achieve. However, the vision provides the organization a unified target to shoot for, and helps to perpetuate the sense of urgency by demonstrating the gap between the *real* and the *ideal*. Armed with a unified vision for a digital organization, the Digital Board can secure resource commitments for beginning the change process.

4. Digital Competency Assessment

When an organization has a vision for change and digital leaders with the ability and charisma to lead that change, leaders have a tendency to begin attacking bureaucracies and attempting to make changes immediately. More often than not, making those changes in a single silo at this point faces substantial opposition, and may create sudden rifts and inconsistencies with long-established policies and procedures still in effect within other parts of the organization. Instead, we recommend effecting change in a much more logical and methodical manner.

Some questions we often ask organizations at this stage are: Where are you now in each functional area, both internally and externally, compared with your digital vision? How does your personnel fare in executing digital strategies compared to where they need to be? Which structural areas and policy topics need reform immediately, and which should be modified in the medium- or long-term?

To help answer these questions, we propose that companies conduct a thorough organizationwide assessment of individual and departmental competencies. For large organizations, it is helpful if the Digital Board enlists the aid of one or more partner companies to help conduct this analysis to provide external insight and perspective. The assessment should analyze three key areas:

1. *Internal organizational structures and procedures.* This typically involves an analysis of org charts and reporting policies, as well as an examination of HR, legal, and compliance principles.
2. *External performance in digital channels.* This study that can be conducted by a third party using publically available data in digital channels to compare the organization's performance to those of its competitors. This is known as *digital benchmarking.* See *L2*'s industry reports (l2thinktank.com) for examples.
3. *Human capital Competency in digital knowledge, perception, and behavior.* This is best accomplished with a short, 10-minute exam taken by everyone within the organization (or a random sample within). It should provide a complete picture of human capital's digital strengths and weaknesses across the organization's functional areas and management levels.

It is tempting for organizations to skip this expensive step altogether—and many do—to their own detriment. How can an organization set on a path to achieve its digital vision when the organization has no idea where it currently stands? These analyses answer the aforementioned questions and set up the organization to create an effective roadmap for change. Furthermore, they arm the Digital Board with incredibly valuable data and insights that help perpetuate the digital vision and improve buy-in throughout the organization.

5. Create a Roadmap for Change

The data gathered during the assessment phase will form the basis for communicating the vision to management, as well as to the rest of the organization. It is much easier for employees (and even *dinosaurs*) to buy into a vision that's backed by hard data, and very clearly highlights internal and external areas of weakness where change is necessary. Now that the Board is armed with copious amounts of data indicating where the organization currently stands, as well as a clear picture for where the organization is supposed to go, the next step is to create a very tangible and granular roadmap for change.

This roadmap starts with the current state of the company, and ends with the digital vision as it pertains to each functional area of the organization. We recommend that the overall process take between one and five years, depending upon the present state, size, and structure of the organization. Several intermediary milestones (at least 3 and as many as 10) between these two endpoints should be devised, along with projected dates of completion. Each of these milestones should portray a fully functional operating department that shows clear improvement from the previous state, as well as clear progress toward the end goal set forth in the digital vision. We suggest fully documenting how these intermediary goals are to be achieved using a *mini-roadmap*. There should also be briefs that detail roles and responsibilities, as well as time and resource allocations. The evolution and roadmaps of complementary departments should be taken into account for policy and procedure congruence.

Phase Two: Implementing the Digital Transformation

6. Digital Education

To aid an organization's functional areas in achieving its digital transformation milestones, we recommend targeted and custom-tailored digital education for employees. The organizationwide assessment should reveal pockets of strength and weakness in digital Competency among human capital, and among functional areas of the organization. This valuable data can be used to set up training programs for particular departments, or can be used to select individuals for more comprehensive training programs. Digital education can be run internally by the organization, or can be brought in from the outside using universities or consultancies as partners.

To illustrate, for our client Johnson & Johnson, we set up a three-tier digital education training curriculum. This comprises a *1.0* online course in *Digital Essentials*, which is introductory in its content, cost-effective, and reaches a large number of employees.

The second tier (which we call *2.0*) is an in-person, intensive, and hands-on four-day course that delves into each digital channel. We've trained more than 400 J&J managers across five continents with the *2.0* course alone. Now, two years after we began the relationship, we are putting plans in place for a *3.0*-level course that dives deep into specific digital channels and strategies to help cultivate digital leaders and experts.

The purpose of the three tiers is to allow employees to be appropriately placed into training based on their competency level, and also allows progression for those who wish to (or need to) take their digital education further. Outside of the three-step process, we run a special two-day crash course for senior executives. Feedback from the *1.0* and *2.0* courses indicated that digital initiatives were held up due to lack of senior manager buy-in. We found that this senior executive course helps to move the digital transformation forward by fostering confidence and understanding with key decision makers. On average, across all training levels, J&J received 26 percent gains in digital knowledge, and 34 percent gains in digital confidence, for those who took one of the training courses.

When conducting training, we recommend ending the programs with participants putting plans in place for actionable digital projects that are inspired by the learning. Many of these projects can turn into actual proposals for new digital initiatives. For the first digital marketing training course we conducted for Sonosite in Seattle, all eight proposed capstone projects were funded that very quarter, for a sum total of over $1 million.

The results of digital education can be eye opening, and it is an important and ongoing part of the digital transformation. In many cases, we recommend using targeted education even earlier in the process to help foster a desire to change, and to cultivate digital leadership.

7. Budget and Resource Allocations

When functional areas of the organization have solidified their milestones toward achieving the digital vision, it is essential that resources be allocated to the process. Budgets must be set aside, and dedicated time must be built into employee schedules, to work toward the goal. The time set aside to achieve these goals absolutely must be held sacred—or it will inevitably be eclipsed by pressing needs individuals face in their core duties. At this stage, more than ever, senior managers must make dedication to the digital vision a priority, and not allow day-to-day operational issues to leech budgets and time away from digital strategies and transformation initiatives. Empowering the competent and dedicated Digital Board with special authority is one way senior management can help to keep all functional areas on track.

During this stage, the Digital Board will manage the overall change process, and may act as a liaison between each functional area and the senior management team. The Digital Board should hold regular meetings where each functional area is represented to discuss progress toward milestones. These meetings will also help foster organizationwide communications, aligning all functional areas so that they evolve simultaneously to minimize conflict and inconsistencies. This will likely cause the Board to slow the evolution of some functional areas, while prodding others to effect change more quickly. The Digital Board, along with senior management, must also hold functional area representatives (and especially division heads) accountable for nonadherence to the digital roadmap and failure to incorporate digital into their operating activities.

8. Pilots Demonstrating Short-Term Successes

In order to generate momentum behind the digital transformation, it is necessary to keep the entire organization informed and excited about the changes. We recommend giving regular updates via e-mail or internal social networks about the digital transformation initiative's progress. Successful changes to stale organization structures and bureaucratic procedures, or impactful education initiatives, should be shared and celebrated. In conjunction with the organizational changes, business units should be implementing digital strategy into their marketing and operations. These innovative and cross-channel campaigns that utilize digital media should be considered pilots, the results of which should be shared organizationwide. Successes in digital, no matter how short-term or how small, should be publicized and celebrated. For large organizations, case studies backed with ROI-based results can be created to help share the learning with other areas of the company.

In Dr. John Kotter's well-established eight-step process for leading change, the sixth step is to "generate short-term wins."[5] We feel strongly that this concept be incorporated into any change management continuum. While some business units may already be utilizing digital strategies with some efficacy, there are likely many more that are further behind. Whether their lack of innovation is to due to stodgy dinosaurs leading the group, or due to the perceived risk of funneling resources toward digital, stories backed by hard data that demonstrate these short-term successes are compelling. These business units can see that others had the courage to take the plunge into digital waters and that it led to success, which is inspiring. They say, "Hey, if they can do it, so can we." They also recognize that innovative, incremental successes of their own can garner the same organizationwide praise and publicity, further motivating them to take action. The concept of shooting for short-term successes and celebrating them is an important building block toward creating a digital culture.

Phase Three: Fostering a Digital Culture

9. A Culture of Bravery and Learning

Publicizing and celebrating short-term successes is important, but only one piece of the puzzle. Organizations prepared for the digital world must foster a culture that celebrates and rewards innovation, risk taking, and even failure. Celebrating failure means having a philosophy in place that doesn't penalize decision makers who take justified, calculated risks. Those risks that pay dividends should be celebrated organizationwide, but those that don't should be viewed as learning experiences. Ultra-effective digital strategy does not happen overnight, and these learning experiences can be leveraged by the risk-takers and others throughout the organization to improve digital strategy moving forward.

Creating a culture of bravery and learning requires an alignment of management philosophies, compensation structures, and HR principles, as well as legal and compliance understanding. Senior management must first perpetuate this culture downward through the organization via its communications. This sets the tone for the entire company, and provides the functional divisions with a license and incentive to effect tangible changes to their operations (in accordance with the digital roadmap).

For example, Human Resources should look for digitally inclined, ambitious, and adventurous talent—and should weigh these factors more heavily when evaluating current staff as well. Furthermore, HR must provide the proper compensation structures that incentivize staff to align with the digital vision. If bonuses are based solely on meeting predetermined revenue, profit, or margin goals, managers may feel that taking risks that don't pan out will harm their year-end compensation. Instead, bonuses should reward successful risk taking more heavily, penalize unsuccessful (yet well-thought-out) risks only minimally, and take into account the overall adherence of the employee to the digital vision. The message from management and from HR should be congruent, and say: "Innovate and be rewarded, take the safe road and be penalized."

Legal and compliance now play a more important role than ever, as these departments are traditionally arms of the organization that hamper innovation. We'll be the first to acknowledge the crucial role these departments play in keeping our organizations aligned and out of legal trouble. However, we've found that when marketers and engineers loosen the reins of their digital horses, legal and compliance teams put up walls to change the horses' course. Some of these walls are justified—but many are not, and are erected out of fear of the unknown, or lack of concrete policies to handle issues surrounding digital channels. In fact, many large companies still try to fit digital strategies into existing guidelines, failing to acknowledge these unique channels and the implications surrounding them. In today's digital world, legal and compliance teams must be present during Digital Board meetings. They must commit themselves to creating flexible internal and external policies that don't hamper innovation needlessly and keep pace with our rapidly evolving digital world. Compliance guidelines not only need to be written especially for digital platforms, but also must be amended and updated constantly to reflect best practices for new innovations. We can't stress enough how important the creation of internal governance policies around digital initiatives are toward achieving a complete digital transformation.

10. A Culture of Data Reliance

In the early chapters of this book, we tried to impart the importance of data-driven decision making. Organizations that use ROI as a bottom-line comparison to make apples-to-apples decisions have a much better chance of surviving in the digital world. That said, marketers should not be the only ones utilizing data to make decisions. In fact, data collection and analysis should be built into the very cultural fabric of the organization, and should be utilized by all departments companywide to make good decisions. Sales teams should use data to optimize their pitch activities. Supply chain and manufacturing departments should use it to improve processes and procedures for efficiency. Creative teams, operating departments, engineers, R&D, communications departments, PR, IT, and even accounting and finance can utilize collected and analyzed data to make good decisions, both big and small. Furthermore, all of this data should be stored, collated, and organized for the entire organization as a whole so that insights from one department can be utilized everywhere else. We often recommend a separate team within the organization responsible for collecting, organizing, and mining big data for the benefit of the entire organization. A culture of data reliance means that when making decisions, employees look at numbers first and use their gut-feelings second. It means that estimates are not based on general guesses, but rather historical and industry data that has real meaning. Finally, it means that proposals made without proper data support are weeded out during the decision-making process. Big data, and data utilization techniques, are going to become more and more important over the next decade, and will help the large organizations of tomorrow compete with more agile and innovative startups contending for market share in their operating spaces.

11. A Unified Organization View

The ideal digital organization of tomorrow has digital competencies evenly distributed throughout the entire organization. Every employee, in every department, has a concrete understanding of our digital world, and in particular how their own roles need to function to stay competitive. Furthermore, operating divisions work together seamlessly and efficiently, without any slowdowns or significant misunderstandings, to swiftly achieve commons goals.

This ideal organization is all but impossible to achieve. In truth, every organizational structure creates silos that reduce nimbleness. There will also be disparities in competency and understanding between teams and divisions that must work together. However, despite reporting hierarchies that exist, employees must view the organization as a single entity, with teams that work together to achieve a particular outcome. Steps should be taken by upper management to foster this view, and structural and policy changes should be made to make good on that vision. If silos ultimately can't be broken down completely, they can at least be brought closer together and tied to one another in their operations.

One way to begin doing this for departments that depend on one another is mandatory cross-functional team meetings. For example, employees can be selected from product development, marketing, sales, and compliance, and meet virtually (or in person) every week or two. At this meeting, they can discuss progress about current initiatives and where they are in the pipeline, and vet potential issues before they arise and cause delays. To take this concept one step further, for large organizations we often recommend the concept of the *cross-functional employee* for each department. This employee should be multitalented, and have a thorough understanding of the operations of two (or more) departments, generally having worked in both before. They interface with the teams and leaders of both departments, but generally report to a single higher authority directly rather than the heads of the two departments for which they bridge. Utilizing talented cross-functional teams and employees effectively helps to bridge the silos created by the organization's structure, and improves efficiency for a variety of complex tasks that require the input of multiple departments to complete.

However your organization decides to go about it, creating structures that allow for organized and efficient communication between functional areas is an absolutely essential part of the digital transformation.

Organizations that successfully implement all eleven of these steps are well on their way toward becoming thought-leading digital companies. We hope that after reading this book, you will become a digital leader for your organization as it transforms itself into one that is able to compete—and thrive—in our digital world.

ENDNOTES

1. http://www.google.com/about/company/
2. http://money.cnn.com/magazines/business2/business2_archive/2005/12/01/8364616/index.htm
3. http://www.cbsnews.com/8301–505124_162–57563359/google-out-patents-apple-in–2012/
4. http://youtube/VcaSwxbRkcE
5. http://www.kotterinternational.com/our-principles/changesteps

CONCLUDING THOUGHTS

The Greek philosopher Heraclitus once purported that, "The only thing that is constant is change." Even in 500 BC, more than two millennia before the industrial revolution, there was a sense that the world was constantly moving forward. Time marches on, and in time, humanity made progress. Even in ancient Greece, *progress* meant that the thinking of today would be obsolete tomorrow—and that those cleaving to it were destined to be ineffectual.

Looking back through time at ancient Greece, change appears to have been incredibly slow by today's standards. Entire centuries separated innovations and cultural shifts. Today, we see more innovation in a single week than the Ancient Greeks collectively saw through the entire rise and fall of their civilization.

With all respect to Heraclitus, change is not a constant. Change is, irrefutably, exponential. It's accelerating. With each passing year, change happens more and more quickly. We cannot blame Heraclitus for not seeing it—after all, something accelerating so slowly appears to move at constant speed when viewed through ephemeral human eyes. Today, we see accelerating innovation with our own eyes each and every day. We take rapid change for granted, but rarely do we stop to consider its implications.

We're in the midst of a digital age that is the culmination of all of this change to date. We've reached a point such that change is now happening so fast, by historical standards, that it's difficult for us to keep pace with it. The implications that accompany this change are incredible.

Consumers are ultraempowered and superinformed, and technology has dramatically changed the needs of businesses and consumers alike. Cultural shifts unique to only the last few years have emerged that necessitate changes to marketing and all other aspects of our businesses. Large businesses, whose experience and organized infrastructure created efficiency and competitive advantage in yesterday's world, are hindered today by their inability to be agile.

To survive in the rapidly evolving business environment of tomorrow, companies must embrace a completely new mindset. This is especially true for marketers, whose job is to effectively carry company messages to the new digital consumer. Our goal in all the training and consulting that we do—and the inspiration for sharing it through this book—is to help people understand our changing world, react to it, and create strategies that let our businesses thrive in today's world.

Our methodology asserts that doing so starts with understanding the new digital paradigm and what makes the digital consumer tick. We must remember that today's consumer is evolving faster than your business, and that she is heavily influenced by the information accessed at the *critical moment* that a decision is made. To achieve favorable outcomes, marketers must utilize digital channels effectively and embrace liquid principles to stay flexible as the landscapes surrounding their brands evolve. We propose a digital strategy framework that incorporates creating stories, feeding and curating channels, and determining ROI—with constant testing, measurement, and refinement at the center of everything.

With a sound understanding of the modern consumer and how he is best reached, learning granular strategy for each digital channel sets us on the right path toward success. Search lets consumers find us, tells us their intent at the moment they do, and directs them to the right content to influence their decisions. Social media allows us to interact with brand advocates and critics publically, and yet also more intimately than ever before. Mobile strategies let us reach our target audience on the go, and in innovative and unique ways that were previously impossible. Video combines rich media with social elements and allows brilliant creativity to shine brighter than ever. Websites remain our most essential owned properties, and represent the ultimate voice and authority when consumers seek to contact us or to learn more about us.

These channels are all important individually, but together, a synergistic marketing mix is far greater than the sum of its parts. Digital channels interact and feed off of one another. Consumers often navigate from one digital channel to another, and a consistent, holistic, multichannel strategy is crucial to digital success. By leveraging digital channels together, and weaving in excellent content strategy throughout, companies today can fabricate more relevant and timely connections with consumers than was ever feasible before the dawn of the digital age.

However, choosing among digital initiatives isn't always easy. We cogently recommend estimating ROI using both internal and external data, and using it as the lowest common denominator among campaign choices to make effective decisions.

Perhaps equally difficult is the actual implementation of digital change within an organization. We've postulated that we're often our own worst enemies in becoming digital leaders, and provided tips for creating a persona that can act as a change agent. We've also developed a three-phase digital transformation framework that spans digital planning, implementation, and cultural shifts. Companies large and small can utilize this methodology to evolve into agile, digitally adept victors in their competitive ecosystems.

The flow and methodology of this book closely mirrors the training we give Fortune 500 companies as consultants and digital educators. We hope that you now feel confident implementing digital innovation, changing your organization for the better, and taking your personal career to new heights. We'd love nothing more than for our readers to close this book, put it down, and feel as though they have become digital marketing experts.

That said, we have one final truth to remind you of. If you've read this entire book cover to cover, you might suspect what we're going to say:

You're a student of digital methodologies. You always will be. We're students too, as are all of our contributing authors. We're all learning. As shifts occur in our ecosystem—which happens fairly constantly nowadays—we all scramble to get our bearings and develop new strategies to counter them. We find solace in not knowing everything by expecting and embracing the unexpected. We find success through observing, testing, measuring, and reacting. We find that our competitive advantage lies in being the absolute best students we can be.

By the time you're reading this book, our authors have probably looked back at their respective chapters and realized that bits and pieces are already outdated. They'll know, as top students of their respective disciplines, that changes have already occurred that render small tidbits of advice obsolete.

This book is only a starting point—a launch pad to set you on your way. As you set forth on your digital journey, retain the student mindset. Read blogs, examine new data, and learn through trial and error. Embrace change. Learn as much as you can. Test and measure everything. Don't be afraid to fail.

We'll leave you with one final quote from our old friend Heraclitus: "No man ever steps in the same river twice, for it's not the same river, and he's not the same man." Bravely evolve alongside our ever-changing world, and digital marketing success will be yours.

INDEX

C

D

F

G

H

I

J

K

L

M

R

S

X

Y

Z

ABOUT THE AUTHORS AND CONTRIBUTORS

Eric Greenberg

Eric serves as managing director of Executive Education for the Center for Management Development at Rutgers University. He is also president of EG Consultants, LLC, a marketing consulting services firm focused on brand management and customercentric strategies. He also manages and mentors for Jersey Angels, LLC., a private angel investing group. Prior to these positions, Eric founded and served as the CEO of MTS, LLC, one of the nation's largest providers of CRM services.

Eric has created several innovative and world-class executive education programs at Rutgers, including Strategic Marketing, Digital Marketing, Social Media Marketing, Mobile Marketing, and more. These programs have been cited in the *New York Times* and other leading publications as representing some of the most innovative, and cutting edge training programs in the world. He has also developed CMD's first suite of online certificate programs, and speaks monthly at conferences and summits around the world. Eric earned BA/BS degrees with honors from the University of Pennsylvania, Wharton School of Business. He earned J.D./L.L.M degrees from New York University School of Law.

Alexander Kates

Alex is an entrepreneur and digital marketing enthusiast. When he's not engrossed in a high-tech venture of his own creation, he works as a marketing consultant to big brands, providing strategic guidance and targeted training to executives around the world. Alex enjoys helping companies develop holistic digital strategies that harness creative emerging media. He speaks in training programs and at conferences on the topics of digital strategy, mobile innovation, gamification, and managing digital transformations.

In partnership with Rutgers University, Alex has developed and led tailored digital training programs for Fortune 500 companies on four continents. He serves as professor for a new Rutgers course entitled *Creating Viral Media*, which aims to help students leverage effective content strategy.

Alex is the founder of several companies, including Planga, a social calendaring and geomapping platform in use at more than a dozen colleges and universities. He cofounded the Jersey Angels investment group, and organized the global GRX network of digital consultants.

Alex graduated *Summa cum Laude* and at the top of his class at Cornell University, earning the prestigious Merrill Presidential Scholarship. He majored in Applied Economics and Management, with coursework concentrations in Strategy, Entrepreneurship, Statistics, and Information Science.

Neil Perkin

Neil is a renowned blogger, writer, and the founder of digital and media consultancy Only Dead Fish. He is a regular keynote speaker across Europe on content strategy, emerging media, digital marketing innovation, and social technologies, and writes regularly for BrandRepublic, FutureLab, Marketing Week and Mediatel amongst others.

Neil curates the quarterly series of Firestarters thought-leadership events on behalf of Google UK, and has worked with market-leading global businesses including Warner Bros, the RSA Group, HBOS, YouTube, Marks And Spencer, and the NSPCC. He is an associate of The Futures Agency, a collaboration of some of the world's leading media thinkers and futurists. For people who like shiny things, he has won more industry awards than just about anyone in UK media, with five awards to his name including a Campaign Award, two Media Week Awards, and an Association of Online Publishers award.

He has over 20 years media owner experience and was previously the director of marketing, strategy and digital for IPC Media, the largest consumer publisher in the UK and publisher of multimedia brands including Wallpaper, Marie Claire, and the NME. In this capacity he ran award-winning strategy, planning and consumer insight functions and was at the center of defining and implementing the digital strategy for one of the largest media owners in the UK.

Mike Moran

Author of the acclaimed book on Internet marketing, *Do It Wrong Quickly*, on the heels of the bestselling *Search Engine Marketing, Inc.*, Mike Moran is the founder and president of Mike Moran Group, a digital consultancy and training organization. Mike also serves as a senior strategist for Converseon, a leading social media consultancy based in New York City. Mike holds an Advanced Certificate in Market Management Practice from the Royal UK Charter Institute of Marketing, and is a Visiting Lecturer at the University of Virginia's Darden School of Business, as well as an instructor at Rutgers, Fairleigh Dickinson, and the University of California at Irvine. He also writes a marketing column for Search Engine Guide and for the Biznology® newsletter and blog. Mike speaks worldwide on digital marketing for marketers, public relations specialists, market researchers, and technologists.

Prior to forming Mike Moran Group, Mike worked for IBM for 30 years, rising to the level of Distinguished Engineer. Mike has more than 20 years' experience in search technology, led the IBM product team that developed the first commercial linguistic search engine in 1989, and has been granted six patents in search and retrieval technology. He led the integration of ibm.com's site search technologies and served as product manager for IBM's search and text analytics products.

Greg Jarboe

Greg Jarboe is president and co-founder of SEO-PR, a content marketing agency that offers search engine optimization, online public relations, social media marketing, and video marketing services. SEO-PR's campaigns for Southwest Airlines, *The Christian Science Monitor*, MarketingSherpa, Harlequin Romance, *Parents* magazine, the SES Conference & Expo series, and the Rutgers Center for Management Development have won awards for generating measurable results.

Jarboe is the author of *YouTube and Video Marketing: An Hour a Day*, which is also part of the *Marketing with Social Media: An Hour a Day Collection*. He is a contributor to *Enchantment: The Art of Changing Hearts, Minds, and Actions* by Guy Kawasaki as well as *Complete B2B Online Marketing* by William Leake, Lauren Vaccarello, and Maura Ginty. Jarboe is also profiled in *Online Marketing Heroes: Interviews with 25 Successful Online Marketing Gurus* by Michael Miller.

Jarboe writes for Search Engine Watch and ReelSEO. He is also a frequent speaker at the SES Conference & Expo series and the PRSA International Conference. The International Search Summit audience voted him the winner of its first Medallion Speaker Award.

STRATEGIC DIGITAL MARKETING

Top Digital Experts Share the Formula for Tangible Returns on Your Marketing Investment

ERIC GREENBERG
AND
ALEXANDER KATES

New York Chicago San Francisco Athens London
Madrid Mexico City Milan New Delhi
Singapore Sydney Toronto

1 2 3 4 5 6 7 8 9 0 QFR/QFR 1 0 9 8 7 6 5 4 3

ISBN 978-0-07-181950-3
MHID 0-07-181950-9

e-ISBN 978-0-07-181951-0
e-MHID 0-07-181951-7

Library of Congress Cataloging-in-Publication Data

Greenberg, Eric.
Strategic digital marketing: top digital experts share the formula for tangible returns on your marketing investment / by Eric Greenberg and Alexander Kates.
pages cm
Includes bibliographical references.
ISBN-13: 978-0-07-181950-3 (alk. paper)
ISBN-10: 0-07-181950-9 (alk. paper)
1. Internet marketing. 2. Marketing—Management. I. Kates, Alexander. II. Title.
HF5415.1265.G7397 2014
658.8'72—dc23 2013022659

McGraw-Hill Education books are available at special quantity discounts to use as premiums and sales promotions or for use in corporate training programs. To contact a representative, please visit the Contact Us pages at www.mhprofessional.com.

Prior to co-founding SEO-PR in 2003, Jarboe was the Vice President of Marketing at WebCT, Director of Corporate Communications at Ziff-Davis, Director of Marketing at *PC/Computing*, and Director of Corporate Communications at Lotus Development Corporation.

Jarboe graduated with distinction from the University of Michigan, attended the University of Edinburgh, and completed all the course work for his Masters in Applied Management at Lesley College.

Stanford Smith

Stanford is the managing director at Pushing Social, a social media and content marketing consultancy, and is author of the bestselling book *Born to Blog* (2013).

Stanford has over 15 year of experience crafting award-winning digital marketing campaigns and social media programs for Fortune 500 brands, state organizations, and startups. Social Media Examiner has recognized the Pushing Social blog as one of the Top 10 social media blogs in the world.

Stanford is a well-known guest contributor to a "who's who" list of top social media blogs including Copyblogger, Problogger, Write to Done, Convince and Convert, and {grow}. You can see his latest work at pushingsocial.com and follow him on Twitter via @pushingsocial.

Glen Gilmore

Two years in row named to the Forbes list of Top 50 Social Media Power Influencers, Glen Gilmore has been called a "man of action" by TIME magazine. Founder of Gilmore Business Network, a digital marketing firm, Gilmore is a social media influencer who uses his skills to help companies understand the art of online community building, brand management, content marketing, influencer relations, and customer communications. Author of *Social Media Law for Business*, Gilmore also brings to the task his training and experience as a lawyer to help clients avoid the legal landmines associated with social media marketing in global commerce. He provides customized social media training to members of the *Fortune 500*. Additionally, Gilmore works with special clients to help them with online reputation management.

Jeremy Floyd

In addition to creating curriculum around the theoretical basis and application of digital marketing for University of Tennessee Chattanooga's MBA program, Jeremy serves as the Chief Marketing Officer at BPV Capital Management. Jeremy has written about social media analytics for a forthcoming MBA textbook. In addition, Floyd blogs about digital marketing and leadership at www.jeremyfloyd.com and can be found on twitter at @jfloyd.

Past President of the marketing firm Bluegill where he built social media strategies and architected complex application development to provide clients a complete digitally integrated solution. Prior to Bluegill, Jeremy ran a digital consulting firm called Eluminare, which provided SEO, social media strategy, virtual marketing management and a full range of marketing consulting.

Jeremy holds a BA in English and Philosophy and a JD from the University of Tennessee College of Law, and he actively maintains his law license.

Rob Petersen

Rob is president of BarnRaisers, a digital and social media solutions company that builds brands using proven principles of relationship marketing. Rob was EVP/Chief Strategy Officer for Omnicom and has held leadership positions at FCB, Euro RSCG, and Saatchi & Saatchi.

Rob has been recognized by the American Marketing Association for building billion dollar businesses multiple times. He has developed game-changing consumer relationship platforms that have propelled brands from Abbott, Coca-Cola, Johnson & Johnson, MasterCard, and Pfizer to market leadership.

Rob is on the MBA faculty at Rutgers CMD where he teaches courses in Digital Marketing, Social Media Marketing, and Measurement and ROI. He is also an instructor and the University of California Irvine.

Bob Pearson

One of the true pioneers of social media marketing, Bob Pearson is globally recognized as a marketing visionary who is driving "pragmatic disruption" in the new world of what is now called "Social Commerce."

Bob is president of W2O Group, an independent network of complementary marketing, communications, research, and development firms focused on integrated business solutions to drive change and growth through "pragmatic disruption of the status quo" for the world's leading brands and organizations. Clients include major brands, such as Intel, Red Bull, and Hewlett Packard, as well as dozens of pharmaceutical, medical device, biotechnology, and health technology clients.

An author, frequent speaker, and blogger on social media, as well as an instructor for Rutgers center for management development, Bob's thoughts can be found at the Common Sense blog at www.wcgworld.com. After the success of his book *Pre-Commerce*, Bob is currently working on a new book on the subject of Social Commerce titled *Storytizing* that will be available by the end of 2013.

Prior to W2O Group, Bob worked directly with Michael Dell as VP of Communities and Conversations at Dell to develop the Fortune 500's first global social media function. Before Dell, Bob was Head of Global Corporate Communications at Novartis. Bob has served on many boards, including the original P&G digital advisory board, and served as chair of the $400 million emerging technology fund for the State of Texas.

Amy Kates

Amy is a managing partner of Kates Kesler Organization Consulting and has served as a trusted advisor to business leaders in successful companies around the world. She works with leaders and their teams to assess organizational issues, reshape structures and processes, and build depth of management capability.

Amy has consulted to a wide range of global clients including General Mills, Nike, PepsiCo, Prudential, Comcast, Bristol-Myers Squibb, Bank of America, Old Mutual South Africa, Discovery, Dell, Wells Fargo, Coty, GMCR/Keurig, Marriott, MetLife, Welch Allyn, Girl Scouts USA, New York University, E&J Gallo, Cemex, Time Warner, Ford Foundation, Intel, and Disney.

Amy has coauthored three of the leading books in organization design and talent management, including the most recent *Leading Organization Design* (2010) with her partner, Greg Kesler and has published numerous articles and book chapters on the topic. Her article, "(Re)Designing the HR Organization," was awarded the 2007 HRPS Walker Prize. She is also an editor of the journal, *People & Strategy*.

In addition to consulting and writing, Amy teaches organization design to MBA students at Danish School of Business in Denmark and Cornell University in New York. The organization design approach Amy developed with Jay Galbraith has become the standard internal design methodology used in dozens of major corporations around the world.